Main Street
Beats
Wall Street

HOW THE TOP INVESTMENT
CLUBS ARE OUTPERFORMING
THE INVESTMENT PROS

Richard J. Maturi

IRWIN
Professional Publishing®
Chicago • London • Singapore

This publication is designed to provide accurate and authoritative information in regard to the subject matter covered. It is sold with the understanding that the author and the publisher are not engaged in rendering legal, accounting, or other professional service.

ISBN 1-55738-804-0

Printed in the United States of America

BB

2 3 4 5 6 7 8 9 0

TAQ/BJS

Dedicated in memory of our beloved Roz
(1950–1994)

Table of Contents

PART 2
Successful Investment Club Profiles

PART 3
Putting It All Together

Preface

Professional money managers arm themselves with sophisticated computer models, extensive research departments, and years of investment experience. Conventional wisdom dictates that the individual investor is at a major disadvantage in the investment arena against these big guns of the investment community.

However, conventional wisdom has been proven wrong numerous times in the past and will be proven wrong again in the future. The thrust behind *Main Street Beats Wall Street* is that individuals can and do outperform their professional counterparts. Investment clubs are the unsung heroes of the investment world. Typical working (or retired) men and women across the nation join forces in investment clubs and use their talents and investigative prowess to outperform Wall Street's top money managers.

The following pages uncover how top investment clubs beat the pros from Main Street, U.S.A. You will learn what strategies they use and how to put them to use to improve your own investment returns. You will discover where to obtain investment information sources and how to ferret out tomorrow's top performers in the stock market. This book shows how average people working together can make better investment decisions than the top-paid money managers on Wall Street.

Finally, you will learn how to start your own investment club and reap the benefits of this tried and true investing technique.

This book is organized into four parts: Investment Club Strategies, Successful Investment Club Profiles, Putting It All Together, and Investment Club Top Picks. Feel free to read ahead or review as you see fit. Ample cross-references help you locate information in other parts of the book. Use this book as a handy guide to build your own portfolio delivering superior returns.

Richard J. Maturi
Cheyenne, Wyoming

Acknowledgments

I extend my thanks to the following, who were kind enough to allow the reprinting of charts and illustrations:

National Association of Investors Corporation
The Moneypaper
Sound Mind Investing
Value Line Publishing, Inc.

Investment Club Strategies

INVESTMENT PHILOSOPHY

Just as individual investment philosophies and strategies vary according to the person's age, financial status, financial commitments, investment goals, and risk posture, the philosophies and strategies of every investment club will also differ depending on its membership.

Similarly, just as individuals adjust their portfolios as they move through their life cycles, investment clubs also adjust their portfolio selection process over time as members age, some people retire from the club, and new blood joins the ranks of club members. For those unfamiliar with life-cycle investing, it is an investment strategy that adjusts the risk posture of portfolio holdings as the person moves through his or her career and life cycle.

For example, young people with many more years until retirement can afford to assume a higher risk position because they have time to recoup from losses suffered early in their investment cycle. On the other hand, people nearing retirement and needing current income to sustain a comfortable lifestyle should assume a more conservative risk posture, moving from a majority of growth investments to a larger percentage of fixed-income securities.

Whether you are an individual investor or a member of an investment club trying to earn respectable portfolio returns, it is crucial to your success that you develop and implement an investment strategy aimed at achieving your investment goals. Too many investors purchase a security on the recommendation of others without any consideration of how it fits into their overall strategy or how it will help achieve their desired investment goals.

With that in mind, the National Association of Investors Corporation (NAIC) encourages its members to adopt an investment philosophy that includes the following points, which will be discussed in further detail later in this chapter:

- Invest a set amount regularly, usually once a month, regardless of market conditions. This helps you obtain lower average costs.

- Reinvest dividends and capital gains immediately. Your money grows faster when earnings are reinvested through the power of compounding.

- Buy growth stocks—companies whose sales are increasing at a rate faster than the industry in general. These stocks offer good prospects for continued growth and higher dividends and stock prices.

- Invest in different industries and different-sized companies. Proper diversification helps reduce risk and increase opportunity for gains.

As can be seen from the club profiles in Part 2, investors who establish an investment philosophy, goals, and specific strategies for implementation can and do outperform Wall Street's top money managers.

KEY INVESTMENT PRINCIPLES

Proper Diversification

As indicated earlier, diversification ranks as a key factor in the successful investing equation. It is important to recognize that diversification can take several forms. The variety of asset classes, financial instruments, geographical locations, companies and industries, and investment options react differently during changing economic scenarios or from one market situation to another.

To illustrate, precious metals have traditionally performed well during periods of high inflation and low investor confidence. However, precious metals fared less well during periods of prosperity and stable economic and political environments.

Inherent in all diversification strategies is the desire to avoid the risks associated with placing all your eggs in one basket and then having that basket turned upside-down by changing economic forces.

A diversified portfolio provides protection against a variety of investment risks, such as economic and industry cycles; technological change adversely impacting a particular company or industry; geographical recessions or contractions; interest rate fluctuations; natural, political, and economic crises; changes in raw materials supplies; and management mistakes.

As mentioned earlier, diversification can be effectively accomplished through a number of investing techniques and, more likely, a combination of techniques designed to reduce risk from investing in an overly narrow range of investment options.

Diversify by Company

With the need for proper diversification established, we'll now look at several specific types of diversification that you need to consider. The most obvious method of adding diversity to your investment portfolio lies in avoiding the investment of all or a bulk of your available financial resources in one company, no matter how much faith you have in that company.

Anyone who invested their whole nest egg in International Gaming Technology when the stock market was hot on gaming issues in late 1993 could have seen their investment drop to less than half of its previous value in less than a year as IGT's stock price plummeted from a high of $41\frac{3}{8}$ per share to $17\frac{1}{4}$ per share by mid-July, 1994.

The "Rule of Eight" diversification strategy requires a minimum of eight stocks to attain proper diversification, thereby reducing risk and increasing capital gains potential. A portfolio of eight different securities should help you build enough protection into your portfolio to prevent an unpredictable event affecting several stocks from devastating the overall value of your investment holdings.

Numerous risks can impact the market performance of any stock. Prolonged labor unrest, natural disasters, technological advances, fraud, and unfavorable legislation are but a few of the misfortunes that can cause a firm's operating and financial performance to falter, sinking the company's stock price in the process.

While any of these events can happen to any one or two of the companies in which you own stock, the odds of them happening to more than one or two at the same time are greatly reduced through proper diversification.

Therefore, limiting the amount of money, by aggregate or percentage, invested in any one stock or investment ranks as a top investment strategy and wealth preserver.

Diversify by Industry

Just as individual companies and their stocks can go through down economic cycles and fall out of favor with investors, whole industries can encounter turbulent times when company and industry revenues and earnings drop drastically and company stock prices experience substantial declines.

The reversals in industry fortunes occur for a variety of reasons. Cyclical industries, such as automobile, metals, paper products, and steel, periodically undergo economic cycles as the economy expands and contracts.

As the economy starts an upturn off the bottom of a recession or stagnant period, cyclical stocks start to come back to life and represent one of the best investment opportunities around. Unfortunately, as the economic and business cycle matures, cyclical stocks once again start to lose steam, eventually falling out of favor again as earnings start to taper off and then decline.

Obviously, investing heavily in a single industry exposes your portfolio to significant risks and investment losses in the event that the economy starts to sour for that industry.

In addition to economic risks of investing in a single industry, political risks also come into play. To illustrate, the stock prices of many defense firms encountered sharp price pullbacks as the Cold War dissipated and the Iron Curtain crumbled. A portfolio heavily weighted in defense stocks would have been devastated as these world political events unfolded.

Domestic political events can also negatively impact the future prospects of market sector portions or even entire sectors. Uncertainties over proposed healthcare reforms and changes in national energy policies put healthcare stocks and some energy and utility stocks in turmoil in 1993 and 1994.

Another example: Utility stocks took a dive in the wake of the Federal Reserve Board's raising of interest rates. The Dow Jones Utility Average dropped precipitiously after September 1993, taking a downward roller coaster ride from a high around of 258 to just a tad over 183 by mid-July 1994 (see Chart 1–1).

Not only does it make sense to diversify by company, but it is also wise to diversify by industry. Keep a close watch on industry health and the economic, political, and other pertinent factors that can negatively affect industry revenues and earnings and subsequently, industry company stock prices.

Chart 1–1   *Dow Jones Utility Average*

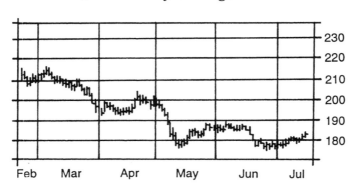

Diversify by Geographical Location

Until relatively recently, geographical diversification mainly referred to making sure your investments were not concentrated too heavily in any one or two regions of the United States. Today, with intense global competition and the explosive growth of overseas investment opportunities, geographical diversification takes on new meaning.

No longer are investors living in the United States confined to domestic securities or possibly a rare venture into Canadian investment opportunities. The proliferation of foreign stocks listed and traded on U.S. stock exchanges and in the over-the-counter market as American Depositary Receipts (ADRs) adds a new dimension to geographical investing. In the same vein, with the explosion of new mutual funds (both open and closed) targeting international and global markets and companies, the geographical diversification choices are practically unlimited.

In fact, in 1992, Glaxco Holdings PLC (a United Kingdom pharmaceutical company) became the first ADR issue to lead the New York Stock Exchange in annual trading volume. Telefonos de Mexico (a Mexican telecommunications company) consistently ranks as one of the New York Stock Exchange's top-traded securities in terms of both share trading volume and dollar trading volume.

Diversify by Company Operations

Another way to protect your portfolio lies in investing in companies with diversified operations. Companies can internally diversify in a number of ways. The firm could develop a broad product line and a variety of services crossing several industries. A company could also have operating divisions that react counter to each other during different economic cycles. Another way for a company to diversify is geographically: by establishing sales branches, facilities, and other operations in various regions of the United States or in foreign countries. Finally, companies can effectively diversify by marketing to different market segments, for example, selling to both consumer and industrial markets or government and commercial markets.

Rubbermaid, Inc. (NYSE: RBD) prides itself on its broad product line in excess of 5,000 items ranging from household products to children's toys. In fact, one of the company's major strengths is its introduction of more than 300 new products each year.

As the world's largest processor of seasonings and spices, McCormick & Company, Inc. (NASDAQ: MCCRK) attains an international geographical diversification second to none both in terms of raw material supply sources and key markets.

Automotive companies diversify in a number of ways. Their broad product lines are sold around the world and serve a wide variety of market segments, including government, industrial, commercial, consumer, upscale, and economy.

RPM, Inc. (NYSE: RPOW), a perennial investment club favorite, spreads its operations across market segments. Its protective-coatings operations serve the industrial market, while its hobby products serve the consumer market. RPM's divisions also tend to be recession resistant. During tough economic times, industry invests in the restoration and protection of existing facilities, using RPM specialty chemical products. An economic upturn also adds to the demand for RPM products as more facilities are built that need protection and as consumers have more spending money for hobbies. (See Chart 1–2.)

In the same vein, to protect themselves from declining Defense Department expenditures, some defense firms, such as General Dynamics (NYSE: GD), have adjusted their production to shift operations more toward the commercial market. This move makes them less susceptible to the ill-effects of downsized military defense program budgets.

To be sure, proper diversification represents a key building block in the construction of your investment program. Don't make the drastic mistake of failing to protect your investment portfolio properly.

FORMULA INVESTMENT PLANS

Dollar Cost Averaging Formula

One of the major cornerstones of the NAIC's successful investment philosophy is the persistent use of dollar cost averaging. The two most attractive features of dollar cost averaging are that it is easy to employ and it works as long as you maintain the discipline to make regular investments regardless of current market conditions.

Simply put, dollar cost averaging is an investment strategy based on purchasing securities over a period of time by investing at specific regular intervals. When the security price is lower, more shares or units of the security can be purchased. On the other hand, when the security price is higher, fewer shares or units can be obtained.

This formula plan eliminates the uncertainty of market timing and the risk of being out of the market at a time when lucrative profit opportunities exist.

Obviously, dollar cost averaging is not for the faint-hearted investor. It takes courage to continue purchasing securities as the market heads south and stocks and bonds are racking up losses. To make the strategy work, the investor must not lose faith and stop buying securities during a bear market. The underlying purpose of dollar cost averaging is to acquire shares at a lower average price than could be accomplished otherwise, such as through

Chart 1–2   RPM, Inc. Stock Chart

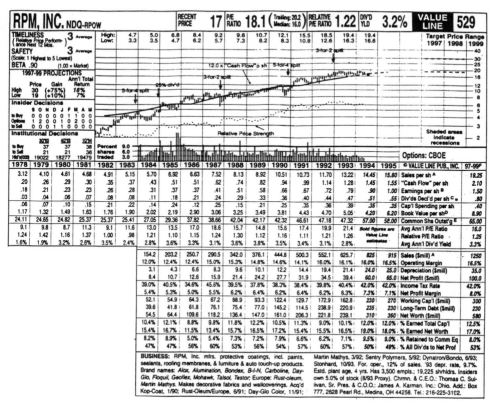

Source: ©1994 by Value Line Publishing, Inc. Reprinted by permission; All Rights Reserved.

market timing. It is during these bear markets that more shares can be purchased, thereby reducing the average price of your portfolio holdings.

There's also the temptation to discontinue purchases after stocks have risen to a high level. You must resist this temptation for several reasons. For one, how high is too high? Investors who stopped purchasing stocks when the Dow Jones Industrial Average broke 2800 in mid-1990 lost the opportunity to participate in the significant upside move in the Dow as the index rose to over 3700 by the last quarter of 1993. There's also the risk that the money might be spent elsewhere and not be available for investment when unique market and stock situations present themselves. Finally, you run the risk of abandoning the program and sabotaging your strategy before it has the chance to work for you.

To review, dollar cost averaging, combined with dividend and capital gain reinvestment, puts the power of compounding to work for you.

The keys to dollar cost averaging are a long-term investment perspective and the discipline to make regular purchases. Benefits come from a lower average cost, elimination of market timing guesswork, and compounding of income and earnings.

Strictly speaking, this investment formula recommends investing a constant sum of money on a regular basis. As a practical matter, the amount invested may vary from period to period as investment club members join or leave the club. Similarly, as an individual investor, you might alter your regular investment amount depending on your financial circumstances.

There are some caveats to mention. First of all, this formula plan works better with stocks and markets that fluctuate, allowing you to average down your cost. Dollar cost averaging may not outperform lump sum investing in markets exhibiting nearly straight-up market moves such as that experienced in the mid-to-late 1980s and early 1990s. Recent studies also suggest that dollar cost averaging of a lump sum amount such as a pension distribution or inheritance may not outperform a single-amount investment due to the trend of the market rising over the long term.

As mentioned earlier, you need to maintain proper diversification; therefore, you will be purchasing a variety of securities. You will also need to periodically evaluate your portfolio and cull out the losers or those that show less promise than alternative investments.

Like all investment programs, dollar cost averaging is not failproof. It will work better in some market environments than others but over the long haul produces attractive results and has the added benefit of promoting regular investing to build up your investment portfolio.

See Table 1–1 for an illustration of how this formula plan works. As shown in the table, the dollar cost averaging price per share totals $21.05 versus $21.88 for the average share price. Based on this information, you can lower your overall cost per share by nearly 4 percent by putting dollar cost averaging to use. This is accomplished by the ability to purchase more shares with your $1,200 investment when the stock price is relatively low. For example, 80 shares can be purchased for $1,200 in Period 2, while only 40 shares can be purchased for $1,200 in Period 8.

By employing dollar cost averaging you also eliminate the risk of investing your lump sum amount at the high prices of $25 per share in Periods five and seven and $30 per share in Period 8.

Value Averaging Formula

Value averaging represents a new twist on the dollar cost averaging formula plan. Instead of investing a fixed amount at specific intervals as in the averaging plan previously discussed, value averaging allows your invest-

Table 1–1 Dollar Cost Averaging

Period	Amount Invested	Share Price	Shares Purchased
1	$1,200	$20	60
2	1,200	15	80
3	1,200	20	60
4	1,200	20	60
5	1,200	25	48
6	1,200	20	60
7	1,200	25	48
8	1,200	30	40
Total	$ 9,600	$175	456

Dollar Cost Average Share Cost: $21.05 ($9,600/456)
Average Share Price: $21.88 ($175/8)

ment to grow by that fixed amount either through appreciation or the investment of new money. In other words, value averaging takes into account the performance of your portfolio in determining the amount of new money to invest.

Michael E. Edleson, a Harvard professor and author of *Value Averaging* (International Publishing Press, 1992), explains how this formula approach helps the investor avoid buying high and selling low to earn a higher return. In addition to positioning you to purchase more shares when prices drop exceptionally low, value averaging forces you to take your gains as the market soars.

Possible disadvantages of using this strategy include excessive transaction costs and the tedious task of periodically recalculating your account value to decide what to invest or sell. Also, the formula performs better with mutual funds than with individual stocks due to the probability of odd-lot and fractional share purchases.

It works like this: Assume you want to increase your investment portfolio by $1,500 each period to reach your goal of accumulating investment holdings of $150,000 at the end of a certain period, perhaps as a fund for college expenses or a house purchase.

In the first period you would invest $1,500. Each subsequent period you would either invest an amount of new money depending on your portfolio's performance or sell some of your holdings to bring your portfolio value to the target amount. To illustrate, if your portfolio increased in value by $500 during the period, you would only need to invest $1,000 of new money to reach the targeted $1,500 increase in the portfolio value per period. This is reflected in Period 2 of Table 1–2. On the other hand, if you are fortunate to have your portfolio value increase by more than $1,500 during any one period, you would then sell enough securities to bring your portfolio value in line with your $1,500 value increase target. This situation occured in Period 5.

Constant Dollar Formula

The underlying feature of the constant dollar formula is to keep a constant amount of dollars invested in stocks regardless of the stock market or individual stock price level. For instance, your target investment amount could be $25,000 invested in equities at all times. While the value averaging strategy seeks to invest a specified amount on a periodic basis, the dollar constant plan strives to adjust the portfolio to return to a desired level of equity investment at periodic intervals.

This strategy helps ensure that the investor has no more than a predetermined amount of money at risk in the equity market at any one time. Table 1–3 illustrates how the plan works.

Assume a target equity investment of $25,000 and a review process on an annual basis. The investor also starts out with a bond portfolio investment of $10,000. At the start of Year 2, the stock portfolio had increased to $30,000 and the bond portfolio to $12,000. To readjust to the desired stock investment target of $25,000, the investor would sell $5,000 worth of stock and purchase a like amount of bonds.

At the start of Year 5, the stock portfolio totals only $20,000, while the bond portfolio now equals $35,000. Under this scenario, the investor would sell $5,000 worth of bonds and purchase the same amount of stocks to bring the equity portfolio back to the $25,000 target.

Table 1–2   Value Averaging

Period	Portfolio Value	Portfolio Target	Amount Invested	Amount Sold	Portfolio Earnings
1	$ -0-	$ 1,500	$1,500	$ —	$ 500
2	2,000	3,000	1,000	—	750
3	3,750	4,500	750	—	(300)
4	4,200	6,000	1,800	—	2,500
5	8,500	7,500	—	1,000	750
...	...	...	...	...	...
99	146,500	148,500	2,000	—	(1,500)
100	147,000	150,000	3,000	—	

Table 1–3 Constant Dollar Formula

Year	Stock Fund Value	Bond Fund Value	Stock Purchase/ (Sales)	Bond Purchase/ (Sales)	Portfolio Value
1	$25,000	$10,000	—	—	$35,000
2	30,000	12,000	($5,000)	$5,000	42,000
...	...	...	...	...	...
5	20,000	35,000	5,000	(5,000)	55,000

Constant Ratio Formula

Instead of trying to maintain a constant dollar amount invested in equities, the constant ratio formula attempts to readjust to a desired target ratio between the value of stocks and bonds in the portfolio. As stock prices rise, stocks are sold and bonds purchased to bring the ratio of stocks to bonds in the portfolio back to the predetermined target. Conversely, as stock prices decline, stocks are purchased and bonds sold to return to the desired portfolio ratios.

This formula reduces the investor's exposure to stocks as they rise, thus reducing risk. It also allows the investor to purchase more stock as prices decline, thereby positioning him or her for the rebound. However, the plan requires judgment of the "correct" ratio. A prolonged market rise could result in investors using this plan underperforming the market.

Table 1–4 shows how the constant ratio strategy works. Assume an initial investment of $25,000 each in stocks and bonds. That calculates out to a 50-50 target ratio. With a 20 percent rise in stock prices, the stock portfolio rises to a total of $30,000; the bond fund stands still at $25,000. To return to the 50-50 target ratio, the investor would have to sell $2,500 worth of stock and purchase bonds as in Period 2.

Table 1–4 Constant Ratio Formula, 50/50 Target Ratio

Period	Stock Portfolio	Bond Portfolio	Stock Purchase/ (Sales)	Bond Purchase/ (Sales)	Portfolio Value
1	$25,000	$25,000	—	—	$50,000
2	30,000	25,000	($ 2,500)	$ 2,500	55,000
...	...	...	...	...	...
5	20,000	40,000	10,000	(10,000)	60,000

If the value of the stock portfolio fell to $20,000 while the bond portfolio increased to $40,000, the investor would have to purchase $10,000 worth of stock and sell the same dollar figure of bonds to rebalance the portfolio as in Period 5.

Variable Installment Formula

Under the variable installment formula, the investor starts out investing an equal amount in stocks and bonds or a money market account. Additional contributions to the stock portfolio are adjusted based on changes in the stock portfolio value.

If the stock portfolio decreases by a predetermined percentage, say 15 percent, the entire contribution amount gets invested in stocks. Likewise, if the stock portfolio increases by a predetermined amount, say 20 percent, you could invest this period's whole amount in bonds or in your money market account and nothing in stocks. Of course, there can be varying degrees of stock investment between 100 percent and zero depending on the parameters you set in advance.

All of the above plans work with mutual funds as well as individual stocks and bonds. In fact, you may incur less transaction charges by using no-load and low-load mutual funds.

DIVIDEND REINVESTMENT PLANS (DRIPs)

The Power of Compounding

Dividend reinvestment plans (DRIPs) are firmly grounded in the investment principle of compounding your investment returns for enhanced portfolio growth. Reinvestment of cash dividends puts more money to work for you, earning additional income.

The power of compounding is clearly illustrated in Table 1–5. For example, if you invested $2,000 a year for 33 years, you would have accumulated $66,000, a fair-sized amount. However, if you let your annual income accumulate in the account and be reinvested at an 8.5 percent return instead of

Table 1–5 Comparison of Compounded and Uncompounded Investment

Annual Investment	Age	Years Invested	Uncompounded Amount at 65	Compounded at Age 65
$2,000	32	33	$66,000	$364,078*

*Exclusive of taxes

taking a distribution, your $2,000 annual investment would have grown to $364,078 (exclusive of taxes).

Here are two simple compounding rules to keep handy for easy reference:

- *The Rule of 72 (Doubling).* To determine how long it takes to double your money, divide the rate of return into 72. For example, an investment earning a return of 8 percent will take nine years to double (72/8).

- *The Rule of 115 (Tripling).* To determine how long it takes to triple your money, divide the rate of return into 115. For example, an investment earning a return of 10 percent will triple in approximately 11½ years (115/10).

Table 1–6 provides information to determine the future value of an amount invested at a given interest rate for a specific number of years.

Table 1–6   Amount of 1 Compounded

Year	3.0%	4.0%	5.0%	6.0%	7.0%	8.0%	9.0%	10.0%	11.0%	12.0%	13.0%	14.0%	15.0%
1	1.03000	1.04000	1.05000	1.06000	1.07000	1.08000	1.09000	1.10000	1.11000	1.12000	1.13000	1.14000	1.15000
2	1.06090	1.08160	1.10250	1.12360	1.14490	1.16640	1.18810	1.21000	1.23210	1.25440	1.27690	1.29960	1.32250
3	1.09272	1.12486	1.15762	1.19101	1.22504	1.25971	1.29502	1.33100	1.36763	1.40492	1.44289	1.48154	1.52087
4	1.12550	1.16985	1.21550	1.26247	1.31079	1.36048	1.41158	1.46410	1.51807	1.57351	1.63047	1.68896	1.74900
5	1.15927	1.21665	1.27628	1.33822	1.40255	1.46932	1.53862	1.61051	1.68505	1.76234	1.84243	1.92541	2.01135
6	1.19405	1.26531	1.34009	1.41851	1.50072	1.58687	1.67709	1.77156	1.87041	1.97382	2.08195	2.19497	2.31305
7	1.22987	1.31593	1.40709	1.50362	1.60578	1.71382	1.82803	1.94871	2.07615	2.21067	2.35260	2.50226	2.66001
8	1.26676	1.36856	1.47745	1.59384	1.71818	1.85092	1.99256	2.14358	2.30453	2.47596	2.65844	2.85258	3.05901
9	1.30477	1.42330	1.55132	1.68947	1.83845	1.99900	2.17189	2.35794	2.55803	2.77307	3.00403	3.25194	3.51787
10	1.34391	1.48024	1.62889	1.79084	1.96714	2.15892	2.36736	2.59374	2.83941	3.10584	3.39456	3.70721	4.04555
11	1.38423	1.53945	1.71033	1.89829	2.10484	2.33163	2.58042	2.85311	3.15175	3.47854	3.83585	4.22622	4.65238
12	1.42575	1.60102	1.79585	2.01219	2.25218	2.51265	2.81265	3.13842	3.49844	3.89597	4.33451	4.81789	5.35024
13	1.46852	1.66506	1.88564	2.13292	2.40983	2.71961	3.06579	3.45226	3.88327	4.36348	4.89800	5.49240	6.15277
14	1.51258	1.73167	1.97992	2.26089	2.57852	2.93718	3.34171	3.79749	4.31043	4.88710	5.53474	6.26133	7.07569
15	1.55796	1.80093	2.07892	2.39654	2.75902	3.17216	3.64247	4.17724	4.78457	5.47355	6.25425	7.13792	8.13704
16	1.60469	1.87297	2.18286	2.54034	2.95215	3.42593	3.97029	4.59496	5.31088	6.13038	7.06731	8.13723	9.35760
17	1.65283	1.94789	2.29201	2.69276	3.15880	3.70000	4.32762	5.05446	5.89507	6.86602	7.98606	9.27644	10.7612
18	1.70242	2.02580	2.40661	2.85432	3.37992	3.99600	4.71710	5.55990	6.54353	7.68995	9.02425	10.5751	12.3754
19	1.75349	2.10683	2.52694	3.02558	3.61651	4.31568	5.14164	6.11589	7.26332	8.61274	10.1974	12.0556	14.2317
20	1.80610	2.19111	2.65328	3.20712	3.86966	4.66094	5.60439	6.72748	8.06228	9.64627	11.5230	13.7434	16.3664
21	1.86028	2.27875	2.78595	3.39954	4.14054	5.03381	6.10878	7.40023	8.94913	10.8038	13.0210	15.6675	18.8214
22	1.91609	2.36990	2.92524	3.60351	4.43038	5.43652	6.65857	8.14025	9.93354	12.1002	14.7137	17.8609	21.6446
23	1.97357	2.46470	3.07151	3.81973	4.74050	5.87144	7.25785	8.95428	11.0262	13.5523	16.6265	20.3615	24.8913
24	2.03278	2.56329	3.22508	4.04891	5.07234	6.34115	7.91105	9.84971	12.2391	15.1785	18.7880	23.2121	28.6250
25	2.09376	2.66582	3.38633	4.29184	5.42740	6.84844	8.62305	10.8346	13.5854	16.9999	21.2304	26.4618	32.9188
26	2.15657	2.77245	3.55565	4.54935	5.80732	7.39632	9.39912	11.9181	15.0798	19.0399	23.9904	30.1664	37.8566
27	2.22127	2.88335	3.73343	4.82231	6.21383	7.98802	10.2450	13.1099	16.7385	21.3247	27.1091	34.3897	43.5351
28	2.28791	2.99868	3.92010	5.11165	6.64880	8.62707	11.1670	14.4209	18.5798	23.8837	30.6333	39.2043	50.0653
29	2.35656	3.11863	4.11611	5.41835	7.11422	9.31723	12.1721	15.8630	20.6235	26.7497	34.6156	44.6929	57.5751
30	2.42724	3.24337	4.32191	5.74345	7.61221	10.0626	13.2676	17.4493	22.8921	29.9597	39.1157	50.9499	66.2114
31	2.50066	3.37311	4.53801	6.08806	8.14507	10.8676	14.4616	19.1942	25.4103	33.5549	44.2007	58.0828	76.1431
32	2.57506	3.50803	4.76491	6.45334	8.71522	11.7370	15.7632	21.1136	28.2054	37.5815	49.9468	66.2114	87.5646
33	2.65231	3.64835	5.00315	6.84054	9.32529	12.6759	17.1819	23.2250	31.3080	42.0912	56.4399	75.4845	100.699
34	2.73188	3.79429	5.25331	7.25097	9.97806	13.6900	18.7283	25.5475	34.7519	47.1422	63.7771	86.0523	115.804
35	2.81383	3.94606	5.51598	7.68603	10.6765	14.7852	20.4138	28.1022	38.5746	52.7993	72.0681	98.0996	133.174
36	2.89825	4.10390	5.79177	8.14719	11.4238	15.9680	22.2510	30.9125	42.8178	59.1352	81.4369	111.833	153.150
37	2.98519	4.26806	6.08136	8.63603	12.2235	17.2454	24.2536	34.0037	47.5277	66.2314	92.0237	127.490	176.123
38	3.07475	4.43878	6.38543	9.15419	13.0791	18.6251	26.4365	37.4041	52.7558	74.1792	103.986	145.338	202.542
39	3.16699	4.61633	6.70470	9.70344	13.9947	20.1151	28.8157	41.1445	58.5589	83.0807	117.505	165.686	232.923
40	3.26200	4.80098	7.03994	10.2856	14.9743	21.7243	31.4092	45.2589	65.0004	93.0503	132.780	188.822	267.861
41	3.35986	4.99302	7.39193	10.9027	16.0225	23.4622	34.2360	49.7848	72.1504	104.216	150.042	215.352	308.040
42	3.46066	5.19274	7.76153	11.5569	17.1441	25.3392	37.3172	54.7633	80.0869	116.722	169.547	245.471	354.247
43	3.56447	5.40045	8.14961	12.2503	18.3442	27.3663	40.6758	60.2396	88.8965	130.728	191.588	279.837	407.384
44	3.67141	5.61647	8.55709	12.9853	19.6282	29.5556	44.3366	66.2636	98.6751	146.416	216.495	319.014	468.491
45	3.78155	5.84113	8.98494	13.7644	21.0022	31.9201	48.3269	72.8900	109.529	163.986	244.639	363.676	538.765
46	3.89500	6.07477	9.43419	14.5903	22.4724	34.4737	52.6763	80.1790	121.577	183.664	276.442	414.591	619.580
47	4.01185	6.31776	9.90590	15.4657	24.0454	37.2316	57.4172	88.1969	134.951	205.704	312.379	472.633	712.517
48	4.13220	6.57047	10.4011	16.3937	25.7286	40.2101	62.5847	97.0166	149.795	230.388	352.989	538.802	819.394
49	4.25617	6.83329	10.9212	17.3773	27.5296	43.4269	68.2173	106.718	166.273	258.035	398.877	614.234	942.303
50	4.38385	7.10662	11.4673	18.4199	29.4567	46.9010	74.3569	117.390	184.563	288.999	450.731	700.227	**1083.64**

Assume you have $10,000 to invest annually for 10 years at a rate of return of 8 percent compounded.

Using the table, you find a factor of 2.15892 where the lines for Year 10 and 8% intersect. Since the factor number is for the amount of 1 compounded, you will need to multiply the number by $10,000 to arrive at the value of the $10,000 annual investment at the end of 10 years, $215,892.00 ($10,000 × 2.15892).

DRIPs

The growing popularity of dividend reinvestment plans (DRIPs) became further evident in July 1994 as industry giant Charles Schwab and discount broker counterpart Quick & Reilly announced enhancements to their DRIP services. Effective August 15, 1994, Charles Schwab eliminated transaction fees it charges clients who reinvest dividends. Likewise, Quick & Reilly launched a DRIP option that enables customers to automatically reinvest their dividends and keep track of all their reinvestment activity as part of their regular monthly statement.

Just what are DRIPs? Simply stated, they are plans in which the cash dividends, instead of being paid out to the shareholder, are reinvested in the company's stock (a few plans allow for investment in other stock as well). In addition, many of the DRIP programs permit the purchase of additional shares of company stock for cash within predetermined limits and specified times during the year. Further, the plans provide for periodic shareholder statements showing account activity, the number of shares purchased, and the balance of shares in the account.

Too many investors miss out on investment compounding opportunities either by not being aware of the significant benefits offered by DRIPs or by not taking advantage of them. Dividend reinvestment plans offer a number of advantages to investors. First of all, many of the corporate sponsors of DRIPs pick up the tab for administration costs and commission charges for stock purchases. The lower your acquisition cost, the quicker you can turn a profit and the higher your return on investment.

Second, being able to sell the stock through the company DRIP program means you can eliminate commissions on both ends of the transaction. When the company does charge a sales fee, the commission may still be smaller than that charged by your broker. Third, as mentioned previously, many companies allow the purchase of additional shares for cash within minimum and maximum ranges. This enables you to build your portfolio faster at a lower cost.

Fourth, some companies allow their shareholders to purchase company stock at a discount from its market price, providing an immediate built-in profit margin. Fifth, some plans allow you to register the shares purchased through dividend reinvestment in an account assigned to another person. For example, your dividend reinvestment purchases could be placed in children's custodial accounts. Finally, the ease of increasing your stock holdings is another selling point for DRIPs. A few moments of paperwork and you are on your way to building your investment portfolio in DRIPs.

A stock yielding 10 percent annually would return your original investment after 10 years. However, if you reinvested those 10 percent cash dividends and allowed them to compound at the same rate, you would earn your original investment back in only seven years and three months.

Vita Nelson, editor of *The Moneypaper,* calls DRIPs "the stock market investor's secret weapon for developing a widely diversified portfolio of stocks purchased via dollar cost averaging."

Of course, you wouldn't purchase a stock just because it offered a dividend reinvestment program. The stock would still have to fit your diversification, investment goal, and risk posture considerations.

But don't worry. There are plenty of companies in a wide variety of industries that offer DRIPs. You can choose from more than 1,000 firms with DRIP programs, around 85 percent of which permit shareholders to purchase additional shares of company stock, above and beyond dividend reinvestments, for cash.

There are some considerations that need to be addressed:

- You will be taxed on the cash dividends even though you did not receive the cash.

- Since dividends are reinvested automatically at periodic intervals, you forgo the option to time your purchases.

- Since the stock acquired through the DRIP is bought at an average price, you will not get the lowest price available.

- You need to determine whether you need the current income stream from cash dividends to maintain your standard of living.

- Some DRIP sponsors have instituted administration fees which make their programs far less attractive. Make sure you read the DRIP agreement carefully before you sign on the dotted line.

- There's another possible tax bite. If you purchase the stock at a discount from market price, you will incur a tax liability for the price difference.

Overall, the benefits far outweigh the minor drawbacks associated with DRIPs. They make good ecomomic sense for the majority of shareholders. Instead of cashing those dividend checks and frivolously spending the money, put those funds to work compounding your investment return. You'll be far better off over the long run.

Where can you find information on dividend reinvestment programs? As a start, check the back page or two of the company's annual report. It typically states whether a dividend reinvestment program is available and how to contact the proper source for material on the DRIP. There's often a toll-free number to call for information.

Your broker can be of help to determine whether a particular company has a DRIP program. Value Line and Standard & Poor's tear sheets list whether DRIPs are available. Both can be located in most city and university libraries.

Another source of DRIP information is Standard & Poor's *Directory of Reinvestment Plans* ($39.95). It includes listings of DRIP programs, listings of DRIPs where $1,000 invested grew to $6,500 or more over the 10-year period ending December 31, 1993, and DRIP companies where dividends have increased 70 percent or more over the five-year period 1989-93. Other helpful features include a listing of American Depositary Receipts (ADRs) with DRIPs and DRIPs stocks with S&P's A+ quality ranking. Standard & Poor's Corporation can be contacted at 25 Broadway, New York, New York 10004, or call 800-221-5277.

Evergreen Enterprises publishes an annual guide, *Directory of Companies Offering Dividend Reinvestment Plans.* It can be purchased for $28.95 plus $2 shipping and handling. You can contact Evergreen Enterprises at P.O. Box 763, Laurel, Maryland 20725-0763, or call 301-549-3939. The company also supplies a software program, *Dividend Reinvestment Plan Portfolio Tracker,* for keeping a running record of dividend reinvestment plan transactions and market value.

The Moneypaper offers *Guide to Dividend Reinvestment Plans* for $25. The guide is published four times a year and *Moneypaper* subscribers can purchase it for $9. Subscribers to *The Moneypaper* can benefit from its Direct Stock Purchase Plan program, which helps investors acquire the first share needed for enrollment in the DRIPs of approximately 520 companies. The investment newsletter features regular coverage of direct purchase plans (see the Buy Direct section later in Part 1), the market outlook, several tracked portfolios, and *The Moneypaper* DRP 63 Index (see Chart 1–3). You can order a one-year subscription at one-half off for $36. Contact *The Moneypaper* at 1010 Mamaroneck Avenue, Mamaroneck, New York 10543, or call 800-388-9993.

The Moneypaper compiles and reports on its unique DRP 63 Index, based on reinvested dividends. It tracks the performance of companies offering dividend reinvestment plans for comparison with other indices such as the Dow Jones Industrial Average (DJIA) and Standard & Poor's 500 (S&P 500). *The Moneypaper* DRP 63 Index follows 63 stocks to represent the universe of companies offering dividend reinvestment plans.

Table 1–7 shows the track record for major stock indices through the first half of June 1994.

Chart 1–3 The Moneypaper DRP 63 Index™

104.09

Company	1/1/94	Now	Value		Company	1/1/94	Now	Value
Abbott Labs	29.63	29.63	101.91		Kmart	21.50	17.25	82.56
AFLAC	28.50	35.63	126.26		Limited (The)	17.00	21.38	126.93
Am. Water Works	30.00	27.38	94.03		MacDonald's	28.50	27.88	97.98
Avery Dennison	29.38	34.38	118.87		MM& Mfg.	54.38	54.38	101.69
Bemis Co.	23.63	24.50	105.45		Mobil	79.13	83.00	107.15
Block (H&R)	40.75	43.50	108.97		Monsanto	73.38	80.88	112.01
Campbell Soup	41.00	38.50	96.02		National Fuel Gas	34.00	30.63	93.41
Caterpillar	89.00	113.25	128.08		New Eng. Elec.	39.13	32.13	85.97
Citicorp	36.88	44.13	120.55		PepsiCo	40.88	33.75	83.36
Coca-cola	44.63	46.25	104.67		Phelps Dodge	48.75	63.00	131.10
ConAgra	26.38	32.38	125.00		Phillip Morris	55.63	60.75	113.42
Diebold	40.17	42.38	106.65		Pitney Bowes	41.38	37.50	91.77
Duke Power	42.38	38.00	91.96		Quaker Oats	71.00	79.88	115.10
Engelhard	24.38	26.88	111.18		Questar	33.00	30.00	92.43
Exxon	63.13	59.25	96.04		Roadway Services	60.00	63.50	107.50
Fed. Nat'l Mtge.	78.50	88.00	114.49		Rochester Tele.	22.56	22.88	104.08
First Union	41.25	46.00	113.66		RPM Inc.	17.38	17.63	103.63
Ford Motor	54.58	29.50	93.55		Rubbermaid	34.75	27.63	80.47
Gannett	57.25	49.75	88.55		St. Paul Cos	44.94	42.13	96.26
General Electric	52.44	49.88	96.46		Sara Lee	25.00	22.00	89.91
Georgia Pacific	68.75	74.25	109.37		SCANA Corp.	49.75	44.63	93.85
Gillette	59.63	71.38	120.98		Schering-Plough	68.50	69.00	103.02
GTE Corp.	35.00	31.50	94.03		SBC Corp.	41.50	41.25	102.22
Hannaford Bros.	21.50	24.00	112.51		Synovus Finan.	18.63	18.88	103.10
Hanson PLC ADRs	20.00	19.63	101.78		Time Warner	44.25	37.50	85.13
Harley-Davidson	44.13	56.13	127.52		TRW Inc.	69.25	73.50	107.53
Hershey Foods	49.00	46.00	95.09		Union Pacific	62.63	58.00	94.54
Home Depot	39.50	44.25	112.31		VF Corp.	46.13	52.13	114.52
Huntington Bank	23.63	20.50	112.00		Walgreen	40.88	37.50	92.48
Intel	62.00	64.23	103.80		Wendy's Int'l	17.38	15.63	90.87
Johns. & Johns.	44.88	50.13	113.23		WMX Tech.	26.38	29.75	114.68
Jostens	19.75	17.88	93.91					

The first column shows the price on 1/1/94, when $100 was invested to create this index. The second column shows the price now, and the third column shows the current value of the shares owned.

Source: *The Moneypaper*

Table 1–7   Stock Indices Performance

(January 1, 1994, through June 16, 1994)

	Moneypaper Drp 63	DJIA	S&P 500	NASDAQ Composite	American Exchange
1-01-94	100.00	3754.09	466.45	776.80	477.15
6-16-94	97.49	3646.65	446.20	706.85	424.72
(LOSS)	(2.51%)	(2.86%)	(4.34%)	(9.00%)	(10.99%)

Source: *The Moneypaper*

Since mid-June, the DRP 63 Index hit a high of 105.03 before settling back to the 104.09 level by the end of August. The DRP 63 Index spent the entire month of August ahead of the DJIA. For the year to date, it outperformed the DJIA by 17 percent and outpaced the S&P 500 and NASDAQ Composite by even greater margins.

Clearly, the power of compounding by reinvesting dividends can help boost your returns and lower your risk posture. Equally important, as the index and its performance indicates, is the ability to pick the right stocks to add to your portfolio. A diversifed portfolio of quality companies offering DRIPs can help boost your overall portfolio performance and add a degree of protection against major downside moves, thus reducing your risk posture.

Charles B. Carlson, CFA, author of *Buying Stocks Without a Broker* (New York: McGraw-Hill, 1992), and editor of *Dow Theory Forecasts*, launched a new investment newsletter, *DRIP Investor*, at an annual subscription price of $59. You can subscribe by contacting *DRIP Investor* at 7412 Calumet Avenue, Hammond, Indiana 46324-2692, or call 219–931–6480.

DRIP Investor informs investors on companies offering dividend reinvestment plans, gives advice on how to start your own DRIP investing program, provides tax strategies for DRIP investors, advises how to dodge the broker on first-time purchases to qualify for the DRIP programs, and discusses DRIP model portfolios. The investment newsletter also provides full-page coverage of individual companies offering DRIPs, complete with important statistical data. A subscription entitles you to a free copy of the annually updated directory of DRIPs.

Buying Stocks Without a Broker sells for $16.95 retail but can be obtained free with a subscription to *DRIP Investor*. This handy and informative reference includes a directory of more than 900 companies with DRIPS, a performance rating of most stocks available through DRIPs, strategies for using the cash investment option to make your portfolio grow, and instructions for getting started in dividend reinvestment plans.

All you need to qualify for DRIP programs is to be a company stock-holder. One share of company stock will get you registered as a shareholder of record in most DRIPs and open the doors to commission savings, compounding earnings, and improved portfolio return. If you currently own shares in a company with a DRIP and are a shareholder of record, you automatically qualify for DRIP enrollment. Some plans permit DRIP enrollment for shareholders who have their shares registered in "street name" at their broker, but there may be some charges to handle the extra paperwork associated with such accounts.

The enrollment process is easy. Just contact the company's Shareholders' or Investors' Relations Department, or the trustee handling the company's DRIP, and request a plan prospectus and enrollment forms. Fill out the forms, send in your payment if making a cash purchase of stock, and you're on the road to increasing your investment return in DRIPs. It's that simple.

Some companies prefer to send you a certificate before they officially enroll you in their plan. Other companies take the book entry route and record your initial share purchase in the plan. The latter method makes more sense from a practical standpoint.

The Moneypaper allows investors to avoid purchasing that first share through a broker and incurring large commissions. Subscribers to the investment newsletter can purchase shares of approximately 520 companies with DRIPs via the Direct Stock Purchase Plan program. *The Moneypaper* will purchase and transfer the share to you and then instruct the plan agent to enroll you in the DRIP for a small fee.

Along similar lines, the National Association of Investors Corporation offers its members its Low Cost Investment Plan, which purchases the initial shares for interested members to gain entry into specific DRIPs. NAIC then instructs the plan trustee or administrator to transfer the shares out of its account and into the names of those making the investment. You do not have to be a member of an investment club to avail yourself of this service. There is a small NAIC administration fee for handling the transaction. The NAIC can be contacted at 711 West Thirteen Mile Road, Madison Heights, Michigan 48071, or call 810-583-6242. For more information on the Low Cost Investment Plan and participating companies, refer to Part 3 of this book.

Still another option for obtaining that first share of company stock is to become a member of First Share. While First Share doesn't sell you shares or purchase them directly, it does connect you with a member willing to sell you the share you desire to purchase. Your cost includes market price for the share and minimal fees for each company to First Share and the member selling you the stock.

There's one catch: You have to agree to sell shares to other First Share members for a small fee. You can recoup part of your cost in this way. First

Share also publishes a directory of 100 top DRIPs for $12.95. Membership costs $15 per year. First Share also has a Buy One Share Before You Join option. You can reach First Share at P.O. Box 222, Westcliffe, CO 81252-0222, or call 800-683-0743.

A limited number of companies at present allow you to purchase that initial share directly from them to avoid any broker commission charges or fees for entering the DRIP. There may be a minimum purchase requirement required by some of these firms. Companies allowing the initial stock purchase directly from them include Arrow Financial Corporation, Atmos Energy, Central Vermont Public Service, Exxon Corporation, W. R. Grace & Company, SCANA Corporation, and Texaco, Inc. In addition, other companies allow residents of their state to make their initial stock purchase directly from the firm. These include Bancorp Hawaii, Florida Progress Corporation, Hawaiian Electric Industries, Inc., and WICOR, Inc. (Wisconsin).

A limited number of companies permit the enrollment in DRIPs through individual retirement accounts (IRAs). This option gives you the opportunity to tax-shelter your compounded earnings. Centerior Energy Company and Exxon Corporation are two firms that provide the IRA DRIP option.

DRIPs in Action

One of the major attractions of long-term DRIP investing is the power of compounding. This feature is further enhanced by corporate growth, because a company's cash dividend payout also increases, making dividend reinvestment a growing percentage of the investor's total return.

This point is clearly illustrated in the November 1993 issue of NAIC's *Better Investing,* the organization's investing magazine.

For example, a $10,000 investment in Peoples Energy Corporation would have purchased 1,000 shares of the company's stock on January 15, 1983. A little over 10 years later, on April 15, 1993, those shares would have grown to a market value of $31,750, repesenting an attractive double-digit return of nearly 12 percent.

However, had the investor belonged to the company's DRIP and had steadfastly reinvested those cash dividends to purchase additional shares of Peoples Energy Corporation stock, the shareholder would have ended up owning another 1,140 shares for a grand total of 2,140 shares worth $67,934, for an annualized return in excess of 20 percent.

Peoples Energy is a representative example of how DRIPs can go to work for you. Of course, not all DRIPs or their companies are created equal, so you must do your investigative work to ferret out the best investment candidates. Review the prospects for the industry in which the company operates, and evaluate which companies are most likely to outperfrom their industry counterparts. Unless a firm's earnings increase, it is unlikely that its stock price will rise substantially or that its cash dividends will rise.

DRIPs at a Discount

A variety of companies offer their shares at a discount from market price to entice DRIP purchases. The average discount ranges from 3 percent to 5 percent off the market price, but there are some discounts as high as 10 percent. A word of caution: Some companies may have to offer discounts to lure funds because a poor performance record and financial risk rendered them unable to attract sufficient capital by more-traditional financing methods.

The following companies represent only a portion of those that give shareholders a price break of 3 percent or more on purchases through the company's dividend reinvestment plan. The discount may only apply to dividend reinvestments and not cash purchases.

Company	*Percent Discount*
American Express Company	3
American Water Works Company	5
Atmos Energy Corporation	3
BC Gas Inc.	5
Bancorp Hawaii, Inc.	5
Bay State Gas Company	3
Blount Inc.	5
Chase Manhattan Bank Corporation	5/3*
Crestar Financial Corporation	5
EnergyNorth Inc.	5
First Interstate Bancorp	3
Fleming Companies	5
HRE Properties	5
Health Care REIT Inc.	4
Hibernia Corporation	5
Kemper Corporation	5
Kennametal Inc.	5
Maxus Energy Corporation	3
National City Corporation	3
Oneida Ltd.	5
Pacific Telesis Group	3.5
Piccadilly Cafeterias Inc.	5
Telephone & Data Systems, Inc.	5
Tenneco Inc.	3
UGI Corporation	5
Wells Fargo & Company	3
York Financial Corporation	10

*5 percent discount on dividend reinvestment and 3 percent discount on cash purchases

DRIP Diversification

As a percentage of organizations offering DRIPs, banks and utility companies rank the highest, but you can see from the listing that a wide variety of companies offer such programs. They range from industrial companies to insurance firms, from consumer products firms to mining companies, and from real estate investment trusts (REITs) to medical services providers. In other words, there are plenty of choices from which to construct a diversified portfolio.

You can take that diversification one step further by investing in Canadian companies having DRIP programs. For example, Bank of Nova Scotia (banking), Dofasco Inc. (steel), Inco Limited (nickel and copper), and Hudson's Bay Company (retail) represent north-of-the-border DRIP opportunities. Taking a global approach, a number of foreign companies traded as American Depositary Receipts (ADRs) on United States stock exchanges also allow their shareholders to purchase additional shares through DRIPs. Among the more prominent foreign companies offering such programs are the United Kingdom's British Airways (transportation), Glaxco Holdings (pharmaceuticals), and SmithKline Beecham (medical instruments and pharmaceuticals), as well as Sweden's Volvo (automobiles).

A final way to diversify using DRIPs is to invest in closed-end funds with a DRIP. Examples include Allied Capital Corp., Blue Chip Value Fund, InterCapital Income Securities Inc., Patriot Global Dividend Fund, Templeton Global Income Fund Inc., Worldwide Value Fund Inc., Zweig Fund Inc., and Zweig Total Return Fund Inc.

Cash Purchase Option

In addition to employing compounding and purchasing stock at a discount to reduce acquisition costs and boost portfolio performance, you can also take advantage of the cash purchase option that is a feature of some company DRIPs. This provision permits you to purchase company stock for cash, above and beyond what you purchase with your reinvested dividends.

The beauty of the cash purchase option is that it allows you to accumulate your investment in the company faster and cheaper. You avoid paying the broker commissions and in some cases can also purchase the stock at a discount from market value. Permitted cash purchases can range from as low as $10 a month to as much as $25,000 or more per quarter.

The following companies are but a few of the firms that make provision for cash purchases of company stock through their DRIP.

Company	Cash Purchase Option	Discount
American Brands Inc.	$100–10,000/Qtr	N/A
Bay State Gas Company	10–2,000/Mo	3%
Burnham Pacific Properties	100–5,000/Qtr	5%
Chase Manhattan Bank Corp.	100–2,000/Mo	3%
Goodyear Tire & Rubber Company	10–15,000/Qtr	N/A
IBM	10–25,000/Qtr	N/A
The Limited, Inc.	30–6,000/Qtr	N/A
Mellon Bank Corporation	100/Mo–50,000/Yr	3%
Nalco Chemical Company	50–15,000/Qtr	N/A
Pfizer, Inc.	10–10,000/Mo	N/A
Questar Corporation	50–15,000/Qtr	N/A
Reynolds Metals Company	25–3,000/Qtr	N/A
SunTrust Banks Inc.	10/Mo–60,000/Yr	N/A
Tambrands, Inc.	25–24,000/Yr	N/A
USX Corporation	50–10,000/Mo	N/A
Whirlpool Corporation	10–3,000/Qtr	N/A

The Moneypaper suggests paying close attention to dividend cycles and using timing to generate extra dividends. The strategy works like this: You can earn an extra 30 days of dividends with a timing device as long as the company accepts investments on a monthly basis and pays dividends on a quarterly basis. It works even better with companies that invest more than once a month.

Send in your optional cash investment the month after the dividend is paid. The money you invest will earn a dividend in 60 days, rather than 90 days. If you invest quarterly, you can take advantage of this strategy four times a year.

For example, Rubbermaid invests optional cash on the first of each month and its quarterly dividend is paid on March 1, June 1, September 1, and December 1. The stock goes ex-dividend around four weeks before the payment dates.

It is best to send in your investment the month after the dividend date. If you send it in to coincide with the dividend, you will get your dividend in 90 days. If you send the investment the month after, you will get the dividend on this investment in 60 days.

Selling DRIP Holdings

There are several ways to dispose of your DRIP investments. For one, you can request the transfer agent to liquidate your shares. This has the advantage of lower costs compared with broker commissions but has the drawbacks of possibly not getting the best price and having to wait for the sale execution, since your stock will be sold at the next date specified in the plan. You may also incur a termination fee for closing your DRIP account.

To sell through your broker, you will need to get a stock certificate if you do not already have it. This can be obtained by requesting one from the transfer agent or plan administrator. Make sure to request your certificate in plenty of time beacuse it may take several weeks or more for the paperwork to be processed and your stock certificate to arrive in the mail.

Uncle Sam's Take

At one time, you could take advantage of tax-sheltering your dividend income until the shares purchased through a DRIP were sold. In 1986 Congress closed that tax loophole, and you are now required to report and pay income taxes on dividends whether received in cash or reinvested in company stock.

In other words, you incur a tax liablility and subsequent outflow of cash to pay taxes on income earned but not yet received in cash (since you reinvested the dividends). Sorry, but those are the tax facts of life. However, you can be reassured that those dividends are working to compound your investment for superior total returns.

When you sell the shares purchased through a DRIP you need only report the increase in value as a taxable gain. Remember, you already paid income tax on the value of the dividend which purchased the shares. For example, if you received a $300 dividend and had it invested in company stock through a DRIP, you pay tax on the $300 dividend income in the year of the dividend payment date. Later, if you sell those shares for $400, you will owe tax only on the $100 gain ($400 − $300).

The tax laws regarding holding periods and short-term and long-term capital gains work the same for sales of DRIP stock as for any other security investment. If you hold the investment property for more than one year, your gain or loss is a long-term capital gain or loss. On the other hand, if you sell the investment within a year or less, your gain is a short-term capital gain, taxed at higher rates. For stock acquired through DRIPs, the acquisition date is the date the bank or other agent purchases the stock. Full shares are considered purchased first and fractional shares purchased last.

You can also run afoul of the IRS if you purchase stock at a discount. The value of the discount (the difference between the market price and the price you paid) is taxable too. When figuring this amount, use the fair market value of the stock on the dividend payment date.

The Company Perspective

Why do companies sponsor dividend reinvestment plans? After all, there must be a mound of paperwork to keep track of and lots of expense to monitor shareholder accounts.

Actually, there are plenty of solid reasons for firms to have a DRIP:

- Firms like a stable shareholder base, which helps cut down on administrative expense and keeps the company's shares safe from potential unfriendly takeover raiders.

- A large shareholder base can also contribute to market support for the company's stock price.

- It's a relatively inexpensive method of raising capital on an ongoing basis.

- DRIPs help build good shareholder relations through the low acquisition costs and other benefits afforded the shareholder.

- Companies look on shareholders as potential long-term customers of their products and services.

Synthetic DRIPs

There's another way to utilize dividend reinvestment to bolster your total return, even if the company does not sponsor a DRIP. Some innovative brokerage firms have adopted the DRIP concept to permit their clients to reinvest cash dividends, even though the company may not have a DRIP in place. This greatly expands the ability to reinvest your dividends and compound your earnings, since you are no longer limited to those companies with DRIPs.

Instead of having your cash dividends placed in a low-interest-bearing money market account or sent directly to you, the synthetic DRIP programs direct your cash dividends into a reinvestment process that allows you to purchase fractional shares in company stock. Typically, the brokerage firm charges a mimimal fee based on a percentage and/or dollar figure. As mentioned earlier, Charles Schwab eliminated transaction fees for customers who use its dividend reinvestment services.

While each brokerage DRIP program may differ slightly, the basics are the same from one firm to another. Dividend reinvestment is available on more than 3,500 stocks traded on U.S. exchanges. A phone call puts the plan into action. Simply tell your broker for which stocks you want the cash dividend reinvested. The firm takes care of the purchase and record-keeping requirements and provides you with dividend reinvestment activity detail on your regular monthly account statement.

To date, none of the synthetic DRIPs allow you to make additional commission-free stock purchases for cash or to purchase stock at a discount from market price.

Brokerage firms offering the synthetic DRIP programs in addition to Charles Schwab include Alex Brown & Sons, Marquette de Bary Company, Merrill Lynch, and Prudential Securities.

Buying Direct

A growing number of companies are opting to sell shares directly to investors with no commission. From just two or three firms providing this money-saving benefit just a few years ago, the list has expanded to nearly 20. In a little over a year, Exxon Corporation attracted more than 187,000 investors to its buy-direct program. It's a win/win situation for everyone involved. The company gains new investors and a cheap source of capital, while the investor reduces his or her investment acquisition costs.

The following companies allow you to avoid the broker's commission bite by buying shares directly from them. Only DQE charges a one-time fee of $5 for administration costs. DQE's direct stock purchase program is not available to residents of Arizona, Florida, Nebraska, North Carolina, North Dakota, Ohio, Oklahoma, or Vermont.

Company	Telephone	Minimum Investment
American Recreation Centers	916-852-8005	$100
Arrow Financial Corporation	518-793-4121	25
Atlantic Energy, Inc.	609-645-4506	250
Barnett Bank Inc.	800-854-5798	250
Central Vermont Public Service	802-747-5406	50
DQE Company	800-247-0400	100
Dial Corporation	800-453-2235	100
Exxon Corporation	800-252-1800	250
First Alabama Bancshares Inc.	205-832-8859	20
Interchange Financial Services	201-703-4508	10
Johnson Controls Inc.	800-828-1489	50
Kellwood Company	314-576-3100	100
Kerr-McGee Corporation	800-786-1556	750
Mobil Corporation	800-648-9291	250
SCANA Corporation	800-763-5891	250
Texaco Inc.	800-283-9785	250
US West, Inc.	800-537-0222	300

There's an old Wall Street adage that "there's no such thing as a free lunch." DRIPs and direct purchase programs may prove that saying obsolete.

Ferreting Out DRIP Candidates

The NAIC recommends the current edition of *Moody's Handbook of Dividend Achievers* as a great place to start your search for excellent DRIP candidates for your portfolio. *Moody's* has already performed the chore of sifting through its 13,000-plus company database of equities. More to the point, *Moody's* provides you with a wealth of business and statistical information with which to begin your search. It supplies company and industry data, historical and current financial information, and more. *Moody's Handbook* also includes a number of handy rankings such as dividend growth over the past 10 years and the firms with the highest number of consecutive dividend increases. The list of 325 companies provides fertile ground for seeking out top dividend performers to add to your dividend reinvestment program.

Periodically, Standard & Poor's *The Outlook* publishes a listing of companies that have paid a cash dividend for at least 50 consecutive years and have increased dividend payments for the past five years. Other criteria include possessing a yield matching or exceeding that of the S&P 500 and receiving an S&P rank of four or five stars. The 29 firms ranked as 1993 Dividend Achievers are listed below.

Company	*Industry*
American Express Company	Financial and travel services
Anheuser-Busch Companies, Inc.	Beverage and food products
Beneficial Corporation	Financial services
EI Du Pont de Nemours & Company	Chemical
Dun & Bradstreet Corporation	Publishing
First of America Bank Corporation	Banking
First Tennessee National Corp.	Banking
First Union Corporation	Banking
Florida Progress Corporation	Utility
GATX Corporation	Railcar leasing/transportation
H.J. Heinz Company	Food products
Johnson & Johnson Company	Healthcare products
Mercantile Stores Company, Inc.	Department Stores
Minnesota Mining & Mfg. Company	Industrial and consumer tapes
Monsanto Company	Chemical
Norfolk Southern Corporation	Railroad
Ohio Casualty Corporation	Insurance

Company	Industry
Old Kent Financial Corporation	Banking
PPG Industries Inc.	Glass/paint
Peoples Energy Corporation	Utility
Pfizer, Inc.	Pharmaceutical
Quaker Oats Company	Food products
SAFECO Corporation	Insurance
Thomas & Betts Corporation	Electrical/electronics
Transamerica Corporation	Insurance
UST, Inc.	Tobacco
U.S. Trust Corporation	Banking
Washington Gas Light Company	Utility
Wilmington Trust Corporation	Banking

The NAIC Computer Group developed a Dividend Superscreen to aid investors. It includes approximately two dozen key pieces of dividend information on each of the 200 companies in the NAIC's *Better Investing* magazine's annual Top 100 and Second 100 listings of companies held by investment clubs. See Part 4, Investment Club Top Picks.

The group identified and selected database items that should prove invaluable to investors seeking dividend information. Examples of data provided for each of the 200 stocks include dividend indicated rate, indicated dividend yield, dividend payout rate, dividend five-year growth, number of dividend increases in the last five years, and S&P ranking.

The computer screen also provides information on related fundamentals such as long-term debt to capital, earnings stability, and cash flow to earnings, which could have an impact on a specific company's ability to continue to pay or grow its dividends.

AUSTIN PRYOR'S DIVIDENDS/ VALUE BENCHMARK TECHNIQUE

Austin Pryor, publisher of the investment newsletter *Sound Mind Investing* in Louisville, Kentucky, suggests employing dividends as a benchmark for value. According to Pryor, common sense dictates that the value of a company should derive, at least in part, from the following three items: (1) the assets owned by the business, (2) the level of annual profits earned, and (3) the dividends paid to shareholders.

When assessing the market as a whole, Pryor uses the level of dividends paid to shareholders each year as a benchmark. Chart 1–4 shows the price movement of the Dow Jones Industrial Average from 1967 to 1992 with a corresponding graph of the price-to-dividends ratio over the same time frame. The price-to-dividends ratio (p/d) represents how much investors are

Chart 1–4   Price-to-Dividends Ratio

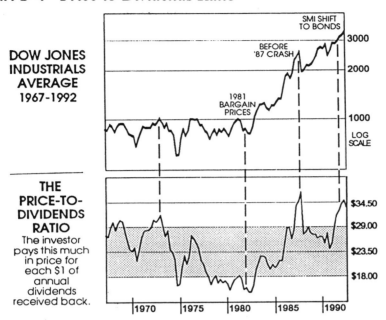

DOW JONES INDUSTRIALS AVERAGE 1967-1992

SMI SHIFT TO BONDS

BEFORE '87 CRASH

1981 BARGAIN PRICES

3000

2000

1000

LOG SCALE

THE PRICE-TO-DIVIDENDS RATIO
The investor pays this much in price for each $1 of annual dividends received back.

$34.50

$29.00

$23.50

$18.00

1970   1975   1980   1985   1990

Source: Sound Mind Investing

willing to pay for each $1 in annual dividends they receive in return for their investment.

The p/d is calculated by dividing the current price level by the dividends received by shareholders over the past 12 months. When the Dow stood as 3397 in mid-1992, the amount of cash dividends paid out during the previous 12 months totaled $101.61. Thus, the p/d ratio calculated out to $33.43 (3397/$101.61).

The p/d for an individual stock can also be determined as follows. For example, if a stock currently commands a market price of $45 per share and that company's shareholders earned cash dividends totaling $2 per share over the past 12 months, that company's stock would have a price-to-dividends (p/d) ratio of 22½ (45/2).

Historically, the ratio for the market as a whole has been between $18 and $29 roughly one-half of the time (as indicated by the shaded area on Chart 1–4). Pryor calls this shaded area the fair value range. Approximately one-fourth of the time, the p/d ratio is below $18, falling into bargain territory. The other approximately one-fourth of the time, the p/d ratio rises above $18, making stocks relatively expensive in terms of the price-to-dividends ratio benchmark.

Excursions into expensive territory are typically brief. The p/d ratio returns to the fair range as stock prices fall, dividends rise, or a combination of both takes place. A research project published in the Stock Market Logic newsletter showed how the S&P 500 performed in the past once the p/d ratio reached an extreme reading of $34. On average, the stock market declined 5 percent within the end of a one year period and 10 percent by the end of two years. Historically, investors have experienced a drop in their shares' value during the first two years when purchasing at overvalued levels as indicated by the p/d ratio.

A free sample of Austin Pryor's investment newsletter, *Sound Mind Investing*, can obtained by writing to SMI, P.O. Box 22128-E, Louisville, KY 40252-0128. An annual subscription costs $59.

Of course, there's a wealth of investment information sources to help you narrow down your investment candidates search. Check out the following in your local or university library, or order your own subscription to the ones which work best for you. Of the myriad of investment newsletters and investment publications on the market, I find those listed below especially helpful in uncovering growth and value companies having the ability to generate higher earnings and excess cash for steadily increasing dividends.

Barron's
200 Burnett Road
Chicopee, MA 01020
Annual subscription $129
26-week trial $66

Investor's Business Daily
P.O. Box 66370
Los Angeles, CA 90066-0370
800-443-3113
Annual subscription $169
Six-month trial $94

Moody's Handbook of Div. Achievers
Moody's Investors Service
99 Church Street
New York, NY 10007
212-553-0300

Standard & Poor's *The Outlook*
25 Broadway
New York, NY 10004
800-852-1641
Annual subscription $289

United & Babson Inv. Report
101 Prescott Street
Wellesley Hills, MA 02181
617-235-0900
Periodic specials

The Wall Street Journal
200 Liberty Street
New York, NY 10281
800-JOURNAL
Annual subcription $149

Morningstar ADRs
Morningstar
225 West Wacker Drive
Chicago, IL 60606
800-876-5005
Annual subscription $195

The Value Line Investment Survey
Value Line Publishing Company
220 East 42nd Street
New York, NY 10017-5891
800-833-0046
Annual subscription $525
10-week Trial $55

Wall Street Transcript
Wall Street Transcript Corp.
100 Wall Street
New York, NY 10005
212-490-3258
Annual subscription $1,890

Your Money
Consumers Digest, Inc.
5708 N. Lincoln Avenue
Chicago, IL 60659
312-275-3590
Annual subscription $15.97
Periodic specials

Now that we've seen the profiles of successful investment clubs and discussed investment philosophy and key investment principles such as compounding and diversification, it's time to turn to Part 2, Successful Investment Club Profiles.

Successful Investment Club Profiles

THE INVESTMENT CLUB ADVANTAGE

Looking for a good way to beat those paltry returns now being offered by certificates of deposit, savings accounts, and money market accounts? If so, then consider joining an investment club. You would be putting yourself in good company. Today, around 25,000 investment clubs operate in the United States, 10,000 more than in 1980. The National Association of Investors Corporation (NAIC) sports a membership of nearly 12,000 investment clubs with over 217,000 members. In addition, the NAIC has approximately 43,000 individual members not belonging to a specific club. The personal portfolio of all NAIC members combined totals in excess of $20 billion, and the average personal portfolio is around $109,000.

The average NAIC investment club has been investing in common stocks for approximately $9\frac{1}{4}$ years with an investment portfolio around $89,000. More than 1,000 of the NAIC investment clubs are 20 years old. More than 53 percent of investment club members have a college education, and more than 36 percent have studied for advanced degrees. Around 90 percent have family incomes exceeding $25,000. The majority of club members, 50.4 percent, are female.

Members derive a number of benefits:

- The low monthly cash outlay is affordable by just about anybody, enabling one to build up an investment portfolio in small, easy pieces.

- There's safety in numbers. Several people evaluating a stock purchase are less likely to make that big wrong decision that decimates the portfolio.

- Sharing investment knowledge and research with others covers a lot more ground than an individual can.

- The pooling of investment money allows investors to own a wider range of stocks than otherwise possible.

Investment meetings can be quite informative. Members can present potential stock purchase candidates, or the club can invite a special speaker such as an investment broker, tax accountant, estate planner, or other investment or personal finance specialist.

However, one of the best, and most profitable, advantages of belonging to an investment club lies in the disciplined investment approach taken by most investment clubs, dollar cost averaging. Dollar cost averaging consists of investing the same amount of money on a regular basis.

The beauty of dollar cost averaging is that it prevents poor market timing and making a major investment at an inopportune time (at market peaks, for instance). Dollar cost averaging allows the purchase of shares at an average price that would be lower than if the shares were purchased at once through market timing. Dollar cost averaging and other formula investment programs were discussed in great detail in Part 1, Investment Club Strategies.

There's also the social aspect of club membership. Some clubs hold periodic get-togethers, such as a wine and cheese party or an annual meeting in Las Vegas or other intriguing spot, in addition to regular club investment meetings. Combining the serious investment and social aspects make for a great way to increase your wealth, in terms of both your financial performance and new friendships.

Where can you turn for information on how to set up an investment club and run it efficiently? The National Association of Investors Corporation, 711 West Thirteen Mile Road, Madison Heights, Michigan (810-583-6242), is a nonprofit organization dedicated to educating the individual investor and investment club members.

The association provides stock study materials and pamphlets that discuss starting your investment club. In addition, it sponsors investment seminars and publishes the investment magazine *Better Investing*. Informative articles help investors improve their investment skills. Topics such as understanding bank stocks, analyzing the management ingredient, and mutual fund investing aid in broadening members' investment perspectives and options. Other regular magazine features include Stocks to Study, Growth Stock Outlook, Technically Speaking, Undervalued Stocks, 5 Years Ago Stock to Study, and a cover story on timely investment topics. Regional notices inform members of upcoming seminars, workshops, and conferences.

Better Investing BITS is published 10 times a year and focuses on the use of computers in investing. The organization's Computer Group produces a Dividend Superscreen tool for uncovering investment candidates, while other NAIC investment software is also available for an additional charge. See Part 3, Putting It All Together, for a review of the investment software programs and information on how to order.

The NAIC also sponsors national, regional, and state investment seminars. Major benefits of the NAIC's investment seminars are their low cost structure, informative speakers, and their proximity to where you live. If you can't attend the national conference, there are regional and state conferences nearby for your convenience.

For example, in 1994 NAIC held its Investors Congress and Expo'94 on August 19-21 in Denver, Colorado. Seminar sessions included a discussion of the "Lease versus Purchase Option" by Ford Motor Company, "How to Turn $100 into $1,000 with Investment Clubs" by the NAIC, and "Playing the Market to Win" by Lewis J. Horowitz, executive vice president of the New York Stock Exchange. In addition, a variety of companies were on hand to answer questions and provide published information on their firm to prospective investors.

Other exhibitors included financial planning firms and investment counselors. Publishers such as Probus Publishing presented upcoming investment books. I and Don Cassidy, author of *Plugging into Utilities* and *It's Not What Stocks You Buy, It's When You Sell That Counts,* teamed up with Probus to discuss our investment books with Expo participants.

In October of 1994, the Denver Area Council hosted the Thirteenth Rocky Mountain Investors Fair in Aurora, Colorado, with four featured corporations giving presentations. The state and regional meetings provide a great opportunity to meet new people, trade investment ideas, and learn more about investing alternatives and products. There are state and regional seminars and workshops held across the country throughout the year. You do not have to be a club member to avail yourself of this tremendous opportunity.

In today's global investment environment, you can also opt to attend an investment conference overseas to gain a better perspective on international and global investment opportunities and information sources. For example, the 16th Congress of the World Federation of Investment Clubs met for four days in Innsbruck, Austria, in June 1994. Among seminar presentations by member organizations and corporations were country and regional reports and investment lectures. Corporations also put on exhibitions.

INDIVIDUAL INVESTOR INFORMATION

Another source of investment information for the individual investor or investment club is the American Association of Individual Investors (AAII), which can be contacted at 625 North Michigan Avenue, Chicago, Illinois 60611-3110, or call 312-280-0170. Membership privileges include an investment journal, discounts on investment publications and software, and investment seminars at reduced cost.

Annual membership dues are only $49 and include subscription to the association's *AAII Journal,* which comes out 10 times per year. Members also receive a free copy of *The Individual Investor's Guide to Low-Load Mutual Funds.* The association has in excess of 170,000 members in more than 60 local chapters throughout the United States.

The AAII assists individuals in becoming effective managers of their own investments. Obviously, their investment principles and information can be put to good use by individuals and investment clubs alike to outperform the market. According to an AAII survey, its members have earned an annual investment return 4.4 percent above that of the stock market as a whole.

Tools that the AAII provides the investor include stock screens that save time when searching for undervalued stocks; a year-end tax strategy guide to help reduce the tax bite; the AAII Quoteline to obtain real-time quotes on stocks, options, and mutual funds; reduced-cost investment seminars and study programs; *The Individual Investor's Guide to Computerized Investing;* and a listing of companies offering dividend reinvestment plans (DRIPs) and how to take advantage of them. For an extra fee, AAII members can purchase Stock Investor, a quarterly updated investment software program enabling investors to screen and analyze more than 7,000 stocks using 130 predetermined financial variables or custom made variables.

The *AAII Journal* provides subscribers with a wealth of investment information on a wide variety of topics, such as annuities, global portfolios with American Depositary Receipts (ADRs), special considerations of sector investing, the impact of currency changes on your investment portfolio, and financial planning. Regular features include articles on stock investing basics, mutual funds, and investor surveys.

Each year the AAII sponsors its Investment Education National Meeting. In 1994, it was held in Washington, D.C., and featured workshops on investigating how best to make asset allocations and manage your portfolio, understanding the critical financial decisions for retirement and estate planning, examining the various methods of valuing stocks and bonds, and learning how to select mutual funds to meet your financial needs and goals.

Across the border, the Canadian Shareowners Association (CSA) assists individual investors and investment clubs in achieving superior returns. The association teaches members proven strategies for successful, long-term investing in stocks and provides a Stock Selection Guide Manual to help investors ferret out quality growth stocks. In addition, the CSA provides listings of Canadian and U.S. companies participating in their Commission-Free Investing Program.

The CSA members receive the *Canadian Shareowner* magazine bi-monthly. The investment magazine provides basic investing information as well as in-depth analysis of individual stocks and mutual funds. CSA also publishes the *Guide Data Book 400* with ready-to-use company information on more than 400 Canadian and U.S. companies. Their database is also available in MS-DOS format.

To contact the Canadian Shareowners Association, write to 1090 University Avenue West, P.O. Box 7337, Windsor, Ontario, Canada N9C 4E9, or call 519-252-1555.

Whether or not you belong to an investment club, it is imperative that you take advantage of the best resources available. Search out investment information and resources just as you search out investment candidates. The better informed you are, the better investment decisions you will make.

SUCCESSFUL INVESTMENT CLUB PROFILES

Investment clubs are the unsung heroes of the investment world. Often, investment clubs outperform Wall Street's top money managers and the market averages. Indeed, as reported in *The Wall Street Journal,* more than 60 percent of investment clubs produced lifetime average compounded annual returns equal to or better than the stock market. Annual samples of NAIC investment club members reflect that NAIC members outperformed the Standard & Poor's 500 (S&P 500) Index two-thirds of the time in the past 18 years through 1993. That's even more impressive when you consider that 75 percent of all professional money managers fail to beat the S&P 500 every year.

The following NAIC investment clubs represent a good crosssection of top-performing investment clubs from across the nation. They range from relatively new clubs to clubs that have been in existence for 30 years or more. Further, each club membership is rich in diversity. You will meet people from all walks of life.

You will learn from the experience of several West Coast clubs in existence for more than 20 years as well as profit from younger clubs sporting respectable returns despite their recent arrival in the investment world. Diversity adds an important dimension to the investing equation.

In the balance of Part 2, we will look at how the top investment clubs are outperforming the pros. With a review of each club's investment philosophy and strategies, we will uncover how a group of amateur investors working together can make better investment decisions than the highest paid Wall Street professionals. The purchases and sales that made each club a top performer will be analyzed to uncover the investment rationale behind the transactions. In Part 4, Investment Club Top Picks, we will look at top investment club holdings.

Read on to learn how you, too can beat the big players on Wall Street at their own game. Investment clubs are a great way for beginning investors to learn investment strategy fundamentals without putting a large amount of money at stake. In effect, you earn while you learn. The regular periodic investing approach allows you to build up a substantial portfolio over a period of time without having to make a large investment at any one time.

Become a top investment performer in your own right by learning from the amateurs that beat the pros over and over again. Even more important than improved investment club performance is your opportunity to transfer what you've learned in your club meetings to your larger personal portfolio to improve its performance too.

The diversity of most investment club memberships brings a breadth of investment experience and knowledge to the group. In addition, individual members benefit from the research and investment candidates brought to the club by other members. Frequently this information would not have been available to a specific investor on his or her own. After all, there is only so much research and analysis that one person can perform. It's a win/win situation for everyone involved in the investment club process.

GRQ Investment Club

San Francisco, California

CLUB MAKEUP

Number of members	14
Member age range	60–85
Age of club	More than 30 years
Average number of securities in portfolio	20
$ value of portfolio	$214,000 (July 1994)
Amount invested per member/per month	$35

Membership consists mostly of retired people with previous occupations ranging from secretaries and clerical workers to professors and middle-level managers.

MAJOR CURRENT HOLDINGS

Company	Purchase Date	Original Cost	Value
Home Depot	1988	$2,209	$21,438
U.S. Healthcare	1991	5,309	24,806
Wal-Mart	1982	418	14,775

CLUB INVESTMENT PHILOSOPHY

GRQ strives for long-term capital gains rather than concentrating on generating income. The club uses a buy-and-hold strategy, seeking growth companies. As indicated by the major holdings listed above, GRQ will hold a solid stock indefinitely.

"We don't tend to sell our winners, we hold them. It's the losers that we sell," explains GRQ Club member Henry Clay Lindgren, Ph.D., an emeritus professor of psychology at San Francisco State University.

The GRQ Investment Club is an excellent example of how a portfolio can grow with an investment of as little as $35 per month per member. The club has built up its portfolio to nearly $215,000 over the years, despite members cashing in shares for vacations, home repairs, and other personal needs.

GRQ also illustrates how club objectives can change over time. The club started out in 1963 with a value of $1 per share and a speculative philosophy. After bottoming around 27 cents per share in 1975, the club shed its speculative approach for a long-term investment strategy. The value of the GRQ Investment Club peaked over $14 per share before settling back to the $11–$12 per share range in July 1994.

"After we stopped speculating, we did much better," says Lindgren.

GRQ employs a three-pronged approach to its investment club. First of all, the members consider the social aspect of the club very important to its success. The club has never missed a scheduled meeting in its 30-plus years of existence, even when the value of the club dropped to less than one-third of its original value. The club meets once a month and serves refreshments after the business portion of the meeting to minimize disruptions.

To promote investment education, the club asks that each member report on at least one stock a year. The reports are brief and to the point, and are preferably accompanied by information distributed to the other members. Performance data include earnings per share over the past five years, price/earnings ratio, price movement of the stock over the past year, closing price of the stock on the most recent trading day, financial status of the company (assets/liabilities comparison) with Standard & Poor's and/or Value Line rating for safety, market where the stock is traded, prospects for the stock's rise in value (including Value Line rating for capital appreciation), and experts' opinions regarding the stock's future prospects.

Finally, GRQ's investment strategy avoids the "big" stocks, such as those that comprise the Dow Jones Industrial Average (DJIA or DOW), and searches out smaller growth companies with consistent yearly earnings increases, a clear indication of superior management.

To ferret out potential investment candidates, GRQ uses the quarterly and annual earnings reports that appear in financial publications. Companies with per share earnings increases of 20 percent or more make the first cut. Further investigation typically eliminates four out of five of these candidates for one reason or another. The balance receive additional review to see how they perform in the market.

The club also employs a unique Sweepstakes Game to investigate likely candidates for the club's portfolio. The game players all begin with a mythical $10,000, which they invest in no more than three stocks that they anticipate will show major gains during the next 12 months. The Gamekeeper calculates the value of each player's holdings prior to each monthly club meeting and reports on the percentage change in each portfolio for the previous and current months. Comparison with stock market average benchmarks such as the DJIA, S&P 500, and Value Line are also provided. Discussion of the stocks becomes an important part of the monthly business meeting.

"The game not only helps club members become familiar with a wide range of stocks, it also helps members identify stocks that might be included in the club's portfolio or their own personal portfolio. The Sweepstakes Game instills an element of competition to achieve the best return and livens up our meetings," says Lindgren.

GRQ uses an Australian ballot process for portfolio choices. Each member ranks all stocks presented at a meeting, with first-choice stocks receiving the rank of 1, and so forth. The stock receiving the lowest total points is designated as the preferred stock. Ranked stocks are tracked until the time arrives for stock purchase.

As evidence of the variety of investments brought to the table by GRQ club members, consider the following partial list of Sweepstakes Game stocks for 1994:

Company	*Industry*
Abbott Laboratories	Pharmaceuticals
Ben & Jerry's Homemade, Inc.	Ice cream
Brunswick Corporation	Recreational products
Burlington Coat Factory Ware. Corp.	Apparel stores
Caterpillar, Inc.	Heavy machinery
Hong Kong Telecommunications, Ltd.	Telecommunications
Intel Corporation	Semiconductors
Newmont Mining Corporation	Gold mining
Nortek, Inc.	Building products
Sante Fe Pacific Corporation	Railroad/Natural resources
Scitex Corporation	Imaging/Computer graphics
Southwest Gas Corporation	Natural gas
Stanley Works	Hardware
Universal Health Services, Inc.	Acute-care hospitals
William Wrigley Jr. Company	Chewing gum

Big winners in 1993 included the club's positions in American Power Conversion Corporation (+58%), U.S. Healthcare, Inc. (+29%), and Wal-Mart Stores, Inc. (+28%). On the downside: CML Group, Inc., Walgreen Company, and Lands' End, Inc. declined in value during 1993 and were subsequently removed from the portfolio.

Like many other investors, GRQ entered the foreign investment arena in late 1993 and 1994 with the purchase of several country closed-end funds. Toward the end of August 1994, its investments in the First Philippine Fund $(+5\frac{1}{8})$ and Thai Fund $(+5\frac{1}{4})$ were showing strong gains, while the Mexico Fund $(-3\frac{3}{4})$ reflected a loss.

The club recognized Home Depot and Wal-Mart's potential early, establishing stakes in the companies well before they became top performers and market favorites.

A recent addition to the club's portfolio is Pacific Scientific Company, a manufacturer of specialty motors based in Newport Beach, California. According to Lindgren, the major attractions of Pacific Scientific that can make it a winner include sound finances, a good price/earnings ratio, favorable outside recommendations and ratings, and a rising stock price.

NEW PORTFOLIO PURCHASE PROFILE

Pacific Scientific Company   Stock Exchange: NYSE
620 Newport Center Drive   Ticker Symbol: PSX
Newport Beach, California 92660   Telephone: 714-720-1714

Company Business

Pacific Scientific Company manufactures electrical equipment (70 percent of revenues) and safety equipment (30 percent of revenues). The company serves the aviation, electric utility, factory automation, hydraulic equipment, pharmaceutical, and semiconductor markets. Export sales, primarily to Asia and Europe, contributed approximately $9.5 million, or nearly 5 percent, of annual revenues in 1993.

Shareholder Information

Outstanding shares	5,575,000
Insider ownership	More than 7 percent
DRIP program	No

Financial Information (July 1994)

Total assets	$169 million
Cash and temporary investments	$5 million
Working capital	$57 million
Long-term debt	$31 million
Equity ratio	65 percent
Book value	$15.00 per share
Dividend rate	12 cents per share on annual basis
Yield	.5 percent
Price/earnings ratio	19

Stock Price History (through mid-September 1994)

	1992	*1993*	*1994*
Low	$9\frac{1}{4}$	$12\frac{1}{8}$	$21\frac{3}{8}$
High	$15\frac{5}{8}$	$23\frac{7}{8}$	$28\frac{1}{2}$

Revenue And Earnings History (through July 1994)

	1992	*1993*	*1st Half 1993*	*1st Half 1994*
Revenue	$173	$196	$91	$109
Net income	5	7*	3*	4
Earnings per share	1.10	1.53*	.51*	.70

In millions, except per-share amounts
* Excluding positive impact of accounting change in the amount of $1.1 million, or 20 cents per share.

Key Growth Rates (past 5 years)

Revenues	5.5%
Cash flow	14.5%
Earnings	43.0%

Company Prospects

Pacific Scientific Company is experiencing record revenues in its 75th year of operation. Even more impressive, earnings continue to surge ahead at an incredible double-digit pace in excess of 40 percent. Gross margins are also on the rise, improving to more than 32 percent during the second quarter of 1994 versus less than 30 percent for the same period in 1993.

To remain a technological leader, Pacific Scientific devotes approximately 4 percent of revenue annually to research and development efforts. An estimated 25 percent and 50 percent of annual revenues are derived from products developed in the past three and five years, respectively.

The company also keeps a keen eye out for strategic acquisitions. For example, during 1993, Pacific Scientific purchased all the remaining outstanding shares of common stock of Powertree Industrial Corporation, a manufacturer of brushless motors and controls, and Automation Intelligence, Inc., a developer of automation software and systems using the company's motors. It also purchased operating assets of Unidynamics/Phoenix, Inc., a pyrotechnic subsidiary of John Crane Corporation.

During 1994, Pacific Scientific reconfigured its Motor & Control Division into two separate ones to sharpen its focus on specialized market opportunities for complex-motion automation systems.

The company's financial position remains strong, with a current ratio of 2.9 to 1. An improving cash flow adds to the firm's flexibility in acquiring new businesses and introducing new products.

Temporary problems in the firm's automation of its outdoor lighting control operations appear to have been ironed out. The division now operates close to targeted production levels and has stemmed its losses. Continued improvement will add to the company's overall bottom line.

Pacific Scientific is well positioned to post higher revenues and earnings in the years ahead. See Chart 2–1 for an analysis of the company's stock price potential.

Section 1 of the Stock Selection Guide shows a visual analysis of Pacific Scientific's sales, earnings, and stock price. Section 2 evaluates management based on trends in percentage of pretax profit on sales and percentage earned on invested capital. Section 3 reflects the company's stock price history as an indicator of the future. For example, the firm's current price/earnings ratio stands at 17.2 versus an average price/earnings ratio of 23.5.

Section 4 evaluates risk and reward potential over the next five years. With an average high P/E of 31.5 and estimated high earnings of $1.78 per share, the stock could command a price as high as $56 per share ($31.5 \times 1.78$).

Chart 2–1   *Pacific Scientific Stock Selection Guide*

STOCK
SELECTION
GUIDE

**The most widely used aid
to good investment judgment**

NATIONAL ASSOCIATION
OF INVESTORS CORPORATION

INVESTMENT EDUCATION
SINCE 1951

Company	PACIFIC SCIENTIFIC	Date 9/9/94
Prepared by	SPC	Data taken from S & P ()
Where traded	NYSE	Main product/service MOTORS

CAPITALIZATION	Authorized		Outstanding
Preferred		0.0	0.0
Common		0.0	5.4
Other Debt	49.7	Potential Dilution	None

1 VISUAL ANALYSIS of Sales, Earnings and Price

PSX

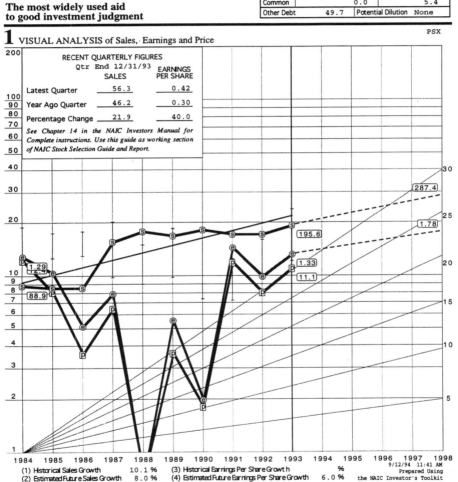

RECENT QUARTERLY FIGURES
Qtr End 12/31/93

	SALES	EARNINGS PER SHARE
Latest Quarter	56.3	0.42
Year Ago Quarter	46.2	0.30
Percentage Change	21.9	40.0

*See Chapter 14 in the NAIC Investors Manual for
Complete instructions. Use this guide as working section
of NAIC Stock Selection Guide and Report.*

(1) Historical Sales Growth   10.1 %
(2) Estimated Future Sales Growth   8.0 %
(3) Historical Earnings Per Share Growth   %
(4) Estimated Future Earnings Per Share Growth 6.0 %

9/12/94 11:41 AM
Prepared Using
the NAIC Investor's Toolkit

Source: National Association of Investors Corporation

Chart 2–1   Pacific Scientific Stock Selection Guide

2 EVALUATING MANAGEMENT Company ___PACIFIC SCIENTIFIC___   9/9/94

		1984	1985	1986	1987	1988	1989	1990	1991	1992	1993	LAST 5 YEAR AVE.	TREND UP	DOWN
A	% Pre-tax Profit on Sales (Net Before Taxes + Sales)	13.9	9.5	4.2	4.2	-2.6	2.2	1.0	6.9	4.7	5.7	4.1	↑	
B	% Earned on Invested Capital (E/S + Book Value)	13.0	9.9	4.9	7.2	-8.4	4.9	1.7	11.2	7.4	8.9	6.8	↑	

3 PRICE-EARNINGS HISTORY as an indicator of the future

PRESENT PRICE ___22.875___   HIGH THIS YEAR ___28.500___ LOW THIS YEAR ___14.625___

	Year	A PRICE HIGH	B PRICE LOW	C Earnings Per Share	D Price Earnings Ratio HIGH A÷C	E Price Earnings Ratio LOW B÷C	F Dividend Per Share	G % Payout F÷C X 100	H % High Yield F÷B X 100
1	1989	18.5	9.8	0.56	33.0	17.4	0.000	0.0	0.0
2	1990	16.4	7.4	0.20	81.9	36.8	0.000	0.0	0.0
3	1991	12.5	7.2	1.46	8.6	5.0	0.030	2.1	0.4
4	1992	16.0	9.8	1.00	16.0	9.8	0.120	12.0	1.2
5	1993	23.9	12.1	1.33	17.9	9.1	0.120	9.0	1.0
6	TOTAL								
7	AVERAGE		9.2		31.5	15.6		7.7	
8	AVERAGE PRICE EARNINGS RATIO	23.5			**9** CURRENT PRICE EARNINGS RATIO		17.2		

Current P/E Based upon Last 12 mo. Earnings [1.33]
Proj. P/E [16.2] Based upon Next 12 mo. Earnings [1.41]

4 EVALUATING RISK and REWARD over the next 5 years

A HIGH PRICE - NEXT 5 YEARS
Avg. High P/E ___31.5___ (3D7) x Estimated High Earnings/Share ___1.78___ = Forecast High Price B-1 $ ___56.0___ (4A1)

B LOW PRICE - NEXT 5 YEARS
(a) Avg. Low P/E ___15.6___ (3E7) x Estimated Low E/Share ___1.33___ = $ ___20.8___
(b) Avg. Low Price of Last 5 Years = ___9.2___ (3B7)
(c) Recent Severe Market Low Price = ___7.2___
(d) Price Dividend Will Support $\dfrac{\text{Present Divd.}}{\text{High Yield (H)}}$ = $\dfrac{0.120}{1.2}$ = ___9.8___

Selected Estimated Low Price _____   B-2 $ ___9.2___ (4B1)

C ZONING
___56.0___ (4A1) High Forecast Price Minus ___9.2___ (4B1) Low Forecast Price Equals ___46.8___ (C) Range. ¹/₃ of Range = ___15.6___ (4CD)

Lower ¹/₃ = ___9.2___ (4B1) To ___24.8___ (Buy) (4C2)
Middle ¹/₃ = ___24.8___ To ___40.4___ (Maybe) (4C3)
Upper ¹/₃ = ___40.4___ To ___56.0___ (4A1) (Sell) (4C4)
Present Market Price of ___22.9___ is in the --- **Buy** --- (4C5) Range

D UP-SIDE DOWN-SIDE RATIO (Potential Gain vs. Risk of Loss)
High Price ___56.0___ (4A1) Minus Present Price ___22.9___ = $\dfrac{33.2}{13.6}$ = ___2.4___ (4D) =To 1
Present Price ___22.9___ Minus Low Price ___9.2___ (4B1)

Relative Value: 73.0 %

5 5-YR POTENTIAL

Projected Relative Value: 68.9 %

A Present Full Year's Dividend $ ___0.120___ / Present Price of Stock $ ___22.9___ = ___0.005___ x100 = ___0.5___ Present Yield or % Returned on Purchase Price

B AVERAGE YIELD OVER THE NEXT 5 YEARS
Avg. Earn. Per Share Next 5 Years ___1.58___ x Avg % Payout ___7.7___ (3G7) = ___0.5___ %

Present Price $ ___22.9___   Total Return: 19.9 %

Source: National Association of Investors Corporation

On the other hand, with an average low P/E of 15.6 and estimated low earnings of $1.33 per share, the stock price could drop to a low of $20.8 per share (15.6 × 1.33). Running through the zoning calculation shows that Pacific Scientific falls into the buy range at its current market price of $22.9 per share.

Section 5 uses dividend information to compute future yield and the total return expected on Pacific Scientific stock over the next five years.

With a projected total return of 19.9 percent over the next half-decade, Pacific Scientific rates a strong buy based on current estimations of the company's prospects. For a more detailed discussion of the Stock Selection Guide, refer to Part 3, Putting It All Together.

MAJOR PORTFOLIO HOLDING PROFILE

The Home Depot, Inc.   Stock Exchange: NYSE
2727 Paces Ferry Road   Ticker Symbol: HD
Atlanta, Georgia 30339   Telephone: 404-433-8211

Company Business

Home Depot ranks as the leading retailer in the home improvement building industry, with more than 288 stores operating in 24 states plus another 10 stores located in Canada. Revenues are derived from lumber and building materials (33%); plumbing, heating, and electrical supplies (29%); seasonal and specialty items (15%); tools and hardware (12%); and paint and furniture (11%). Home Depot stores carry around 30,000 different items in inventory and average approximately 102,000 square feet. Overall, the company maintains in excess of 29 million square feet of selling space.

Taking an aggressive expansion stance, the Atlanta-based company announced plans in May 1994 to triple its home improvement outlets over the next four years. This growth will include further expansion in the Midwest and Canada, markets the company entered in 1994. Home Depot also intends to join the international arena by entering the Mexican market.

Shareholder Information

Outstanding shares   475,900,000
Insider ownership   Approx. 9 percent
DRIP program   Yes

Financial Information (July 1994)

Total assets $5.4 billion
Cash and temporary investments $421 million
Working capital $998 million
Long-term debt $841 million
Equity ratio   78 percent

Book value	$6.61 per share
Dividend rate	16 cents per share on annual basis
Yield	.4 percent
Price/earnings ratio	37

Stock Price History (through mid-September 1994)

	1992	1993	1994
Low	$29\frac{7}{8}$	35	$36\frac{1}{2}$
High	$51\frac{1}{2}$	$50\frac{7}{8}$	$46\frac{3}{8}$

Revenue and Earnings History (through July 31, 1994)

	1992*	1993*	1st Half 1993	1st Half 1994
Revenue	$7,148	$9,239	$4,633	$6,159
Net income	363	457	241	318
Earnings per share	.82	1.01	.53	.69

In millions, except per-share amounts
*Fiscal Year Ended January 31

Key Growth Rates (past five years)

Revenue	29.0%
Cash flow	38.0%
Earnings	38.0%

DRIP Details

Home Depot's dividend reinvestment program permits company shareholders to purchase additional shares of company common stock for cash amounts ranging from $10 to $4,000 per month. Administrative expenses are absorbed by the company. For information regarding this DRIP, contact The First National Bank of Boston, Dividend Reinvestment Unit, P.O. Box 168I, Mail Stop 45-01-06, Boston, Massachusetts 02105-1681, or call 800-442-2001.

Company Prospects

Home Depot's prowess in the retail home improvement industry gains force as the company adds new stores, enters new markets, improves on its average sales per transactions, adds to its average sales per square foot, and keeps revenues growing at a nearly 30 percent clip.

Ever an innovator, Home Depot recently joined forces with QVC Network, Inc. in an agreement to jointly develop home improvement programming for television. The company is also moving ahead on another successful innovation: It plans to open two more EXPO Design Centers (two are in operation currently) in other markets in 1995. The EXPO stores carry upscale merchandise, with higher margins, not available in traditional company home improvement outlets. Expanded product offerings and a new store prototype also promise to keep Home Depot's revenues and earnings rising. Further, the company's acquisition of the Canadian Aikenhead home improvement chain bolsters Home Depot's share of that country's market.

In May 1994, Home Depot directors boosted the company's dividend by 33 percent, to 4 cents per share from 3 cents per share quarterly. Since its initial public offering back in 1981, the company's shares have split 10 times. Adjusting for stock splits, a $1,200 investment in 100 shares of Home Depot common stock in 1981 would be worth approximately $32,300 today (see Chart 2-2).

MAJOR PORTFOLIO HOLDING PROFILE

U.S. Healthcare, Inc.	Stock Exchange: NASDAQ
980 Jolly Road	Ticker Symbol: USHC
P.O. Box 1109	Telephone: 215-628-4800
Blue Bell, Pennsylvania 19422	

Company Business

U.S. Healthcare is a national leader in managed healthcare. The company owns and operates health maintenance organizations (HMOs) in Connecticut, Delaware, Massachusetts, New Hampshire, New Jersey, New York, Pennsylvania, and the District of Columbia. HMO members are also offered dental, pharmacy, vision, mental health, substance abuse, and preventive-care services.

Company subsidiaries also provide services to self-insured employers, quality and outcome measurement and improvement programs, coordination and administration services for multiple health plans of multistate employers, and physician practice management software and electronic interfaces between the company and its participating providers.

U.S. Healthcare's HMO membership rose to nearly 1.7 million people in mid-1994. More importantly, the pace of membership growth is accelerating, up 20 percent over the 1993 rate of increase and the largest six month membership growth in the company's history.

Shareholder Information

Outstanding shares	162,391,000
Insider ownership	More than 2 percent
DRIP program	No

Financial Information (June 1994)

Total assets	$ 1.3 billion
Cash and temporary investments	$ 1.1 billion
Working capital	$651 million

Chart 2–2   The Home Depot, Inc. Stock Chart

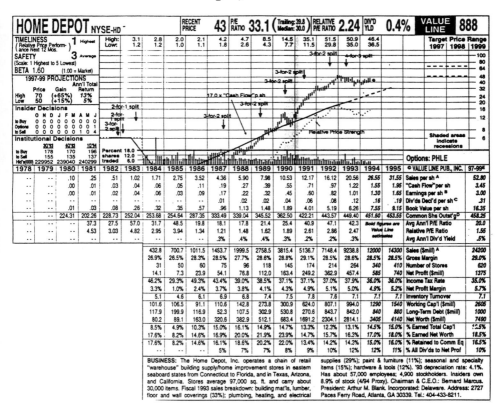

Source: ©1994 by Value Line Publishing, Inc. Reprinted by permission; All Rights Reserved.

Long-term debt	-0-
Equity ratio	100 percent
Book value	$4.79 per share
Dividend rate	84 cents per share on annual basis
Yield	1.9 percent
Price/earnings ratio	20

Stock Price History (through mid-September 1994)

	1992	1993	1994
Low	17⅛	24½	33¾
High	34¼	40⅜	47½

Revenue and Earnings History (through June 30, 1994)

	1992	1993	1st Half 1993	1st Half 1994
Revenue	$2,189	$2,645	$1,290	$1,443
Net income	330	504	130	183
Earnings per share	1.23	1.84	.80	1.12

In millions, except per-share amounts

Key Growth Rates (past 5 years)

Revenue	27.5%
Cash flow	64.5%
Earnings	74.5%

Company Prospects

U.S. Healthcare's strong earnings growth makes the company a healthy cash generator. With more than $1.1 billion in cash and marketable securities, the company's coffers provide plenty of capital to grow the company and expand into new markets.

In addition, strong cash flow provides a solid underpinning for enhanced dividend growth, which is already growing at a compound rate in excess of 43 percent over the past five years.

Plans are in motion to expand HMO operation into Georgia, North Dakota, Rhode Island, and Virginia by the end of 1994. In addition, the company received federal approval to offer its Medicare plans in Connecticut, Delaware, Massachusetts, New Hampshire, and the District of Columbia. This expansion will increase the total population of the areas served by U.S. Healthcare's HMOs to 60 million, up from 40 million in 1993.

An expanded product line brings in added revenues. The firm's new Quality Point of Service product has now been extended to all of the company's major markets.

U.S. Healthcare is improving its operations as well. The firm's medical loss ratio decreased to 70.2 percent for the first half of 1994, compared with 75.2 percent for 1993's first six months.

U.S. Healthcare has its house in order to deliver outstanding earnings in the years ahead. Coupled with a sharply rising dividend payout, this healthcare stock promises superior total returns over the long term. The stock has enjoyed a number of stock splits as the market has pushed the stock price higher with improving revenues and earnings (see Chart 2–3).

MAJOR PORTFOLIO HOLDING PROFILE

Wal-Mart Stores, Inc.
(See the discussion under L-P Investors Investment Club.)

Chart 2–3   U.S. Healthcare, Inc. Stock Chart

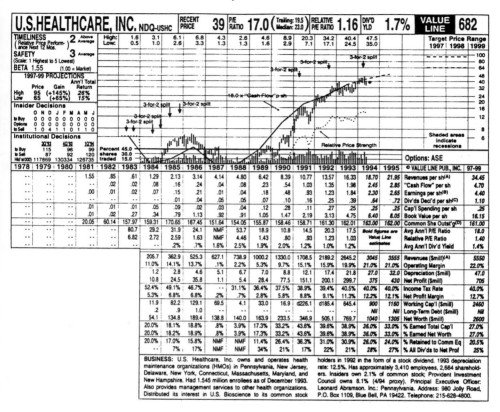

| U.S.HEALTHCARE, INC. NDQ-USHC | RECENT PRICE 39 | P/E RATIO 17.0 (Trailing: 19.5 / Median: 23.0) | RELATIVE P/E RATIO 1.16 | DIV'D YLD 1.7% | VALUE LINE 682 |

TIMELINESS 2 Above Average (Relative Price Performance Next 12 Mos.)
SAFETY 3 Average (Scale: 1 Highest to 5 Lowest)
BETA 1.55 (1.00 = Market)

1997-99 PROJECTIONS
	Price	Gain	Ann'l Total Return
High	95	(+145%)	26%
Low	65	(+65%)	15%

Insider Decisions
	O	N	D	J	F	M	A	M	J
to Buy	0	0	0	0	0	0	0	0	0
Options	0	0	0	0	0	0	0	0	0
to Sell	1	0	4	1	1	0	1	1	0

Institutional Decisions
	2Q93	3Q93	4Q93
to Buy	115	96	99
to Sell	87	92	120
Hld'w(000)	117869	130334	126735

Percent 45.0 shares 30.0 traded 15.0

High: 1.6 3.1 6.1 6.8 4.3 2.6 4.6 8.9 20.3 34.2 40.4 47.5
Low: 0.5 1.0 2.6 3.3 1.3 1.3 1.6 2.9 7.1 17.1 24.5 35.0

Target Price Range 1997 1998 1999

3-for-2 split
3-for-2 split
3-for-2 split
3-for-2 split
18.0 x "Cash Flow" p sh
Relative Price Strength
Shaded areas indicate recessions
Options: ASE

	1978	1979	1980	1981	1982	1983	1984	1985	1986	1987	1988	1989	1990	1991	1992	1993	1994	1995	© VALUE LINE PUB., INC.	97-99
	..	..	..	1.55	.85	.61	1.29	2.13	3.14	4.14	4.80	6.42	8.39	10.77	13.57	16.33	18.70	21.95	Revenues per sh (A)	34.45
	..	..	..	..	.02	.02	.08	.16	.24	.04	.08	.23	.54	1.03	1.35	1.98	2.45	2.85	"Cash Flow" per sh	4.70
	..	..	..	.00	.01	.02	.07	.15	.21	.01	.04	.18	.48	.93	1.23	1.84	2.30	2.65	Earnings per sh (B)	4.40
	..	..	..	..	..	..	..	.01	.04	.05	.05	.07	.10	.16	.25	.39	.64	.72	Div'ds Decl'd per sh (C)	1.10
	..	..	..	.01	.01	.01	.05	.09	.02	.03	.04	.12	.28	.11	.27	.25	.25	.25	Cap'l Spending per sh	.25
	..	..	..	.01	.02	.27	.34	.79	1.13	.92	.91	1.05	1.47	2.19	3.13	4.75	6.40	8.05	Book Value per sh	16.15
	..	..	..	20.05	60.14	157.97	159.31	170.65	167.45	151.64	154.05	155.87	158.46	158.71	161.30	162.01	163.00	162.00	Common Shs Outst'g (D)	161.00
	..	..	..	..	80.7	29.2	31.9	24.1	NMF	53.7	18.9	10.8	14.5	20.3	17.5	Bold figures are			Avg Ann'l P/E Ratio	18.0
	..	..	..	..	6.82	2.72	2.59	1.63	NMF	4.46	1.43	.80	.93	1.23	1.03	Value Line estimates			Relative P/E Ratio	1.40
	..	..	..	..	..	.2%	.7%	1.6%	2.5%	1.9%	2.0%	1.2%	1.0%	1.2%					Avg Ann'l Div'd Yield	1.4%
							205.7	362.9	525.3	627.1	738.9	1000.2	1330.0	1708.5	2189.2	2645.2	3045	3555	Revenues ($mill) (A)	5550
							11.0%	14.1%	13.7%	.1%	2.2%	5.3%	9.7%	15.1%	15.9%	19.9%	21.0%	21.0%	Operating Margin	22.0%
							1.2	2.8	4.6	5.1	6.7	7.0	8.8	12.1	17.4	21.8	27.0	32.0	Depreciation ($mill)	47.0
							10.8	24.5	35.8	4.1	5.4	28.4	77.5	151.1	200.1	299.7	375	430	Net Profit ($mill)	705
							52.4%	49.1%	46.7%	..	31.1%	36.4%	37.5%	38.9%	39.4%	40.5%	40.0%	40.0%	Income Tax Rate	40.0%
							5.3%	6.8%	6.8%	.2%	.7%	2.8%	5.8%	8.8%	9.1%	11.3%	12.2%	12.1%	Net Profit Margin	12.7%
							11.9	82.2	129.1	69.5	4.1	33.0	16.9	d226.1	d185.4	645.4	900	1160	Working Cap'l ($mill)	2460
							.2	.9	1.0	..	..	..	..	..	..	..	Nil	Nil	Long-Term Debt ($mill)	Nil
							54.1	134.8	189.4	138.8	140.0	163.9	233.5	346.9	505.1	769.7	1040	1305	Net Worth ($mill)	2600
							20.0%	18.1%	18.8%	.8%	3.9%	17.3%	33.2%	43.6%	39.6%	38.9%	36.0%	33.0%	% Earned Total Cap'l	27.0%
							20.0%	18.2%	18.9%	.8%	3.9%	17.3%	33.2%	43.6%	39.6%	38.9%	36.0%	33.0%	% Earned Net Worth	27.0%
							20.0%	17.0%	15.8%	NMF	NMF	11.4%	26.4%	36.3%	31.0%	30.9%	26.0%	24.0%	% Retained to Comm Eq	20.5%
							..	7%	17%	NMF	NMF	34%	21%	17%	22%	21%	28%	27%	% All Div'ds to Net Prof	25%

BUSINESS: U.S. Healthcare, Inc. owns and operates health maintenance organizations (HMOs) in Pennsylvania, New Jersey, Delaware, New York, Connecticut, Massachusetts, Maryland, and New Hampshire. Had 1.545 million enrollees as of December 1993. Also provides management services to other health organizations. Distributed its interest in U.S. Bioscience to its common stock holders in 1992 in the form of a stock dividend. 1993 depreciation rate: 12.5%. Has approximately 3,410 employees, 2,664 shareholders. Insiders own 2.1% of common stock; Provident Investment Council owns 8.1% (4/94 proxy). Principal Executive Officer: Leonard Abramson. Inc.: Pennsylvania. Address: 980 Jolly Road, P.O. Box 1109, Blue Bell, PA 19422. Telephone: 215-628-4800.

DISAPPOINTING STOCKS SHED

Company	Industry
CML Group, Inc.	Specialty retailer
Lands' End, Inc.	Mail order clothing
Rubbermaid, Inc.	Plastic and rubber housewares
Walgreen Company	Drug stores

L-P Investors Investment Club

Pleasanton, California

CLUB MAKEUP

Number of members	19
Member age range	40-70
Age of club	More than 21 years
Average number of securities in portfolio	16-20
$ Value of portfolio	$197,000 (mid-July 1994)
Amount invested per member/per month	$20 (except Aug. & Dec.)*

Membership in AAUW (American Association of University Women) required.
*Members may invest more if they so desire.

MAJOR CURRENT HOLDINGS

Company	Purchase Date	Original Cost	Value
Cisco Systems, Inc.	1993	$30,079	$19,625
General Electric Co.	1990	13,143	21,640
Wal-Mart Stores, Inc.	1987	7,199	20,300
Home Depot, Inc.	1989	3,407	18,060

CLUB INVESTMENT PHILOSOPHY

L-P Investors invests in the common stock of growth companies. The club tends to stay fully invested but has the flexibility of not purchasing stocks at any given meeting if the securities presented that month are not to the liking of the majority of club members.

While the GRQ Investment Club considers its first priority as a social club with investment interests, L-P Investors refers to itself as primarily a business group. Its sole social activity is a January potluck luncheon. The monthly meeting covers the secretary's minutes; treasurer's report; a short report from each member about each security held (hold/buy/sell recommendation plus other pertinent information on the company or stock); stock studies for the month's potential buys; and a study topic to expand the members' knowledge about investing.

A few years ago, L-P members voted to reassign the securities tracked and reported on by members for two or three years. This policy provides a broader variety of securities that each member covers over time and allows fresh insight into the review process of current holdings.

The club's use of a deep discount broker cuts transaction costs. Occasionally, club members buy out the outstanding securities of resigning members to prevent ill-timed security sales for generating adequate funds to pay off departing members. Typically, members do not take money out of the club except when they leave the group. However, club bylaws permit bonus distributions when the value of the club portfolio base figure increases by 25 percent or more. Members may elect not to participate in the bonus distribution, thereby retaining the full value of units in the portfolio. The bylaws also permit members to trade or sell units under certain conditions.

In keeping with the businesslike nature of L-P Investors, the club automatically terminates any member who has failed to make an investment payment for a period of two months. In addition, nonattendance for a period of three consecutive meetings or five meetings during the year could be cause for membership termination by a majority consent of the remaining members.

Prospective members must visit club meetings twice before joining. To keep attendance active and prevent absenteeism from impeding club business, a quorom consists of a majority of the membership present at any given meeting. Fines are assessed for absenteeism and tardiness.

A two-member team presents a written and oral presentation on selected stocks. All members, except the treasurer, are expected to give at least one report a year. As noted earlier, member "stockwatchers" present a brief hold/buy/sell recommendation at each meeting. In addition, a comprehensive portfolio evaluation is conducted semiannually. Buy and sell action may be taken after discussion and a majority vote of those members present at the meeting.

The club's bylaws also provide for the evaluation of a security for sale if the investment increased in value by more than 50 percent of its original total cost or decreased by 50 percent of its original total cost.

L-P Investors has come a long way since it began investing more than 21 years ago. At one of the first club meetings back in 1973, the broker handed out forms for the members' husbands to sign giving "permission" for the member to participate in the group. Later, the group carried out its investment transactions with a female broker who was formerly an L-P club member.

In 1986 and 1990, L-P Investors was the top California investment club. The club's 1990 performance also ranked it as fifth runner-up nationwide in the *Better Investing* All Star Investment Clubs.

Club top performers in 1993 included the sale of Pall Corporation for a gain of $3,587 on an original investment of $6,856 for a profit of more than 52 percent. The club also sold a partial interest in its AT&T holdings, generating a profit of $2,269 on an original investment of $4,342 for another 52-plus percent gain. Portfolio holdings as of July 1994 that contained large gains included General Electric Company, Glacier Water Services, Home Depot, Inc., McDonald's Corporation, State Street Boston Corporation, and Wal-Mart Stores, Inc.

The big loser carrying over into the 1994 portfolio was Cisco Systems, Inc. with an original cost of $30,079 and a market value of $19,625 as of mid-July 1994. L-P Investors first purchased 300 shares of Cisco Systems in October 1993 at a price of $53.834 per share (prior to the February 1994 2-for-1 stock split). It later added another 700 shares to its portfolio for an overall average cost of $30.0793 cents per share. Despite the nearly 35 percent loss on Cisco Systems, L-P Investors' portfolio reflected a 23.3 percent gain overall based on its July 1994 holdings.

Twice per year, each member is responsible for preparing a Portfolio Management Review Technique (PERT) report and an in-depth study of the stock that she follows. At the other eight meetings, a stock study is presented by two members who chose six stocks that they consider to be the best in a particular industry under review. They present the information using completed NAIC Stock Selection Guides (adapted for L-P Investors use). Key elements of the form include historical percentage of sales growth, historical percentage earnings per share growth, latest four quarters earnings per share and percentage change from previous four quarters, historical and latest 12-month stock price range, historical price/earnings and current price/earnings ratio, dividends for latest four quarters and current yield, and *Value Line* Beta and *Value Line* Financial Strength ratings.

"We use the following three criteria for comparing specific securities for purchase: 10 percent earnings per share growth rate for past five years, a forecasted price range two or more times current market price, and a current price/earnings ratio equal to or less than the average price/earnings ratio of the past five years," says Patricia Jacobson, L-P Investors treasurer.

Using those stock investigation and selection tools, L-P Investors recently purchased shares in Office Depot, Inc. and Starbucks Corporation.

NEW PORTFOLIO PURCHASE PROFILE

Office Depot, Inc.   Stock Exchange: NYSE
2200 Old Germantown Road   Ticker Symbol: ODP
Delray Beach, Florida 33445   Telephone 407-278-4800

Company Business

Office Depot's more than 380 stores in 33 states, the District of Columbia, and Canadian provinces make the company the largest office supply store chain serving the North American market. Revenues are generated from office supplies (46 percent); computers, business machines, and accessories (41 percent); and office furniture (13 percent).

The company has made significant inroads into the stationery business since mid-1993 with the acquisition of six contract stationers contributing $600 million in annual revenues. Synergistic benefits of consolidating the stationery units' delivery, warehouse, and information systems should help improve that segment's profit contribution.

Office Depot plans to open between 60 to 70 new outlets in 1994 and 1995 in its efforts to garner more market share in the highly fragmented

$80-billion industry. The company opened its first store in 1986 and has stepped up its expansion campaign to the tune of an estimated $4 billion in annual revenues by the end of 1994.

Shareholder Information

Outstanding shares	150,464,000
Insider ownership	More than 2 percent*
DRIP program	No

*Plus French Carrefour S.A. owns 15.7 percent of outstanding shares

Financial Information (June 1994)

Total assets	$1.5 billion
Cash and temporary investments	$99 million
Working capital	$454 million
Long-term debt	$376 million
Equity ratio	62 percent
Book value	$3.96 per share
Dividend rate	—
Yield	—
Price/earnings ratio	45

Stock Price History (through mid-September 1994)

	1992	1993	1994
Low	$8\frac{3}{8}$	$11\frac{7}{8}$	$18\frac{7}{8}$
High	$15\frac{1}{2}$	$23\frac{7}{8}$	$26\frac{1}{2}$

Revenue and Earnings History (through June 25, 1994)

	1992	1993	1st Half 1993	1st Half 1994
Revenue	$1,733	$2,579	$1,195	$1,924
Net income	39	63	27	44
Earnings per share	.28	.45	.19	.29

In millions, except per-share amounts

Key Growth Rates (past 5 years)

Revenue	53.5%
Cash flow	50.5%
Earnings	50.5%

Company Prospects

Strong revenue growth across product lines and geographical operations paces Office Depot's record earnings. Same-store sales rose 26 percent over levels one year ago. Aggressive marketing via national televison advertising will enhance the firm's national exposure. Tight purchasing controls, consolidation of stationery operations, and improved management information systems point to bigger margins down the road.

Office Depot plans to enter two new markets each year, opening 70 new stores annually. Lucrative Midwestern markets are on tap for 1994. Internationally, the company continues to expand its Canadian operations, has inked agreements to open stores in Colombia and Israel, and has its eyes on the Mexican market.

Revenues are expected to rise 50 percent in 1994, while earnings should surge 40 percent. Penetration of the commercial market segment in addition to its leading role in the retail office supplies industry promises to keep Office Depot's money-generating engine on track.

Since 1990, the company's stock price has been on a virtual escalator, peaking in early 1994 at $26½ per share. The key question is whether Office Depot can maintain its lofty price/earnings ratio (see Chart 2–4).

MAJOR PORTFOLIO HOLDING PROFILE

Cisco Systems, Inc.	Stock Exchange: NASDAQ
170 West Tasman Drive	Ticker Symbol: CSCO
San Jose, California 95134	Telephone 408-526-4000

Company Business
Cisco Systems leads the industry as the top supplier of high-performance internetworking systems and software for linking computers. More than 90 percent of the company's business derives from the sale of routers. The balance comes from bridges, communication servers, and router management software applications.

Domestic sales account for 64 percent of annual revenues, while foreign business brings in another 36 percent. Cisco Systems conducts its international sales through approximately 55 international distributors in Africa, Asia, Australia, Canada, Europe, Latin America, and Mexico.

The firm takes a two-pronged approach to marketing its products. It sells directly to end users and also licenses OEMs (original equipment manufacturers) to resell, on a nonexclusive basis, Cisco System's product line under their labels.

Shareholder Information

Outstanding shares	257,697,000
Insider ownership	3 percent*
DRIP program	No

* Plus four institutions own 28 percent of outstanding shares

Chart 2–4   Office Depot, Inc. Stock Chart

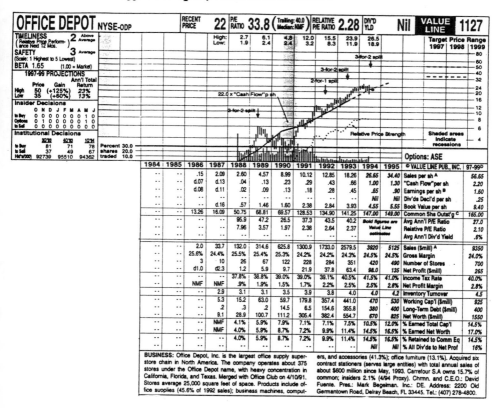

Source: ©1994 by Value Line Publishing, Inc. Reprinted by permission; All Rights Reserved.

Financial Information (July 1994)

Total assets	$1.05 billion
Cash and temporary investments	$183 million
Working capital	$302 million
Long-term debt	-0-
Equity ratio	100 percent
Book value	$3.29 per share
Dividend rate	—
Yield	—
Price/earnings ratio	21

Stock Price History (through mid-September 1994)

	1992	1993	1994
Low	$8\frac{1}{8}$	$19\frac{1}{8}$	$18\frac{3}{4}$
High	$20\frac{1}{4}$	$32\frac{7}{8}$	$40\frac{3}{4}$

Revenue and Earnings History (through fiscal year ended July 31, 1994)

	1992	1993	1994
Revenue	$340	$649	$1,243
Net Income	84	172	315
Earnings per share	.33	.67	1.33

In millions, except per-share amounts

Key Growth Rates (past 5 years)

Revenue	NMF
Cash flow	NMF
Earnings	NMF

Company Prospects

As the L-P Investors Investment Club found out, Cisco Systems' stock price has been buffeted by concerns over the ability of the company to maintain its high growth rates. Despite impressive gains in year-on-year and quarter-on-quarter revenue and earnings comparisons, Cisco Systems shareholders have seen the value of their company stock drop precipitiously. Following a meteoric rise from a tad over $1 per share in 1990 to the high of $40⅞ per share achieved in early 1994, Cisco Systems' stock price has plummeted nearly 35 percent to the $26½ per share level.

To be sure, no company can deliver a 10-fold increase in revenues and earnings every three years as Cisco Systems has done. The key question is what value the market will assign Cisco Systems' future growth prospects.

There are still many positives. The company recently inked a joint venture agreement with 13 leading Japanese companies to provide interoperable internetworking products for the Japanese market. Strengthening its market position, Cisco Systems also completed its first two acquisitions during fiscal 1994.

Financial strength gives Cisco Systems considerable market clout and the ability to capitalize on new opportunites. With more than $180 million in cash and short-term investments and no long-term debt, the company has the resources to pursue additional market share. The current concern over Cisco Systems' growth potential appears to be overblown and provides an opportunity for long-term investors to purchase the stock at a bargain price. See Chart 2–5.

Chart 2–5   CISCO Systems, Inc. Stock Chart

CISCO SYSTEMS NDQ-CSCO	RECENT PRICE **20**	P/E RATIO **13.7** (Trailing: 19.0 Median: NMF)	RELATIVE P/E RATIO **0.93**	DIV'D YLD **Nil**	VALUE LINE **1081**

TIMELINESS 3 Average (Relative Price Performance Next 12 Mos.)
SAFETY 3 Average (Scale: 1 Highest to 5 Lowest)
BETA 1.65 (1.00 = Market)

1997-99 PROJECTIONS
	Price	Gain	Ann'l Total Return
High	55	(+175%)	29%
Low	40	(+100%)	19%

Insider Decisions
	O	N	D	J	F	M	A	M	J
to Buy	0	0	0	0	0	0	0	0	0
Options	0	0	5	2	0	3	1	0	0
to Sell	0	0	6	5	0	2	3	0	0

Institutional Decisions
	2Q'93	4Q'93	1Q'94
to Buy	134	147	143
to Sell	112	86	144
Hds'(000)	206506	208936	206552

High 2.8 / Low 1.1; 8.5/2.5; 20.2/8.1; 32.9/19.1; 40.8/18.8
Target Price Range 1997 | 1998 | 1999
2-for-1 split (multiple)
20.5 x "Cash Flow" p sh
Relative Price Strength
Shaded areas indicate recessions
Options: CBOE, PACE
© VALUE LINE PUB., INC.

	1984	1985	1986	1987	1988	1989	1990	1991	1992	1993	1994	1995	97-99
Revenues per sh A	--	--	--	.02	.03	.13	.33	.80	1.41	2.62	4.85	7.00	9.10
"Cash Flow" per sh	--	--	--	--	--	.02	.07	.20	.38	.75	1.35	1.90	2.35
Earnings per sh B	--	--	--	--	--	.02	.06	.17	.33	.67	1.20	1.70	2.10
Div'ds Decl'd per sh	--	--	--	--	--	--	--	--	--	--	Nil	Nil	Nil
Cap'l Spending per sh	--	--	--	--	--	--	.02	.05	.09	.14	.25	.30	.45
Book Value per sh	--	--	--	--	.02	.04	.32	.56	1.02	1.92	3.25	5.05	8.35
Common Shs Outst'g C	--	--	--	88.42	183.00	207.46	214.18	228.15	240.44	247.42	257.50	264.00	280.00
Avg Ann'l P/E Ratio	--	--	--	--	--	--	25.2	17.1	25.8	30.3	24.0	--	23.0
Relative P/E Ratio	--	--	--	--	--	--	1.87	1.09	1.56	1.79	1.40	--	1.75
Avg Ann'l Div'd Yield	--	--	--	--	--	--	--	--	--	--	--	--	Nil
Revenues ($mill) A	--	--	--	1.5	5.5	27.7	69.8	183.2	339.6	649.0	1245	1850	2550
Operating Margin	--	--	--	10.7%	11.6%	24.9%	32.1%	37.8%	40.1%	42.7%	42.0%	41.0%	39.0%
Depreciation ($mill)	--	--	--	--	.1	.1	1.0	3.1	6.7	13.6	27.5	43.0	74.0
Net Profit ($mill)	--	--	--	.1	.4	4.2	13.9	43.2	84.4	172.0	320	460	590
Income Tax Rate	--	--	--	38.5%	40.0%	39.9%	40.8%	39.0%	38.0%	37.5%	38.0%	38.0%	38.0%
Net Profit Margin	--	--	--	5.4%	7.2%	15.1%	19.9%	23.6%	24.8%	26.5%	25.7%	24.9%	23.1%
Working Cap'l ($mill)	--	--	--	--	2.8	6.7	65.0	114.7	168.8	148.3	375	635	900
Long-Term Debt ($mill)	--	--	--	--	--	--	--	--	--	--	Nil	Nil	Nil
Net Worth ($mill)	--	--	--	--	3.1	7.5	69.2	127.5	245.6	475.2	835	1335	2340
% Earned Total Cap'l	--	--	--	57.1%	12.5%	56.0%	20.1%	33.9%	34.4%	36.2%	38.0%	34.5%	25.0%
% Earned Net Worth	--	--	--	57.1%	12.5%	56.0%	20.1%	33.9%	34.4%	36.2%	38.0%	34.5%	25.0%
% Retained to Comm Eq	--	--	--	57.1%	12.5%	56.0%	20.1%	33.9%	34.4%	36.2%	38.0%	34.5%	25.0%
% All Div'ds to Net Prof	--	--	--	--	--	--	--	--	--	--	--	Nil	Nil

BUSINESS: Cisco Systems, Inc. is the leading supplier of high-performance internetworking products for linking networks of computer systems. Manufactures routers (90% of sales), bridges, and terminal servers; develops software to manage data communications at rapid speeds between networks of computers having a wide variety of operating system protocols. Markets chiefly direct to users, also via OEMs. Foreign business accounts for 36% of sales. R&D, about 7% of sales. Principal facilities are leased. '93 deprec. rate: 19%. Has 1,450 employees, 2,370 shareholders. Mgmt. holds 3% of stock; 4 inst'ns, 28% (10/93 proxy). Pres. & C.E.O.: J.P. Morgridge. Chrmn.: D.T. Valentine. Incorp.: Calif. Address: 170 W. Tasman Drive, San Jose, CA 95134. Tel.: 408-526-4000.

Source: ©1994 by Value Line Publishing, Inc. Reprinted by permission; All Rights Reserved.

MAJOR PORTFOLIO HOLDING PROFILE

General Electric Company
3135 Easton Turnpike
Fairfield, Connecticut 06431

Stock Exchange: NYSE
Ticker Symbol: GE
Telephone 203-373-2211

Company Business

General Electric represents a large, diversified industrial company with worldwide operations. Its main business segments include technology (aircraft engines, factory automation, medical systems, and plastics); financial, communication, and broadcasting services; and core manufacturing (appliances, lighting, industrial and power systems, electrical equipment, and transportation systems).

Seven of GE's 12 business segments experienced double-digit revenue growth in 1993. More importantly, net profit margins have improved dramatically over the past five years, rising to 13.5 percent in 1993 from 8.7 percent back in 1988.

International opportunities represent a significant wild card in the General Electric revenue and earnings picture. In 1993, foreign business accounted for approximately 30 percent of annual revenues.

Shareholder Information

Outstanding shares	1,709,355,000
Insider ownership	Less than 1 percent
DRIP program	Yes

Financial Information (June 1994)

Total assets	$262 billion
Cash and temporary investments	$109 billion
Working capital	NMF
Long-term debt	$32.6 billion
Equity ratio	91 percent
Book value	$15.41 per share
Dividend rate	$1.44 per share on annual rate
Yield	2.9 percent
Price/earnings ratio	16

Stock Price History (through mid-September 1994)

	1992	*1993*	*1994*
Low	36⅜	40½	45
High	43⅞	53½	54⅞

Revenue and Earnings History (through June 30, 1994)

	1992	*1993*	*1st Half 1993*	*1st Half 1994*
Revenue	$57,073	$60,562	$27,617	$30,378
Net income	4,725	5,177*	2,419*	2,590
Earnings per share	2.76	3.03*	1.41*	1.52

In millions, except per-share amounts
*Excluding charge for change in accounting for postretirement benefits totaling $862 million, or 51 cents per share, and gain on discontinued operations of $75 million, or 5 cents per share.

Key Growth Rates (past 5 years)

Revenue	2.0%
Cash flow	8.0%
Earnings	11.0%

DRIP Details
The General Electric DRIP program allows company shareholders to invest between $10 and $10,000 cash in company stock per month in addition to reinvesting their cash dividends. All administration costs are absorbed by the company. For information on this dividend reinvestment program contact GE Securities Ownership Services, P.O. Box 120068, Stamford, Connecticut 06912 or call 203-326-4040.

Company Prospects
The June issue of the NAIC's *Better Investing* magazine covered GE in its 5 Year Ago Stock to Study. At the time of the study, GE generated $1.88 in earnings per share in 1988 on revenues of $39 billion. The stock traded at a price/earnings multiple of 14 and commanded $26⅛ per share in the stock market.

The stock had a five-year doubling target of $78 billion in revenues, $3.76 in earnings per share, and a market price of $52¼ per share. GE failed to meet the higher revenue target. In fact, the company's estimated revenues for 1994 will be around the $39 billion level of six years earlier. However, business restructuring efforts, increased attention to improved efficiency, and rising margins helped the company to achieve estimated earnings around $3.35 in 1994 and a stock price high of $54⅞ in early 1994. Despite the rather flat revenues, GE delivered on its potential to raise earnings and its stock price.

But what does the future hold for GE? Coming off the best year in the company's long history, General Electric enjoys strong cash flow, rising profit margins, and double-digit growth in a majority of its business segments. Over the past 14 years, shareholders have experienced a 20 percent return on their investment, including a 26 percent return in 1993.

Under the savvy tutelage of John F. Welch, Jr., chairman and chief executive officer, look for more of the same in the future.

MAJOR PORTFOLIO HOLDING PROFILE

Wal-Mart Stores, Inc.	Stock Exchange: NYSE
Box 116	Ticker Symbol: WMT
Bentonville, Arkansas 72716	Telephone 501-273-4000

Company Business
Wal-Mart Stores is the world's largest retailer with a chain of discount stores in 47 states. The company stocks its retail outlets from 18 distribution centers located strategically throughout its market area. Wal-Mart also operates Sam's Warehouse Clubs and Supercenters in metropolitan areas.

By the end of 1993, the company operated nearly 1,955 retail outlets and plans to expand with another 110 new stores in 1994. In addition, Wal-Mart will enlarge or relocate 70-plus Wal-Marts and remodel 60 to 70 stores during 1994.

Shareholder Information

Outstanding shares	2,299,156,000
Insider ownership	42 percent
DRIP program	No

Financial Information (July 1994)

Total assets	$30.3 billion
Cash and temporary investments	$10 million
Working capital	$ 4.7 billion
Long-term debt	$ 6.9 billion
Equity ratio	56 percent
Book value	$4.68 per share
Dividend rate	17 cents per share annual rate
Yield	.7 percent
Price/earnings ratio	23

Stock Price History (through mid-September 1994)

	1992	*1993*	*1994*
Low	$25\frac{1}{8}$	23	$22\frac{3}{8}$
High	$32\frac{7}{8}$	$34\frac{1}{8}$	$29\frac{1}{4}$

Revenue and Earnings History (through fiscal year ended July 31, 1994)

	1993	*1994*	*1st Half 1994*	*1st Half 1995*
Revenue	$55,483	$76,345	$30,157	$38,048
Net income	1,995	2,333	947	1,063
Earnings per share	.77	1.02	.42	.46

In millions, except per-share amounts

Key Growth Rates (past five years)

Revenue	27.5%
Cash flow	26.5%
Earnings	25.0%

Company Prospects

No stranger to investment clubs, Wal-Mart ranks as the second most widely held stock by NAIC clubs (trailing only McDonald's Corporation). At the end of 1993, 3,566 NAIC investment clubs held nearly 2.5 million shares of Wal-Mart stock worth more than $60 million.

Some minor missteps and public relations blunders have caused investor concern about the price of Wal-Mart stock. From a high of $34⅛ in early 1993, the stock price trended downward to $23 per share late in the year. Through mid-September 1994, the stock bounced between $22 per share and $29 per share, most of the time in the lower end of that price range.

If an investor were savvy enough to have purchased 100 shares of Wal-Mart stock when the company went public in 1970, he or she would have a nest egg worth over $2.7 million for every 100 shares. That scenario is not likely to repeat. However, the fundamentals still look good for Wal-Mart.

Earnings are expected to post better than 20 percent gains over the next few years as Wal-Mart captures market share against weaker retailers. The company's operating costs on a percentage basis are much lower than the industry average and gross margins are improving. Use the market's disenchantment with Wal-Mart to purchase the stock at prices and price/earnings ratios below their historical averages. There's still a lot of growth left in this growth company. See Chart 2–6.

DISAPPOINTING STOCKS SHED

Company	*Industry*
Ogden Projects, Inc.	Waste-to-energy

Chart 2–6 Wal-Mart Stores, Inc. Stock Chart

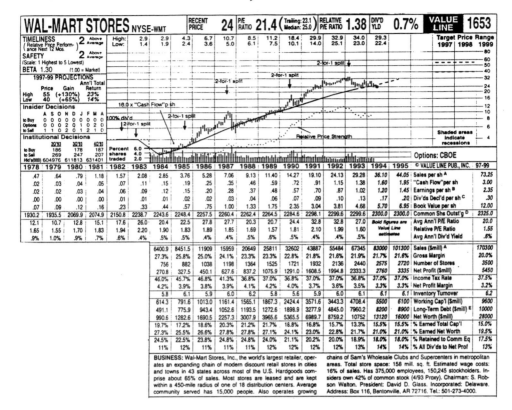

Source: ©1994 by Value Line Publishing, Inc. Reprinted by permission; All Rights Reserved.

Arrow Investment Club

Dayton, Ohio

CLUB MAKEUP

Number of members	16
Member age range	29–83
Age of club	More than seven years
Average number of securities in porfolio	16
$ value of portfolio	$35,393
Amount invested per member/per month	$25*

Note: Club membership includes 3 men and 13 women from all walks of life.
*$200 initial investment

MAJOR CURRENT HOLDINGS 8/20/94

Company	Purchase Date	Original Cost	Value
Becton Dickinson	1991 and 1993	$3,509	$4,363
Mylan Laboratories	1987	1,435	5,200
Synovus Financial	1992	2,413	2,850

CLUB INVESTMENT PHILOSOPHY

Arrow Investment Club follows the NAIC investment principles of regular investment in growth companies (for a more detailed examination of the NAIC investment principles, refer to Part I, Investment Club Strategies).

In addition to using investment criteria for selecting stock purchases, the club tries to invest in companies that produce ethically acceptable products. The investment club also targets stocks that have the potential to double in five years.

Each club member is responsible for following at least one stock and giving a short report on it each month. On top of that, every member is expected to take part in investment discussion and stock selection decision making. An attendance policy helps ensure regular attendance and maximum member participation. The club does not meet in members' homes in order to create a more businesslike atmosphere and keep interruptions to a mimimum.

A commitment to investment education is a key priority. The club occasionally invites outside speakers to its meetings to present information on various investment and financial topics of interest to club members. Other ways the club educates itself on investing include attending regional and national investment club conferences and seminars, viewing video presentations supplied by individual companies, and encouraging individual studies of interest to a member.

The Arrow Investment Club searches for investment candidates by various methods. It uses the NAIC's *Better Investing* magazine as one source of such information. The NAIC Investor Service also provides suggestions or recommendations on companies. As mentioned earlier, individual members with specific interests analyze individual stocks for presentation to the club. Use of member computers and club investment software as well as *Value Line* helps streamline investment analysis.

From January 1, 1993, through August 1994, Arrow Investment Club raised the value of its portfolio to $35,393 from $26,240, an increase of nearly 35 percent (including monthly contributions). The club earned a gain of nearly 18 percent on its Quaker Oats Company investment and currently holds a paper gain in Mylan Laboratories in excess of 262 percent. Disappointing purchases included losses on Liz Claiborne, Inc. and Figgie International, Inc.

Arrow Investment Club further diversified its portfolio recently by adding technology stocks such as Intel Corporation and Microsoft Corporation. Other additions included the purchases of Mobil Corporation and Bay State Gas Company through the NAIC's Low Cost Investment Plan (See Part 3, Putting It All Together for a discussion of the NAIC Low Cost Investment Plan).

NEW PORTFOLIO PURCHASE PROFILE
Intel Corporation
(See discussion under Women of Vested Interest Investment Club.)

NEW PORTFOLIO PURCHASE PROFILE
Microsoft Corporation   Stock Exchange: NASDAQ
One Microsoft Way   Ticker Symbol: MSFT
Redmond, Washington 98052-6399   Telephone 206-882-8080

Company Business
Microsoft Corporation, the leading independent producer of personal computer software, finished its 19th consecutive year of revenue and earnings growth despite a costly litigation settlement, which trimmed 10 cents per share of fiscal 1994 results ended June 30, 1994.

The ongoing proliferation of personal computers in both the business and home environments bodes well for Microsoft. The firm's Windows software product continues to sell at a good pace, and follow-on software applications promise to keep Microsoft's revenues and earnings on their upward trend.

Shareholder Information
Outstanding shares	617,000,000
Insider ownership	More than 45 percent
DRIP program	No

Financial Information (June 1994)

Total assets	$5.5 billion
Cash and temporary investments	$3.6 billion
Working capital	$3.4 billion
Long-term debt	-0-
Equity ratio	100 percent
Book value	$7.21 per share
Dividend rate	—
Yield	—
Price/earnings ratio	30

Stock Price History (through mid-September 1994)

	1992	1993	1994
Low	$32\frac{7}{8}$	$35\frac{1}{4}$	39
High	$47\frac{1}{2}$	49	$59\frac{1}{4}$

Revenue and Earnings History (through fiscal year ended June 30, 1994)

	1992	1993	1994
Revenue	$2,759	$3,753	$4,649
Net income	708	953	1,146*
Earnings per share	1.21	1.57	1.88*

In millions, except per-share amounts
*After-effects of charge for litigation settlement in the amount of $90 million, or 10 cents per share.

Key Growth Rates (past five years)

Revenue	45.0%
Cash flow	51.0%
Earnings	49.0%

Company Prospects

Microsoft's launching of its Chicago software opens up new opportunities for tapping its large base of Windows users, estimated at more than 50 million. Likewise, the company's Office software has been well received by the market. Currently, year-to-year revenue comparisons are up 24 percent for fiscal 1994. This pace should hold for the foreseeable future as the new products take hold. Expansion of the Microsoft Home brand of software via new product introductions also continued, with nine new consumer products in fiscal 1994.

Extending its market share and geographical base further, Microsoft acquired Montreal, Canada-based SOFTIMAGE, Inc., a leading developer of high-performance computer animation and visualization software.

Microsoft's strong financial position with no long-term debt and more than $3.6 billion in cash and short-term investments gives the firm a significant advantage over its competitors.

The company's solid fundamentals provide ample opportunity for a significantly higher stock price over the next five years. Using the NAIC Stock Selection Guide, Microsoft is well within the buy range and, barring any major unforeseen negatives, could deliver a better than 43 percent return over the next five years (see Chart 2–7).

MAJOR PORTFOLIO HOLDING PROFILE

Becton, Dickinson & Company	Stock Exchange: NYSE
1 Becton Drive	Ticker Symbol: BDX
Franklin Lakes, New Jersey 07417	Telephone 201-847-6800

Company Business

Becton, Dickinson manufactures and markets a broad range of medical supplies and devices and diagnostic systems for use by healthcare professionals, medical research institutions, and the general public.

A global company, Becton, Dickinson derives 44 percent of annual revenues and 32 percent of operating income from foreign business. On the international front, the company operates in Canada, Europe, Latin America, Japan and the Asian Pacific, and Puerto Rico.

The medical segment delivers 55 percent of annual revenues while the diagnostic systems segment contributes another 45 percent. Management targets a return of 20 percent on shareholder equity over the next few years.

Shareholder Information

Outstanding shares	72,700,000
Insider ownership	More than 1 percent
DRIP program	Yes

Financial Information (June 1994)

Total assets	$3 billion
Cash and temporary investments	$112 million
Working capital	$601 million
Long-term debt	$706 million
Equity ratio	63 percent
Book value	$20.08
Dividend rate	74 cents on annual basis
Yield	1.7 percent
Price/earnings ratio	16

Chart 2–7 *Microsoft Corporation Stock Selection Guide*

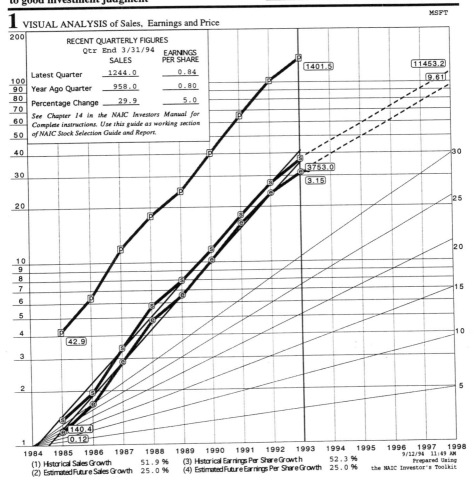

STOCK SELECTION GUIDE

NATIONAL ASSOCIATION OF INVESTORS CORPORATION

INVESTMENT EDUCATION SINCE 1951

The most widely used aid to good investment judgment

Company	MICROSOFT CORP	Date	9/9/94
Prepared by	SPC	Data taken from	S & P ()
Where traded	OTC	Main product/service	PREPACKAGE

CAPITALIZATION	Authorized		Outstanding
Preferred		0.0	0.0
Common		0.0	4926.0
Other Debt	0.0	Potential Dilution	None

MSFT

1 VISUAL ANALYSIS of Sales, Earnings and Price

RECENT QUARTERLY FIGURES

Qtr End 3/31/94

	SALES	EARNINGS PER SHARE
Latest Quarter	1244.0	0.84
Year Ago Quarter	958.0	0.80
Percentage Change	29.9	5.0

See Chapter 14 in the NAIC Investors Manual for Complete instructions. Use this guide as working section of NAIC Stock Selection Guide and Report.

1401.5

11453.2

9.61

3753.0

3.15

42.9

140.4

0.12

(1) Historical Sales Growth 51.9 % (3) Historical Earnings Per Share Growth 52.3 %
(2) Estimated Future Sales Growth 25.0 % (4) Estimated Future Earnings Per Share Growth 25.0 %

9/12/94 11:49 AM

Prepared Using the NAIC Investor's Toolkit

Source: National Association of Investors Corporation

Chart 2–7 *Microsoft Corporation Stock Selection Guide*

2 EVALUATING MANAGEMENT Company _____ MICROSOFT CORP _____ 9/9/94

		1984	1985	1986	1987	1988	1989	1990	1991	1992	1993	LAST 5 YEAR AVE.	TREND UP	TREND DOWN
A	% Pre-tax Profit on Sales (Net Before Taxes ÷ Sales)			30.5	33.4	35.1	31.1	31.2	34.7	36.4	37.7	37.3	35.5	↑	
B	% Earned on Invested Capital (E/S ÷ Book Value)			42.9	27.9	28.7	31.6	29.3	29.0	31.9	29.9	27.4	29.5		↓

3 PRICE-EARNINGS HISTORY as an indicator of the future

PRESENT PRICE ___56.875___ HIGH THIS YEAR ___59.250___ LOW THIS YEAR ___37.125___

	Year	A PRICE HIGH	B PRICE LOW	C Earnings Per Share	D Price Earnings Ratio HIGH A ÷ C	E Price Earnings Ratio LOW B ÷ C	F Dividend Per Share	G % Payout F ÷ C X 100	H % High Yield F ÷ B X 100
1	1989	19.8	10.2	0.67	29.6	15.2	0.000	0.0	0.0
2	1990	35.9	18.7	1.04	34.5	18.0	0.000	0.0	0.0
3	1991	74.7	32.4	1.65	45.3	19.7	0.000	0.0	0.0
4	1992	95.0	65.8	2.41	39.4	27.3	0.000	0.0	0.0
5	1993	98.0	70.4	3.15	31.1	22.3	0.000	0.0	0.0
6	TOTAL								
7	AVERAGE		39.5		36.0	20.5		0.0	
8	AVERAGE PRICE EARNINGS RATIO	28.2							
9				CURRENT PRICE EARNINGS RATIO				16.5	

Current P/E Based upon Last 12 mo. Earnings [3.45]
Proj. P/E [13.2] Based upon Next 12 mo. Earnings [4.31]

4 EVALUATING RISK and REWARD over the next 5 years

A HIGH PRICE - NEXT 5 YEARS
Avg. High P/E ___36.0___ (3D7) x Estimated High Earnings/Share ___9.61___ = Forecast High Price B-1 $ ___345.9___ (4A1)

B LOW PRICE - NEXT 5 YEARS
(a) Avg. Low P/E ___20.5___ (3E7) x Estimated Low E/Share ___3.15___ = $ ___64.5___
(b) Avg. Low Price of Last 5 Years = ___39.5___ (3B7)
(c) Recent Severe Market Low Price = ___32.4___
(d) Price Dividend Will Support Present Divd. / High Yield (H) = ___0.0___ =
Selected Estimated Low Price _____ B-2 $ ___39.5___ (4B1)

C ZONING
___345.9___ (4A1) High Forecast Price Minus ___39.5___ (4B1) Low Forecast Price Equals ___306.4___ (C) Range. ¹/₃ of Range = ___102.1___ (4CD)
Lower ¹/₃ = ___39.5___ To ___141.6___ (Buy) (4C2)
Middle ¹/₃ = ___141.6___ To ___243.7___ (Maybe) (4C3)
Upper ¹/₃ = ___243.7___ To ___345.9___ (4A1) (Sell) (4C4)
Present Market Price of ___56.9___ is in the --- Buy --- (4C5) Range

D UP-SIDE DOWN-SIDE RATIO (Potential Gain vs. Risk of Loss)
High Price ___345.9___ (4A1) Minus Present Price ___56.9___
Present Price ___56.9___ Minus Low Price ___39.5___ (4B1) = 289.0 / 17.4 = 16.6 (4D) = To 1

5 5-YR POTENTIAL

Relative Value: 58.4 %
Projected Relative Value: 46.7 %

A Present Full Year's Dividend $_____
Present Price of Stock $ ___56.9___ = _____ x100 = _____ Present Yield or % Returned on Purchase Price

B AVERAGE YIELD OVER THE NEXT 5 YEARS
Avg. Earn. Per Share Next 5 Years ___6.15___ x Avg % Payout ___0.0___ (3G7) = 0.0 %
Present Price $ ___56.9___

Total Return: 43.5 %

Source: National Association of Investors Corporation

Stock Price History (through mid-September 1994)

	1992	*1993*	*1994*
Low	32¼	32⅝	34
High	42⅛	40¾	44¾

Revenue and Earnings History (through June 30, 1994)

	1992	*1993*	*9 Months 1993*	*9 Months 1994*
Revenue	$2,365	$2,465	$1,798	$1,842
Net income	201	72*	(5)*	141
Earnings per share	2.57	.88*	(.10)*	1.87

In millions, except per-share amounts
*After charges for accounting changes totaling $141 million, or $1.83 per share

Key Growth Rates (past five years)

Revenue	10.0%
Cash flow	13.0%
Earnings	10.5%

DRIP Details

Becton, Dickinson shareholders can automatically reinvest their cash dividends plus invest up to an additional $3,000 per month in company stock without incurring any administrative or commission costs. Information on the dividend reinvestment plan may be obtained by contacting First Chicago Trust Company of New York, Dividend Reinvestment Plan, Becton, Dickinson, P.O. Box 2598, Jersey City, New Jersey 07303-2598, or call 800-446-2617.

Company Prospects

As a leader in developing products that improve safety in the healthcare industry and help hospitals lower healthcare delivery costs, Becton, Dickinson stands to benefit from the drive to reform the nation's healthcare system.

The company is placing increased emphasis on new diagnostic equipment for better diagnostic information on cancer and AIDS, two diseases triggering a rapid increase in healthcare product development. Other new product development thrusts include methods for diagnosing infectious disease information more quickly; safer and easier drug delivery systems; and safer and improved medical techniques. Becton, Dickinson backs up its commitment to new product development with a nearly 6 percent boost in research and development expenditures.

An ongoing share repurchase program will add to per-share earnings as will lowered operating costs and improving gross margins. The company's growing international presence adds another dimension to revenue and earnings growth. Look for Becton, Dickinson to continue its steady progress over the years ahead. Another plus: Excess cash from reduced capital expenditures will be available to increase the dividend, boosting total shareholder return.

MAJOR PORTFOLIO HOLDING PROFILE

Mylan Laboratories, Inc.
1030 Century Building
130 Seventh Street
Pittsburgh, Pennsylvania 15222

Stock Exchange: NYSE
Ticker Symbol: MYL
Telephone 412-232-0100

Company Business

Mylan Laboratories manufactures generic pharmaceutical products and brand-name dermatological products. Its prescription drugs serve antibiotic, anti-inflammatory, cardiovascular, and central nervous system medical needs. Mylan ranks as the leading generic drug manufacturer, with a product line of 73 drugs covering more than 22 therapeutic categories.

The company operates two distribution centers plus eight regional sales offices throughout the United States. Operating facilities and subsidiaries are located in Morgantown, West Virginia; Caguas, Puerto Rico; Sugar Land, Texas; and St. Albans, Vermont.

Shareholder Information

Outstanding shares	79,218,000
Insider ownership	More than 4 percent
DRIP program	No

Financial Information (June 1994)

Total assets	$447 million
Cash and temporary investments	$93 million
Working capital	$206 million
Long-term debt	-0-
Equity ratio	100 percent
Book value	$5.10
Dividend rate	20 cents per share annual basis
Yield	.6 percent
Price/earnings ratio	24

Stock Price History (through mid-September 1994)

	1992	*1993*	*1994*
Low	15⅞	19⅝	15⅝
High	31⅞	37⅝	25¼

Revenue and Earnings History (through June 30, 1994)

	1993	1994	3 Months 1994	3 Months 1995
Revenue	$212	$251	$59	$85
Net income	71	73	16	27
Earnings per share	.92	.93	.21	.34

In millions, except per-share amounts

Key Growth Rates (past five years)

Revenue	14.5%
Cash flow	21.5%
Earnings	21.0%

Company Prospects

Mylan Laboratories is the premier generic pharmaceutical company, with a solid reputation for quality, an excellent distribution system, and strong revenue and earnings growth predicted for fiscal 1995 and beyond.

First-quarter fiscal 1995 results ended June 30, 1994, reflected revenue growth in excess of 45 percent and an earnings per-share surge in excess of 61 percent (34 cents per share versus 21 cents per share for last fiscal year's first three months).

New product introductions capturing a significant market share accounted for the impressive showing. High research and development expenditures will keep Mylan Laboratories' product pipeline full. Currently, the company has more than 15 new drug applications under review by the FDA and 25 drugs in development.

Another major market push included an agreement with Eli Lilly regarding marketing Mylan's Cimetidine (the generic for SmithKline Beecham's popular Tagamet) to the managed healthcare market. Mylan also formed a strategic alliance with Ferrer International of Barcelona, Spain, for the exclusive license agreement for Sentaconazole, a topical antifungal.

Given the number of drugs in the works and market acceptance of its current products, Mylan's growth potential remains great. Mylan's current stock price level adds to this firm's attractiveness as a solid long-term investment. The stock price fell nearly 40 percent in early 1994 before recovering a bit (see Chart 2–8). Buy for exceptional total return.

MAJOR PORTFOLIO HOLDING PROFILE

Synovus Financial Corporation	Stock Exchange: NYSE
P.O. Box 120	Ticker Symbol: SNV
Columbus, Georgia 31902-0120	Telephone 706-649-5220

Chart 2–8   Mylan Laboratories, Inc. Stock Chart

MYLAN LABS. NYSE-MYL	RECENT PRICE **22**	P/E RATIO **19.0** (Trailing: 20.8 Median: 23.0)	RELATIVE P/E RATIO **1.29**	DIV'D YLD **0.9%**	VALUE LINE **1274**

| TIMELINESS **2** Above Average (Relative Price Perform-ance Next 12 Mos.) | High: | 1.8 | 6.2 | 8.8 | 9.0 | 8.7 | 6.6 | 12.7 | 12.4 | 21.3 | 31.9 | 37.6 | 25.1 | Target Price Range 1997 1998 1999 |
| | Low: | 0.7 | 1.4 | 4.0 | 5.0 | 3.8 | 4.0 | 3.8 | 6.9 | 8.6 | 15.8 | 19.6 | 15.6 | |

SAFETY **3** Average
(Scale: 1 Highest to 5 Lowest)
BETA 1.40 (1.00 = Market)

2-for-1 split
3-for-2 split
20.0 x "Cash Flow" p sh
3-for-2 split   2-for-1 split
3-for-2 split
2-for-1 split
Relative Price Strength
Shaded areas indicate recessions
Options: ASE

1997-99 PROJECTIONS
	Price	Gain	Ann'l Total Return
High	55	(+150%)	26%
Low	30	(+35%)	9%

Insider Decisions
	O	N	D	J	F	M	A	M	J
to Buy	0	0	0	0	0	0	1	0	
Options	0	1	2	0	0	0	0	0	
to Sell	0	1	2	0	0	0	0	1	

Institutional Decisions
	2Q'93	4Q'93	1Q'94
to Buy	86	87	59
to Sell	90	55	91
Hld's(000)	35911	33840	28491

Percent 24.0 / 16.0 / 8.0 shares traded

	1978	1979	1980	1981	1982	1983	1984	1985	1986	1987	1988	1989	1990	1991	1992	1993	1994	1995	© VALUE LINE PUB, INC.	97-99
Sales per sh A	.33	.36	.33	.47	.45	.51	.74	1.11	1.32	1.33	1.22	1.32	1.26	1.72	2.71	3.18	4.15	5.00		8.25
"Cash Flow" per sh	.02	.03	.02	.06	.06	.08	.18	.30	.34	.37	.28	.40	.49	.59	.97	1.06	1.40	1.75		2.75
Earnings per sh B	.02	.02	.01	.06	.05	.07	.17	.29	.33	.35	.25	.36	.45	.53	.92	.93	1.25	1.55		2.50
Div'ds Decl'd per sh C	..	..	..	..	..	.00	.02	.02	.04	.05	.05	.05	.10	.10	.12	.15	.20	.24		.40
Cap'l Spending per sh	.02	.01	.02	.01	.01	.03	.03	.05	--	.13	.04	.07	.06	.13	.16	.25	.25	.25		.50
Book Value per sh D	.05	.08	.09	.14	.19	.25	.41	.65	.94	1.24	1.44	1.76	2.11	2.65	3.79	4.80	5.85	7.15		12.25
Common Shs Outst'g D	66.82	67.12	67.12	68.02	70.21	72.12	72.05	72.67	72.23	72.28	72.29	72.41	72.55	76.82	78.19	79.20	79.50	80.00		81.00
Avg Ann'l P/E Ratio	4.9	6.2	11.8	3.5	8.2	19.4	22.9	22.4	21.8	17.7	19.8	22.2	22.8	29.6	27.4	28.0	Bold figures are Value Line estimates			18.0
Relative P/E Ratio	.67	.90	1.57	.43	.90	1.64	2.13	1.82	1.48	1.18	1.64	1.68	1.69	1.89	1.66	1.65				1.40
Avg Ann'l Div'd Yield	..	..	..	..	..	.3%	.6%	.4%	.6%	.8%	1.0%	.6%	1.0%	.6%	.5%	.6%				1.0%

						Sales ($mill) A	53.6	80.8	95.1	96.0	87.9	95.4	91.1	131.9	212.0	251.8	330	400	675

Sales ($mill) A	53.6	80.8	95.1	96.0	87.9	95.4	91.1	131.9	212.0	251.8	330	400	675
Operating Margin	43.0%	45.9%	45.3%	40.4%	26.5%	24.4%	23.5%	23.8%	36.6%	26.4%	36.5%	36.0%	34.0%
Depreciation ($mill)	.8	.9	1.2	1.8	2.1	3.0	2.9	5.1	5.1	11.2	12.0	13.0	19.0
Net Profit ($mill)	12.5	20.7	23.3	25.2	18.3	26.2	32.7	40.1	70.6	73.1	100	125	200
Income Tax Rate	45.8%	45.8%	44.2%	32.6%	22.0%	18.5%	16.0%	20.0%	27.4%	16.1%	28.0%	25.0%	20.0%
Net Profit Margin	23.3%	25.6%	24.5%	26.3%	20.8%	27.5%	35.9%	30.4%	33.3%	29.0%	30.3%	31.3%	29.6%
Working Cap'l ($mill)	23.1	38.9	51.2	64.1	61.2	55.7	71.5	102.1	154.0	191.7	275	300	500
Long-Term Debt ($mill)	2.3	1.9	4.6	6.3	.5	1.1	2.1	--	--		Nil	Nil	Nil
Net Worth ($mill)	29.2	47.6	68.0	89.7	104.3	127.2	153.3	203.5	296.0	380.0	465	570	1000
% Earned Total Cap'l	40.0%	42.1%	32.2%	26.5%	17.6%	20.4%	21.1%	19.7%	23.9%	19.2%	21.5%	22.0%	20.0%
% Earned Net Worth	42.7%	43.6%	34.3%	28.1%	17.5%	20.6%	21.4%	19.7%	23.9%	19.2%	21.5%	22.0%	20.0%
% Retained to Comm Eq	37.3%	38.5%	29.9%	24.0%	14.0%	17.7%	17.8%	16.1%	21.0%	16.3%	18.0%	18.5%	16.5%
% All Div'ds to Net Prof	13%	12%	13%	15%	20%	14%	17%	16%	12%	15%	16%	16%	16%

BUSINESS: Mylan Laboratories Inc. manufactures prescription generic drugs (primarily antibiotic, anti-inflammatory, cardiovascular, and central nervous system agents) and brand-name dermatological products. In 1989, acquired a 50% stake in Somerset Pharmaceuticals, manufacturer of anti-Parkinson's drug, *Eldepryl*, which accounted for 27% of FY '93 pre-tax profits. *Maxzide*, an anti-hypertensive agent, licensed to Lederle Labs. Acquired Dow B. Hickam (dermatol. products), 10/91; Bertek (drug delivery systems), 2/93. 1993 deprec. rate: 9.7%; R&D: 8.6% of sales. Has 1,240 employees; 83,637 shareholders. Insiders own 4.3% of stock (5/94 proxy). Inc.: Pennsylvania. Chairman & C.E.O.: M. Puskar. Address: 130 Seventh St., Pittsburgh, PA 15222. Tel.: 412-232-0100.

Company Business

Synovus Financial is a multifinancial services company with 32 community banks in Georgia, Alabama, and Florida. The company's banks rank either first or second in their respective primary markets.

Synovus Financial also owns nearly 81 percent of Total Systems Services, Inc. (NYSE: TSS), the world's second largest credit card processing company. Total Systems Services generates 22 percent of Synovus Financial's net income. The credit card processing operation has long-term agreements with such players as AT&T Universal Card Services and Bank of America. The credit card operations has experienced a nearly 26 percent compound growth rate over the past 10 years.

Shareholder Information

Outstanding shares	66,958,000
Insider ownership	Nearly 12 percent
DRIP program	Yes

Financial Information (June 1994)

Total assets	$5.8 billion
Cash and temporary investments	$1.5 billion
Net interest margin	5.16 percent
Nonperforming assets ratio	1.02 percent
Net charge-off ratio	.33 percent
Long-term debt	$137 million
Book value	$7.24 per share
Dividend rate	45 cents per share annual basis
Yield	2.4 percent
Price/earnings ratio	16

Stock Price History (through mid-September 1994)

	1992	1993	1994
Low	$11\frac{1}{8}$	15	$16\frac{5}{8}$
High	$16\frac{5}{8}$	$20\frac{3}{8}$	$19\frac{1}{4}$

Revenue and Earnings History (through June 30, 1994)

	1992	1993	1st Half 1993	1st Half 1994
Net income	$61	$74*	$34	$40
Earnings per share	.92	1.11*	.52	.59

In millions, except per share amounts
* Before extraordinary item

Key Growth Rates (past five years)

Loans	16.0%
Earnings	12.0%

DRIP Details

Synovus Financial's dividend reinvestment plan provides for automatic reinvestment of cash dividends plus additional cash purchases of company common stock in amounts up to $2,000 per month. There are no administrative or commission charges. For information on this DRIP, contact Investor Relations, Synovus Financial Corporation, P. O. Box 120, Columbus, Georgia 31902-0120, or call 706-649-5220.

Company Prospects

Synovus Financial has a lot going for it. Its asset quality is strong, and its nonperforming assets are lower than those of the Southeastern peer group it competes against. Both nonperforming assets and charge-offs are at their lowest level in 10 years. Adding to earnings stability, 50 percent of Synovus Financial's Total Systems revenues are fee based.

The financial institution's prospects have not gone unnoticed. *U.S. Banker* ranked Synovus as the eighth-safest and most profitable banking company in the nation in May 1994, and *Financial World* listed Synovus as one of America's 50 Best Mid-Cap Companies in June 1994. *Fortune* ranks Synovus's total return to shareholders between 1983 and 1993 of 21.7 percent yearly as the 12th best among the nation's 100 largest banks.

This financial institution is no stranger to investment clubs either. It ranks 41st in the number of shares held by NAIC investment clubs and 48th in the number of investment clubs owning the stock. Adding to total return, over the 10-year period ended 1993, the firm's dividend grew at a compounded rate in excess of 16 percent.

Total Systems enhanced its growth potential with a recently signed joint venture with PROSA, Mexico's largest credit card processor. Also, banking acquisitions will enhance loan growth and improved margins through operating efficiencies and enlarged market share.

NAIC's *Better Investing* featured Synovus Financial as an undervalued stock in its May 1994 issue. Strong profit potential in both the banking and credit card operations could spur Synovus Financial's stock price in the years ahead, providing superior returns to patient investors. The stock dropped from its record high of $20\frac{3}{8}$ per share in early 1993 to as low as $16\frac{7}{8}$ per share in 1994 before recovering a bit (see Chart 2–9).

DISAPPOINTING STOCKS SHED

Company	Industry
Cincinnati Bell, Inc.	Telecommunications
Liz Claiborne, Inc.	Cosmetics

Chart 2–9 Synovus Financial Corporation Stock Chart

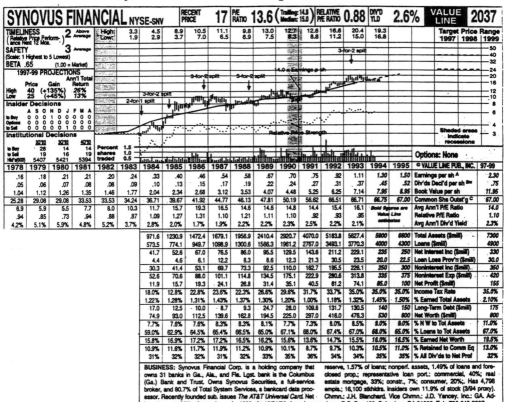

| **SYNOVUS FINANCIAL** NYSE-SNV | **RECENT PRICE** 17 | **P/E RATIO** 13.6 (Trailing: 14.8 Median: 15.0) | **RELATIVE P/E RATIO** 0.88 | **DIV'D YLD** 2.6% | **VALUE LINE** 2037 |

	1978	1979	1980	1981	1982	1983	1984	1985	1986	1987	1988	1989	1990	1991	1992	1993	1994	1995	© VALUE LINE PUB., INC.	97-99
	.16	.18	.21	.21	.20	.24	.33	.40	.46	.54	.58	.67	.70	.75	.92	1.11	1.30	1.50	Earnings per sh A	2.30
	.05	.06	.07	.08	.08	.09	.10	.13	.15	.17	.19	.22	.24	.27	.31	.37	.45	.52	Div'ds Decl'd per sh B■	.75
	1.04	1.12	1.26	1.35	1.46	1.77	2.04	2.34	2.68	3.12	3.53	4.07	4.48	5.25	6.25	7.14	7.95	8.95	Book Value per sh	11.95
	25.28	29.08	29.08	33.53	33.53	34.24	36.71	39.67	41.92	44.77	46.13	47.81	50.19	56.62	66.51	66.71	66.75	67.00	Common Shs Outst'g C	67.00
	6.9	5.9	5.5	7.7	8.0	10.3	11.7	15.7	19.3	16.5	14.6	14.6	14.8	14.4	15.4	16.1	Bold figures are		Avg Ann'l P/E Ratio	14.0
	.94	.85	.73	.94	.88	.87	1.09	1.27	1.31	1.10	1.21	1.11	1.10	.92	.93	.95	Value Line estimates		Relative P/E Ratio	1.10
	4.2%	5.1%	5.9%	4.8%	5.2%	3.7%	2.8%	2.0%	1.7%	1.9%	2.2%	2.2%	2.3%	2.5%	2.2%	2.1%			Avg Ann'l Div'd Yield	2.3%
							971.6	1230.9	1472.4	1679.1	1956.9	2410.4	2920.7	4070.0	5183.8	5627.4	5900	6600	Total Assets ($mill)	7300
							573.5	774.1	949.7	1098.9	1300.6	1586.3	1961.2	2767.0	3493.1	3770.3	4000	4300	Loans ($mill)	4900
							41.7	52.6	67.0	76.5	86.0	95.5	129.5	143.6	211.2	229.1	235	250	Net Interest Inc ($mill)	330
							4.4	4.6	6.1	12.2	8.3	8.6	12.3	21.3	30.5	23.5	20.0	22.5	Loan Loss Prov'n ($mill)	30.0
							30.3	41.4	53.1	69.7	73.3	92.5	110.0	162.7	195.5	226.1	250	300	Noninterest Inc ($mill)..	350
							52.6	70.6	88.0	101.1	114.8	134.5	175.1	222.9	280.6	313.8	335	375	Noninterest Exp ($mill)	420
							11.9	15.7	19.3	24.1	26.8	31.4	35.1	40.5	61.2	74.1	85.0	100	Net Profit ($mill)	155
							18.0%	12.8%	22.8%	23.6%	22.3%	26.6%	29.6%	31.7%	33.7%	35.0%	35.0%	35.0%	Income Tax Rate	35.0%
							1.22%	1.28%	1.31%	1.43%	1.37%	1.30%	1.20%	1.00%	1.18%	1.32%	1.45%	1.50%	% Earned Total Assets	2.10%
							17.0	12.5	10.0	8.7	9.3	24.7	28.0	109.8	131.7	130.5	140	150	Long-Term Debt ($mill)	175
							74.9	93.0	112.5	139.6	162.8	194.5	225.0	297.0	416.0	476.3	530	600	Net Worth ($mill)	800
							7.7%	7.6%	7.6%	8.3%	8.3%	8.1%	7.7%	7.3%	8.0%	8.5%	9.0%	9.0%	% N W to Tot Assets	11.0%
							59.0%	62.9%	64.5%	65.4%	66.5%	65.0%	67.1%	68.0%	67.4%	67.0%	68.0%	65.0%	% Loans to Tot Assets	67.0%
							15.8%	16.9%	17.2%	17.2%	16.5%	16.2%	15.6%	13.6%	14.7%	15.5%	16.0%	16.5%	% Earned Net Worth	19.5%
							10.9%	11.6%	11.7%	11.9%	11.2%	10.9%	10.1%	8.7%	9.7%	10.3%	10.5%	11.0%	% Retained to Comm Eq	13.0%
							31%	32%	32%	31%	32%	33%	35%	36%	34%	34%	35%	35%	% All Div'ds to Net Prof	32%

TIMELINESS 2 Above Average (Relative Price Perform- ance Next 12 Mos.)

SAFETY 3 Average (Scale: 1 Highest to 5 Lowest)

BETA .65 (1.00 = Market)

1997-99 PROJECTIONS
	Price	Gain	Ann'l Total Return
High	40	(+135%)	26%
Low	25	(+45%)	13%

Insider Decisions
	A	S	O	N	D	J	F	M	A
to Buy	0	0	0	1	0	0	0	0	0
Options	0	0	0	0	0	0	0	0	0
to Sell	0	0	0	0	0	1	0	0	0

Institutional Decisions
	2Q'93	3Q'93	4Q'93
to Buy	28	14	14
to Sell	19	16	19
Hld's(000)	5407	5421	5394

Percent shares traded: 1.5 / 1.0 / 0.5

Options: None

BUSINESS: Synovus Financial Corp. is a holding company that owns 31 banks in Ga., Ala., and Fla. Lgst. bank is the Columbus (Ga.) Bank and Trust. Owns Synovus Securities, a full-service broker, and 80.7% of Total System Services, a bankcard data processor. Recently founded sub. issues *The AT&T Universal Card*. Net loan losses, .50% of avg. loans in 1993. At 12/31/93, loan loss reserve, 1.57% of loans; nonperf. assets, 1.49% of loans and foreclosed prop.; representative loan port.: commercial, 40%; real estate mortgage, 33%; constr., 7%; consumer, 20%;. Has 4,798 emple.; 16,100 stkhldrs. Insiders own 11.9% of stock (3/94 proxy). Chrmn: J.H. Blanchard. Vice Chrmn.: J.D. Yancey. Inc.: GA. Address: P.O. Box 120, Columbus, GA 31902. Tel.: 706-649-2387.

Women of Vested Interest Investment Club

Kirkland, Washington

CLUB MAKEUP

Number of members	7
Member age range	39-52
Age of club	More than seven years
Average number of securities in portfolio	14
$ value of portfolio	$42,400 (August 1994)
Amount invested per member/per month	$50*

*Bylaws require minimum of $30 per month.

MAJOR CURRENT HOLDINGS 9/20/90

Company	Purchase Date	Original Cost	Value
McDonald's Corp.	1988	$2,908	$5,250
Microsoft Corp.	1987	739	6,720
Quality Food Centers	1991	4,995	3,581

CLUB INVESTMENT PHILOSOPHY

"Our goal is to learn while having fun. We search for growth companies at the 'right' price," says Bonnie Berry, club treasurer. "We are not opposed to taking on a little higher risk with new issues (IPOs) that make sense to us, but they do not dominate our portfolio."

The Women of Vested Interest Club prepares the Stock Selection Guides recommended by the NAIC for use in the decision-making process. Stock selection candidates come from a variety of sources, including newspapers and business publications such as *Barron's, The Wall Street Journal, The New York Times, Forbes, Fortune*, and *Business Week*. The *Value Line* High Growth Stock Index listings provide another rich place to find companies for purchase consideration.

Club members make good use of NAIC-sponsored investment conferences and seminars as well as NAIC investment software products to enhance their investigative work and portfolio performance. As promulgated by the NAIC, investment gains are reinvested to achieve higher returns through compounding.

The sale of McCaw Cellular in 1993 more than doubled the club's investment in the largest cellular telephone company. The club also enjoys a large gain on its Microsoft Corporation stake, up more than 554 percent since its purchase back in 1987. On the downside, in July 1994 the club shed its interest in troubled merchandiser Price/Costco, Inc. for a loss in excess of $17 per share.

Looking ahead, the Women of Vested Interest Club recently purchased semiconductor manufacturer Intel Corporation and have already scored a $6 per share gain in just over one month. "Intel Corporation fits all the NAIC guidelines for a stock capable of doubling in five years. It operates in an exciting industry, and all the business media are very favorable on the company," Berry says.

NEW PORTFOLIO PURCHASE PROFILE

Intel Corporation   Stock Exchange: NASDAQ
2200 Mission College Boulevard   Ticker Symbol: INTC
Santa Clara, California 95052-8119   Telephone 408-765-8080

Company Business

Intel Corporation is a leading producer of integrated circuits for personal computers, communications, other electronic equipment, industrial automation, and military applications. Intel sells microprocessors, microcontrollers, memory chips, computer models, computer boards, and networking products. A global company, it generates half of its annual revenues from foreign business.

Intel is staking its reputation on developing core logic chip sets (PCI sets). The company has invested more than $100 million in developing PCI local bus architecture, designing PCI sets, and promoting PCI sets as an industry standard. The stakes are huge. Intel estimates that PCI-based system usage will grow to 50 million units by 1997, up substantially from the fewer than 10 million units in use in 1994. Overall, Intel invests 11 percent of revenues in research and development efforts annually.

Shareholder Information

Outstanding shares	437,000,000
Insider ownership	7 percent
DRIP program	Yes

Financial Information (July 1994)

Total assets	$12 billion
Cash and temporary investments	$ 2.3 billion
Working capital	$ 2.9 billion
Long-term debt	$303 million
Equity ratio	96 percent
Book value	$19.06 per share
Dividend rate	20 cents per share annual basis
Yield	.4 percent
Price/earnings ratio	12

Stock Price History (through mid-September 1994)

	1992	*1993*	*1994*
Low	23¼	42¾	56
High	45⅞	74¼	73½

Revenue and Earnings History (through July 2, 1994)

	1992	*1993*	*1st Half 1993*	*1st Half 1994*
Revenue	$5,844	$8,782	$4,153	$5,430
Net income	1,067	$2,295	1,117	1,257
Earnings per share	2.49	5.20	2.53	2.86

In millions, except per-share amounts

Key Growth Rates (past five years)

Revenue	22.0%
Cash flow	36.0%
Earnings	51.0%

DRIP Details

Intel Corporation established its dividend reinvestment plan in 1994. The plan allows company shareholders to automatically reinvest cash dividends in Intel stock. In addition, it permits additional cash investments in amounts ranging from $25 to $15,000 quarterly. For information on the Intel DRIP, contact Harris Trust and Savings Bank, Intel Dividend Reinvestment Stock Purchase Plan, P.O. Box A3309, Chicago, Illinois 60690, or call 800-298-0146.

Company Prospects

Intel Corporation has embarked on a stock repurchase program. During the first half of 1994, the company repurchased 8.6 million shares. Another 5.4 million shares remain available for repurchase under the program authorization. When completed, the program will have reduced outstanding shares of common stock by more than 3 percent, making year-to-year comparisons more favorable for remaining shareholders.

Intel posted its eighth consecutive quarter of record revenues and earnings for the three months ended July 2, 1994. For the first half of 1994, revenues grew by 31 percent while earnings increased 12½ percent.

Despite gross margins under pressure from price reductions caused by stiff industry competition, Intel has the management savvy, financial clout, and product line to beat out the competition over the long term. New manufacturing facilities coming on line promise to bring relief to gross margins and promote record bookings for future delivery.

Market acceptance of the new Pentium processor could add a significant increase to company earnings and revenues in coming years. NAIC's Stock

Selection Guide for Intel reflects an estimated five-year return potential of 21.2 percent, with the stock currently in a buy range (see Chart 2–10).

MAJOR PORTFOLIO HOLDING PROFILE

McDonald's Corporation	Stock Exchange: NYSE
1 McDonald's Plaza	Ticker Symbol: MCD
Oak Brook, Illinois 60521	Telephone 708-575-7428

Company Business

McDonald's Corporation licenses and operates a chain of nearly 14,000 fast-food restaurants throughout the United States, Canada, and overseas in a total of 70 countries. The company has added a new restaurant every 14 hours over the past 10 years and plans to open another 900 to 1,200 over the next few years, at an accelerated pace of one every eight or nine hours.

McDonald's is building a global network of fast-food chains to enhance shareholder value. Foreign operations generate approximately 40 percent of annual revenues and 45 percent of operating profits.

Shareholder Information

Outstanding shares	712,500,000
Insider ownership	Less than 1 percent*
DRIP program	Yes

*Plus corporate profit sharing program owns 3.1 percent of outstanding shares of common stock

Financial Information (June 1994)

Total assets	$12.8 billion
Cash and temporary investments	$147 million
Working capital	NMF
Long-term debt	$ 3 billion
Equity ratio	56 percent
Book value	$9.21 per share
Dividend rate	24 cents per share annual basis
Yield	.9 percent
Price/earnings ratio	18

Stock Price History (through mid-September 1994)

	1992	*1993*	*1994*
Low	19¼	22¾	26¼
High	25⅛	29⅝	31½

Chart 2–10 Intel Stock Selection Guide

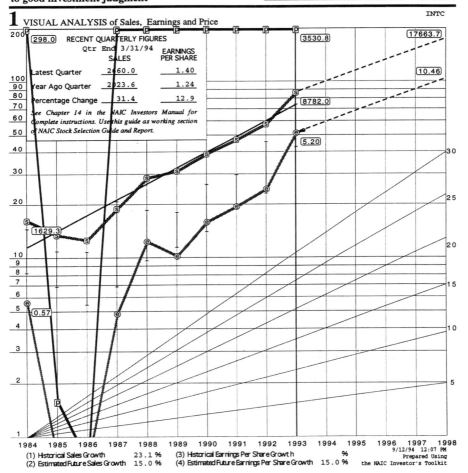

STOCK
SELECTION
GUIDE
**The most widely used aid
to good investment judgment**

NATIONAL ASSOCIATION
OF INVESTORS CORPORATION

NAIC

INVESTMENT EDUCATION
SINCE 1951

| Company | INTEL CORP | Date | 9/9/94 |

Prepared by ___ SPC ___ Data taken from __ S & P () __

Where traded __ OTC __ Main product/service SEMICONDUC

CAPITALIZATION	Authorized	Outstanding
Preferred	0.0	0.0
Common	0.0	418.0
Other Debt	826.0	Potential Dilution None

1 VISUAL ANALYSIS of Sales, Earnings and Price

INTC

(298.0) RECENT QUARTERLY FIGURES
Qtr End 3/31/94

	SALES	EARNINGS PER SHARE
Latest Quarter	2660.0	1.40
Year Ago Quarter	2023.6	1.24
Percentage Change	31.4	12.9

See Chapter 14 in the NAIC Investors Manual for Complete instructions. Use this guide as working section of NAIC Stock Selection Guide and Report.

(3530.8) (17663.7)

(8782.0)

(5.20)

(1629.3)

(0.57)

1984	1985	1986	1987	1988	1989	1990	1991	1992	1993	1994	1995	1996	1997	1998

9/12/94 12:07 PM

(1) Historical Sales Growth   23.1 %
(2) Estimated Future Sales Growth 15.0 %
(3) Historical Earnings Per Share Growth   %
(4) Estimated Future Earnings Per Share Growth 15.0 %

Prepared Using
the NAIC Investor's Toolkit

Source: National Association of Investors Corporation

Chart 2–10 Intel Stock Selection Guide

2 EVALUATING MANAGEMENT Company ——— INTEL CORP ——— 9/9/94

		1984	1985	1986	1987	1988	1989	1990	1991	1992	1993	LAST 5 YEAR AVE.	TREND UP	TREND DOWN
A	% Pre-tax Profit on Sales (Net Before Taxes ÷ Sales)	18.3	0.1	-14.5	15.1	21.9	18.6	25.2	25.0	26.8	40.2	27.2	↑	
B	% Earned on Invested Capital (E/S ÷ Book Value)	14.3	0.0	-14.4	12.6	21.7	14.9	17.8	18.1	19.1	29.0	19.8	↑	

3 PRICE-EARNINGS HISTORY as an indicator of the future

PRESENT PRICE __65.750__   HIGH THIS YEAR __74.250__   LOW THIS YEAR __56.000__

	Year	A PRICE HIGH	B PRICE LOW	C Earnings Per Share	D Price Earnings Ratio HIGH A ÷ C	E Price Earnings Ratio LOW B ÷ C	F Dividend Per Share	G % Payout F ÷ C X 100	H % High Yield F ÷ B X 100
1	1989	18.0	11.4	1.03	17.5	11.1	0.000	0.0	0.0
2	1990	26.0	14.0	1.60	16.2	8.8	0.000	0.0	0.0
3	1991	29.6	18.9	1.96	15.1	9.6	0.000	0.0	0.0
4	1992	45.8	23.2	2.48	18.4	9.4	0.050	2.0	0.2
5	1993	74.2	42.8	5.20	14.3	8.2	0.200	3.8	0.5
6	TOTAL								
7	AVERAGE		22.1		16.3	9.4		2.9	
8	AVERAGE PRICE EARNINGS RATIO		12.9		9 CURRENT PRICE EARNINGS RATIO			12.2	

Current P/E Based upon Last 12 mo. Earnings [5.38]
Proj. P/E [10.6] Based upon Next 12 mo. Earnings [6.19]

4 EVALUATING RISK and REWARD over the next 5 years

A HIGH PRICE - NEXT 5 YEARS
Avg. High P/E __16.3__ (3D7) x Estimated High Earnings/Share __10.46__ = Forecast High Price B-1 $ __170.6__ (4A1)

B LOW PRICE - NEXT 5 YEARS
(a) Avg. Low P/E __9.4__ (3E7) x Estimated Low E/Share __5.20__ = $ __49.0__
(b) Avg. Low Price of Last 5 Years = __22.1__ (3B7)
(c) Recent Severe Market Low Price = __18.9__
(d) Price Dividend Will Support $\frac{\text{Present Divd.}}{\text{High Yield (H)}} = \frac{0.200}{0.5} = $ __42.8__
Selected Estimated Low Price   B-2 $ __22.1__ (4B1)

C ZONING
__170.6__ (4A1) High Forecast Price Minus __22.1__ (4B1) Low Forecast Price Equals __148.6__ (C) Range. 1/3 of Range = __49.5__ (4CD)
Lower 1/3 = __22.1__ (4B1) To __71.6__ (Buy) (4C2)
Middle 1/3 = __71.6__ To __121.1__ (Maybe) (4C3)
Upper 1/3 = __121.1__ To __170.6__ (4A1) (Sell) (4C4)
Present Market Price of __65.8__ is in the --- **Buy** --- (4C5) Range

D UP-SIDE DOWN-SIDE RATIO (Potential Gain vs. Risk of Loss)
$\frac{\text{High Price } \underline{170.6}\ (4A1)\ \text{Minus Present Price } \underline{65.8}}{\text{Present Price } \underline{65.8}\ \text{Minus Low Price } \underline{22.1}\ (4B1)} = \frac{104.9}{43.7} = $ __2.4__ (4D) = To 1

Relative Value: 95.0 %
Projected Relative Value: 82.6 %

5 5-YR POTENTIAL

A Present Full Year's Dividend $ __0.200__ / Present Price of Stock $ __65.8__ = __0.003__ x100 = __0.3__ Present Yield or % Returned on Purchase Price

B AVERAGE YIELD OVER THE NEXT 5 YEARS
Avg. Earn. Per Share Next 5 Years __7.91__ x Avg % Payout __2.9__ (3G7) = __0.4__ %
Present Price $ __65.8__

Total Return: 21.2 %

Source: National Association of Investors Corporation

Revenue and Earnings History (through June 30, 1994)

	1992	1993	1st Half 1993	1st Half 1994
Revenue	$7,133	$7,408	$3,532	$3,825
Net income	959	1,083	507	566
Earnings per share	1.30	1.46	.67	.77

In millions, except per-share amounts

Key Growth Rates (past five years)

Revenue	8.5%
Cash flow	13.5%
Earnings	12.5%

DRIP Details

McDonald's DRIP allows for automatic cash dividend reinvestment plus additional cash investment in company stock in amounts ranging from $50 to $75,000 per calendar year. For information on this dividend reinvestment program contact McDonald's Corporation, 1 McDonald's Plaza, Oak Brook, Illinois, 60521-2278, or call 800-621-7825.

Company Prospects

McDonald's Corporation holds top ranking among NAIC investment clubs both in terms of the number of clubs holding the stock (4,273) and the number of shares owned by clubs (2,277,785). Investment clubs flock to McDonald's for good reason. Over the 10-year period ended December 31, 1993, McDonald's provided a compound annual return to its shareholders of 19.8 percent—that compares with a compound annual return of only 17.5 percent for the Dow Jones Industrial Average and 14.9 percent for the S&P 500 over the same time frame.

McDonald's global strategy will keep revenues and earnings on the upswing. Since 1988, the company has increased the foreign share of its business from 29 percent to 45 percent. Look for this trend to accelerate. Two-thirds of the 900 to 1,200 McDonald's restaurants scheduled to be opened in the next few years will be overseas.

McDonald's NAIC Stock Selection Guide reflects a potential total compound annual return in excess of 10 percent over the next five years with a five-year high price over $43 per share within the realm of possibility. See Chart 2–11.

MAJOR PORTFOLIO HOLDING PROFILE

Microsoft Corporation
(See the discussion under Arrow Investment Club.)

Chart 2–11 McDonald's Corporation Stock Selection Guide

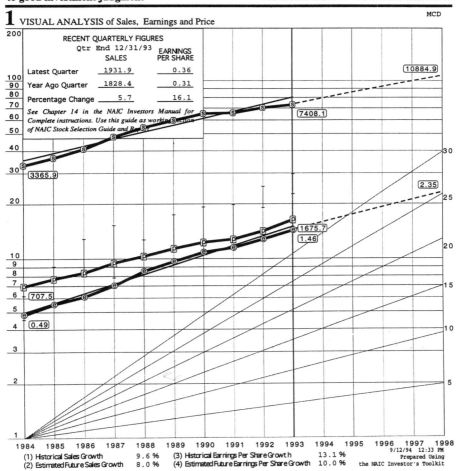

STOCK
SELECTION
GUIDE
**The most widely used aid
to good investment judgment**

NATIONAL ASSOCIATION
OF INVESTORS CORPORATION

NAIC

INVESTMENT EDUCATION
SINCE 1951

Company	MCDONALDS CORP	Date	9/9/94

Prepared by ___SPC___ Data taken from ___S & P ()___

Where traded ___NYSE___ Main product/service ___EATING PLA___

CAPITALIZATION	Authorized	Outstanding
Preferred	0.0	0.0
Common	0.0	707.4
Other Debt	3712.7	Potential Dilution None

MCD

1 VISUAL ANALYSIS of Sales, Earnings and Price

RECENT QUARTERLY FIGURES

Qtr End 12/31/93

	SALES	EARNINGS PER SHARE
Latest Quarter	1931.9	0.36
Year Ago Quarter	1828.4	0.31
Percentage Change	5.7	16.1

See Chapter 14 in the NAIC Investors Manual for Complete instructions. Use this guide as working section of NAIC Stock Selection Guide and Re

10884.9

7408.1

3365.9

2.35

1675.7

1.46

707.5

0.49

1984 1985 1986 1987 1988 1989 1990 1991 1992 1993 1994 1995 1996 1997 1998

9/12/94 12:33 PM

(1) Historical Sales Growth   9.6 %
(2) Estimated Future Sales Growth   8.0 %

(3) Historical Earnings Per Share Growth   13.1 %
(4) Estimated Future Earnings Per Share Growth   10.0 %

Prepared Using
the NAIC Investor's Toolkit

Source: National Association of Investors Corporation

Chart 2–11 McDonald's Corporation Stock Selection Guide

2 EVALUATING MANAGEMENT Company ____ MCDONALDS CORP ____ 9/9/94

		1984	1985	1986	1987	1988	1989	1990	1991	1992	1993	LAST 5 YEAR AVE.	TREND UP	TREND DOWN
A	% Pre-tax Profit on Sales (Net Before Taxes ÷ Sales)	21.0	21.2	20.5	19.7	19.0	19.1	18.8	19.4	20.3	22.6	20.0	↑	
B	% Earned on Invested Capital (E/S ÷ Book Value)	19.1	19.2	18.8	18.7	18.9	20.0	18.9	17.4	16.0	16.5	17.7		↓

3 PRICE-EARNINGS HISTORY as an indicator of the future

PRESENT PRICE ____ 27.375 ____ HIGH THIS YEAR ____ 31.375 ____ LOW THIS YEAR ____ 25.500

	Year	A	B	C	D	E	F	G	H
		PRICE		Earnings Per Share	Price Earnings Ratio		Dividend Per Share	% Payout F ÷ C X 100	% High Yield F ÷ B X 100
		HIGH	LOW		HIGH A ÷ C	LOW B ÷ C			
1	1989	17.4	11.5	0.98	17.8	11.7	0.150	15.3	1.3
2	1990	19.2	12.5	1.10	17.5	11.4	0.165	15.0	1.3
3	1991	19.9	13.1	1.17	17.0	11.2	0.180	15.4	1.4
4	1992	25.2	19.1	1.30	19.4	14.7	0.195	15.0	1.0
5	1993	29.6	22.8	1.46	20.2	15.6	0.210	14.4	0.9
6	TOTAL								
7	AVERAGE		15.8		18.4	12.9		15.0	
8	AVERAGE PRICE EARNINGS RATIO		15.7		9 CURRENT PRICE EARNINGS RATIO			18.8	

Current P/E Based upon Last 12 mo. Earnings [1.46]
Proj. P/E [17.0] Based upon Next 12 mo. Earnings [1.61]

4 EVALUATING RISK and REWARD over the next 5 years

A HIGH PRICE - NEXT 5 YEARS
Avg. High P/E ___18.4___ (3D7) x Estimated High Earnings/Share ___2.35___ = Forecast High Price B-1 $ ___43.3___ (4A1)

B LOW PRICE - NEXT 5 YEARS
(a) Avg. Low P/E ___12.9___ (3E7) x Estimated Low E/Share ___1.46___ = $ ___18.9___
(b) Avg. Low Price of Last 5 Years = ___15.8___ (3B7)
(c) Recent Severe Market Low Price = ___13.1___
(d) Price Dividend Will Support $\frac{\text{Present Divd.}}{\text{High Yield (H)}}$ = $\frac{0.220}{1.4}$ = ___16.0___

Selected Estimated Low Price ____ B-2 $ ___15.8___ (4B1)

C ZONING
___43.3___ (4A1) High Forecast Price Minus ___15.8___ (4B1) Low Forecast Price Equals ___27.5___ (C) Range. $^1/_3$ of Range = ___9.2___ (4CD)
Lower $^1/_3$ = ___15.8___ (4B1) To ___25.0___ (Buy) (4C2)
Middle $^1/_3$ = ___25.0___ To ___34.1___ (Maybe) (4C3)
Upper $^1/_3$ = ___34.1___ To ___43.3___ (Sell) (4C4)
Present Market Price of ___27.4___ (4A1) is in the --- Hold --- (4C5) Range

D UP-SIDE DOWN-SIDE RATIO (Potential Gain vs. Risk of Loss)
$\frac{\text{High Price } 43.3 \text{ (4A1) Minus Present Price } 27.4}{\text{Present Price } 27.4 \text{ Minus Low Price } 15.8 \text{ (4B1)}}$ = $\frac{15.9}{11.6}$ = ___1.4___ (4D) = To 1

Relative Value: 119.8 %
Projected Relative Value: 108.9 %

5 5-YR POTENTIAL

A Present Full Year's Dividend $ ___0.220___
$\frac{}{\text{Present Price of Stock } \$ \, 27.4}$ = 0.008 x100 = 0.8 Present Yield or % Returned on Purchase Price

B AVERAGE YIELD OVER THE NEXT 5 YEARS
Avg. Earn. Per Share Next 5 Years ___1.94___ x Avg % Payout ___15.0___ (3G7) = 1.1 %
Present Price $ ___27.4___

Total Return: 10.4 %

Source: National Association of Investors Corporation

MAJOR PORTFOLIO HOLDING PROFILE

Quality Food Centers, Inc.
10116 N.E. Eighth Street
Bellevue, Washington 98009

Stock Exchange: NASDAQ
Ticker Symbol: QFCI
Telephone: 206-455-3761

Company Business

Quality Food Centers is a leading grocery retailer operating nearly 40 stores in the Seattle metropolitan area under the QFC umbrella. The company competes head to head with industry giants Albertson's and Safeway.

In addition to offering traditional food items, QFC stores also contain major departments: bakery, deli/salad bar, seafood, floral, video, and even a full-service bank. This one-stop-shop strategy helps draw customers away from competitor stores that offer customers less.

Shareholder Information

Outstanding shares	19,547,000
Insider ownership	More than 46 percent
DRIP program	No

Financial Information (June 1994)

Total assets	$198 million
Cash and temporary investments	$ 35 million
Working capital	$ 24 million
Long-term debt	-0-
Equity ratio	100 percent
Book value	$7.44 per share
Dividend rate	20 cents per share annually
Yield	.9 percent
Price/earnings ratio	17

Stock Price History (through mid-September 1994)

	1992	1993	1994
Low	$29\frac{7}{8}$	$22\frac{3}{4}$	$19\frac{1}{2}$
High	46	$38\frac{1}{4}$	$25\frac{1}{4}$

Revenue and Earnings History (through September 3, 1994)

	1992	1993	9 Months 1993	9 Months 1994
Revenue	$460	$518	$355	$384
Net income	25	26	19	18
Earnings per share	1.28	1.35	.95	.91

In millions, except per-share amounts

Key Growth Rates (past five years)

Revenue	16.0%
Cash flow	33.5%
Earnings	39.0%

Company Prospects

Quality Food Centers faces increased competition from bigger industry players. In addition, the company's aggressive expansion in the past few years now faces limited new opportunities in its service area due to a number of factors. First of all, the Seattle area has experienced an economic slowdown with defense-related layoffs at Boeing. Second, real estate development has also tapered off with decreased economic activity, limiting attractive new store site locations. Finally, industry consolidation in the area also promises to decrease its pace, as many of the choice acquisitions have already been made. While QFC acquisitions will continue, the rate is likely to slow, thus hampering the company's growth rate. Future earnings gains will be hard won.

The above realities are starting to show up in QFC's 1994 earnings. For the first nine months, earnings per share declined to 91 cents per share versus 95 cents per share for 1993's first three quarters.

The sober facts are starting to reflect in the company's stock price as well. QFC's stock hit a high of $46 per share in 1992 before drifting steadily lower (with brief upturns) to a low of $19½ per share in April 1994. The stock has rebounded but still trades more than 40 percent below its 1992 high (see Chart 2–12). Better investment opportunities exist elsewhere.

DISAPPOINTING STOCKS SHED

Company	*Industry*
Price/Costco	Wholesale merchandise

Chart 2–12 Quality Food Centers, Inc. Stock Chart

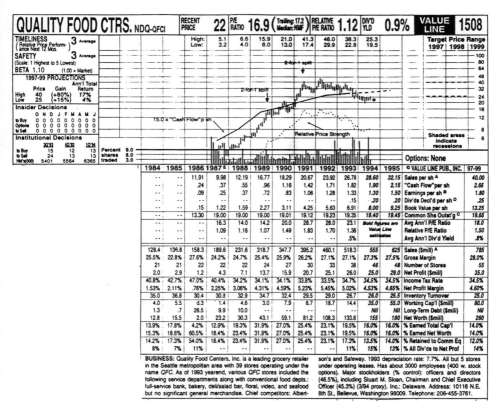

QUALITY FOOD CTRS. NDQ-QFCI		RECENT PRICE **22**	P/E RATIO **16.9** (Trailing: 17.2 / Median: NMF)	RELATIVE P/E RATIO **1.12**	DIV'D YLD **0.9%**	VALUE LINE **1508**

TIMELINESS 3 Average (Relative Price Perform-ance Next 12 Mos.)

SAFETY 3 Average (Scale: 1 Highest to 5 Lowest)

BETA 1.10 (1.00 = Market)

1997-99 PROJECTIONS

	Price	Gain	Ann'l Total Return
High	40	(+80%)	17%
Low	25	(+15%)	4%

Insider Decisions

	O	N	D	J	F	M	A	M	J
to Buy	0	0	0	0	0	0	0	0	0
Options	0	0	0	0	0	0	0	0	0
to Sell	0	0	0	0	0	0	0	0	0

Institutional Decisions

	3Q'93	4Q'93	1Q'94
to Buy	15	12	13
to Sell	24	13	13
Hld'g(000)	5401	5564	6365

Percent shares traded 9.0 6.0 3.0

High: 5.1 6.6 15.9 21.0 41.3 46.0 38.3 25.3
Low: 3.2 4.0 6.0 13.0 17.4 29.9 22.8 19.5

2-for-1 split

15.0 x "Cash Flow" p sh

Relative Price Strength

Shaded areas indicate recessions

Options: None

Target Price Range 1997 1998 1999

1984	1985	1986	1987 E	1988	1989	1990	1991	1992	1993	1994	1995	© VALUE LINE PUB., INC.	97-99
--	--	11.91	9.98	12.19	16.77	18.29	20.67	23.92	26.78	28.60	32.15	Sales per sh A	40.00
--	--	.24	.37	.55	.96	1.16	1.42	1.71	1.82	1.90	2.15	"Cash Flow" per sh	2.65
--	--	.09	.25	.37	.72	.83	1.06	1.28	1.33	1.30	1.50	Earnings per sh B	1.80
--	--	--	--	--	--	--	--	--	.15	.20	.20	Div'ds Decl'd per sh D	.25
--	--	.15	1.22	1.59	2.27	3.11	4.25	5.63	6.91	8.00	9.25	Book Value per sh	13.25
--	--	13.30	19.00	19.00	19.00	19.01	19.12	19.23	19.35	19.40	19.45	Common Shs Outst'g C	19.65
--	--	--	16.3	14.0	14.2	20.0	28.7	28.0	23.1	Bold figures are Value Line estimates		Avg Ann'l P/E Ratio	18.0
--	--	--	1.09	1.16	1.07	1.49	1.83	1.70	1.36			Relative P/E Ratio	1.50
--	--	--	--	--	--	--	--	--	.5%			Avg Ann'l Div'd Yield	.8%
128.4	136.8	158.3	189.6	231.6	318.7	347.7	395.2	460.1	518.3	555	625	Sales ($mill) A	785
25.5%	22.8%	27.6%	24.2%	24.7%	25.4%	25.9%	26.2%	27.1%	27.1%	27.3%	27.5%	Gross Margin	28.0%
21	21	22	22	22	24	27	30	33	38	46	48	Number of Stores	55
2.0	2.9	1.2	4.3	7.1	13.7	15.9	20.7	25.1	26.0	25.0	29.0	Net Profit ($mill)	35.0
40.8%	42.7%	47.0%	40.4%	34.2%	34.1%	34.1%	33.8%	33.5%	34.7%	34.5%	34.5%	Income Tax Rate	34.5%
1.53%	2.11%	.76%	2.25%	3.06%	4.31%	4.59%	5.23%	5.45%	5.02%	4.53%	4.65%	Net Profit Margin	4.60%
35.0	36.8	30.4	30.8	32.9	34.7	32.4	29.5	29.0	26.7	26.0	25.5	Inventory Turnover	25.0
4.0	5.5	d.3	1.4	4.6	3.0	7.9	6.7	18.7	14.4	55.0	55.0	Working Cap'l ($mill)	80.0
1.3	.7	26.5	9.9	10.0	--	--	--	--	--	Nil	Nil	Long-Term Debt ($mill)	Nil
12.8	15.5	2.0	23.2	30.3	43.1	59.1	81.2	108.3	133.6	155	180	Net Worth ($mill)	260
13.9%	17.8%	4.2%	12.9%	19.3%	31.9%	27.0%	25.4%	23.1%	19.5%	16.0%	16.0%	% Earned Total Cap'l	14.0%
15.3%	18.6%	60.5%	18.4%	23.4%	31.9%	27.0%	25.4%	23.1%	19.5%	16.0%	16.0%	% Earned Net Worth	14.0%
14.2%	17.3%	54.0%	18.4%	23.4%	31.9%	27.0%	25.4%	23.1%	17.3%	13.5%	14.0%	% Retained to Comm Eq	12.0%
8%	7%	11%	--	--	--	--	--	--	11%	15%	13%	% All Div'ds to Net Prof	14%

BUSINESS: Quality Food Centers, Inc. is a leading grocery retailer in the Seattle metropolitan area with 39 stores operating under the name *QFC*. As of 1993 yearend, various *QFC* stores included the following service departments along with conventional food depts.: full-service bank, bakery, deli/salad bar, floral, video, and seafood but no significant general merchandise. Chief competitors: Albert-son's and Safeway. 1993 depreciation rate: 7.7%. All but 5 stores under operating leases. Has about 3000 employees (400 w. stock options). Major stockholders (% control): officers and directors (46.5%), including Stuart M. Sloan, Chairman and Chief Executive Officer (45.3%) (3/94 proxy). Inc.: Delaware. Address: 10116 N.E. 8th St., Bellevue, Washington 98009. Telephone: 206-455-3761.

Source: ©1994 by Value Line Publishing, Inc. Reprinted by permission; All Rights Reserved.

Flandreau Investment Club

Flandreau, South Dakota

CLUB MAKEUP

Number of members	15
Member age range	35–49
Age of club	four years
Average number of securities in portfolio	15
$ value of portfolio	$22,758 (August 1994)
Amount invested per member/per month	$25*

*Plus initial $250 within six months of joining

MAJOR CURRENT HOLDINGS

Company	Purchase Date	Original Cost	Value
FNMA	1991	$1,374	$3,660
Intl. Game Tech.	1991	586	2,464
Microsoft	1992	833	2,219

CLUB INVESTMENT PHILOSOPHY

"Our number-one goal is capital appreciation through investment in growth stocks. Our second goal is preservation of capital," says Patrick Powers, of the Flandreau Investment Club. The Flandreau Investment Club often uses the Peter Lynch approach to investing...investing in what you know about. Therefore it's not surprising that International Game Technology and Federal National Mortgage Association (FNMA) are major holdings in the club's portfolio when you learn that one club member is a tribal employee (many Native American tribes own and operate casinos; in fact, there's an Indian casino located right in Flandreau) and another club member is involved in real estate.

Club members also keep an eye on the business press and financial newsletters in their efforts to uncover undervalued stocks with promising possibilities. Periodically, the club will invite guest speakers from the financial community or view videos on companies and industries.

The club earned an enviable 32 percent in 1992 and followed that up with a more modest 5 percent gain in 1993. Past big winners in addition to the major holdings listed above include Utah Medical Products, Inc.; Wendy's International, Inc.; and WMS Industries, Inc. (another gaming industry stock). On the downside, Flandreau Investment Club lost money on waste management companies, Laidlaw Inc. Class B and Chambers Development Company, Inc.

NEW PORTFOLIO PURCHASE PROFILE
The Home Depot, Inc., (See the discussion under GRQ Investment Club)

MAJOR PORTFOLIO HOLDING PROFILE

Federal National Mortgage Association   Stock Exchange: NYSE
3900 Wisconsin Avenue, N.W.   Ticker Symbol: FNM
Washington, D.C. 20016   Telephone 202-752-7000

Company Business
Federal National Mortgage Association (FNMA) is the nation's largest provider of residential home mortgages. The company's debt is not guaranteed by the federal government, but it does have favorable government agency status.

Shareholder Information

Outstanding shares	274,700,000
Insider ownership	Less than 1 percent
DRIP Program	Yes

Financial Information (June 1994)

Total assets	$243 billion
Mortgage portfolio	$207 billion
Long-term debt	$137 billion
Equity ratio	4 percent
Book value	$32.28 per share
Dividend rate	$2.40 per share annual basis
Yield	2.8 percent
Price/earnings ratio	11

Stock Price History (through mid-September 1994)

	1992	1993	1994
Low	$55\frac{1}{8}$	$72\frac{7}{8}$	$75\frac{5}{8}$
High	$77\frac{3}{8}$	$86\frac{1}{8}$	$90\frac{3}{8}$

Revenue and Earnings History (through June 30, 1994)

	1992	1993	1st Half 1993	1st Half 1994
Net interest income	$2,058	$2,533	$1,236	$1,384
Net income	1,649*	2,042*	982*	1,053*
Earnings per share	6.00*	7.44*	3.57*	3.84*

In millions, except per-share amounts

*Before extraordinary items

Key Growth Rates

Mortages	6.5%
Earnings	32.5%

DRIP Details

The FNMA dividend reinvestment program permits the automatic reinvestment of cash dividends and additional cash investment in company shares in amounts between $10 to $1,000 per month. There is a $5 service fee for cash purchases and a brokerage fee. For information on the FNMA DRIP, contact Federal National Mortgage Association DRIP, c/o Chemical Bank, P.O. Box 24850 Church Street Station, New York, New York 10249-0007, or call 212-613-7147.

Company Prospects

FNMA is entering a tough interest rate environment that may temper mortgage growth. However, the company is issuing more debt overseas, where it should be able to attract more favorable interest rates.

Management has proven adept at successfully adjusting to changing economic scenarios in years past. Look for continued earnings increases and dividend hikes.

MAJOR PORTFOLIO HOLDING PROFILE

International Game Technology	Stock Exchange: NYSE
5270 Neil Road	Ticker Symbol: IGT
P.O. Box 10120	Telephone 702-686-1200
Reno, Nevada 89510-0120	

Company Business

International Game Technology is the undisputed gaming industry leader in the design, manufacture, and marketing of gaming machines and proprietary software systems for computerized wide-area gaming machine networks.

The IGT-North America division maintains manufacturing facilities in Reno, Nevada, and Winnipeg, Manitoba, Canada. IGT's International Division handles manufacturing and sales for all jurisdictions outside of North America, including Australia, Asia, Europe, Latin America, and Africa. International manufacturing facilities are located in Sydney, Australia.

Shareholder Information

Shares outstanding	136,481,000
Insider ownership	7 percent
DRIP program	No

Financial Information (June 1994)

Total assets	$765 million
Cash and temporary investments	$138 million
Working capital	$370 million
Long-term debt	$135 million*
Equity ratio	100 percent
Book value	$3.58 per share
Dividend rate	12 cents per share annual basis
Yield	.5 percent
Price/earnings ratio	23

*Long-term jackpot liabilities

Stock Price History (through mid-September 1994)

	1992	1993	1994
Low	$6\frac{1}{4}$	$23\frac{3}{4}$	$17\frac{1}{4}$
High	$22\frac{1}{8}$	$41\frac{3}{8}$	34

Revenue and Earnings History (through June 30, 1994)

	1992	1993	9 Months 1993	9 Months 1994
Revenue	$364	$478	$214	$387
Net income	63*	106*	70*	102*
Earnings per share	.53*	.85*	.56*	.78*

* Earnings from continuing operations only
In millions, except per-share amounts

Key Growth Rates (past five years)

Revenue	32.5%
Cash flow	57.0%
Earnings	118.5%

Company Prospects

International Game Technology is on its way to yet another year of record revenues and earnings. For the nine months ended June 30, 1994, revenues spurted ahead 58 percent while income from continuing operations surged 46 percent. With such a stellar track record, the stock market rewarded IGT with a stock price that skyrocketed to $41\frac{3}{8}$ per share (adjusted for stock splits) in 1993 from less than $2 per share as recently as 1991.

Stock market jitters combined with the gaming industry, with its high price/earnings ratios, falling out of favor caused IGT's lofty stock price to plummet over 45 percent before staging a recovery. See Chart 2–13.

IGT's fundamentals are still strong, however. The company is hard at work enlarging its market share and expanding overseas; gaming continues to expand worldwide as cities, states, and countries seek additional revenue

Chart 2–13 International Game Technology Stock Chart

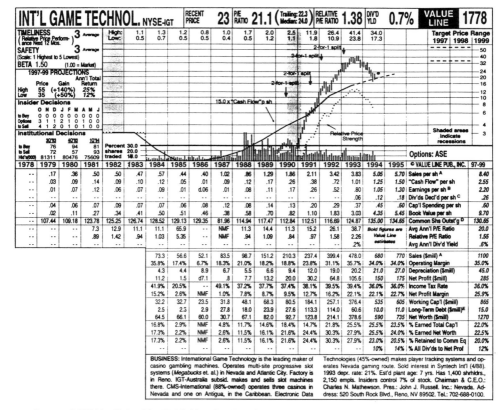

sources to combat budget deficits and slow economies; and IGT's product innovativeness creates new demand in existing markets.

For the long-term investor not concerned about the fickleness of the market, IGT remains a solid long-term investment as the premier company in the gaming industry.

MAJOR PORTFOLIO HOLDING PROFILE
Microsoft Corporation
(See discussion under Arrow Investment Club.)

DISAPPOINTING STOCKS SHED

Company	*Industry*
Electric utilities	Utilities facing new competition

SOUND ADVICE

Every investor has investments that don't turn out as expected. The real trick is to know when to sell as well as what to purchase; for excellent advice on selling, refer to Don Cassidy's book, *It's Not What Stocks You Buy, It's When You Sell That Counts* (Chicago: Probus Publishing Co., 1991). A study of the most successful investment clubs shows that they make a practice of shedding their losses quickly, taking their lumps and moving on to more attractive investment opportunities. Likewise, savvy investment clubs let their winners run. The result: superior overall returns, returns the professionals would love to achieve.

Putting It All Together

In Part 1 of this book, we looked at the strategies and investment tactics that have made investment clubs successful. In Part 2, we reviewed various investment clubs and evaluated their major holdings to determine how they achieve superior investment returns. Now it's time to take that knowledge and put it all together in developing your own investment strategy to beat Wall Street.

STARTING YOUR OWN INVESTMENT CLUB

As mentioned earlier, an investment club represents an excellent way to learn the market and how to successfully pick stocks for your own portfolio. You benefit from the combined knowledge and investigative resources of the group as a whole, and the group's diversity brings you into contact with a wide variety of investment options. In addition, the group decision-making process helps reduce the likelihood of purchasing a stock that could decimate the portfolio's returns. Obviously, it's harder to convince several people of the merits of a particular stock.

The actions of the group help temper any rash action an individual investor might make on his or her own. You don't fall victim to the temptation to purchase those "hot tips" that can turn into major disasters. Remember, the key word is "hot." You can get burned by "hot tips."

Starting an investment club is easy, though it does take some time to get it off to a good start. Careful advance planning and thoroughly thinking through your investment club philosophy and objectives can head off trouble and hard feelings down the road. Certainly, as in any organization of diverse individuals, minor disagreements will occur over time. But, by planning ahead and providing for ways to handle potential contentions, you can make your investment club experience a pleasant and profitable one.

Club Philosophy

Obviously, one of the first steps in starting an investment club involves getting members to join. Begin by discussing the club with your friends or business associates. Other fertile ground for finding prospective members include the neighborhood and religious or social organizations to which you belong. The investment club's philosophy and investment goals should be put down in writing and clearly understood by prospective members before they join.

"Disagreements over what the club invests in cause the most problems in and sometimes end with the breakup of the club. Therefore, it's very important to settle this issue at the outset," advises Barry Murphy, the NAIC's director of marketing. "You need to agree on the investment time frame, risk posture, size of portfolio (number of stocks invested in), and the regular investment amount."

For example, an investor seeking conservative, long-term growth opportunities will not be comfortable with the purchases of an investment club seeking to maximize returns based on purchases of junior gold mining stocks. However, as the membership changes over time, the club can modify or change its investment philosophy and strategies to reflect its new investment goals.

If the club's proposed investment philosophy does not match an investor's investment philosophy and goals, then he or she may need to pursue a different investment club to join. You want to find an investment club in tune with your strategy. After all, you will want to transfer the knowledge gained via the investment club and the discovery of prospective superior performing stocks to your larger personal portfolio for additional gains. Typically, the individual's personal portfolio is two to three times larger than the club's portfolio.

Invite prospective members to an organization meeting to discuss these important issues and hash out any misunderstandings or differences in approach before people join the investment club.

Other Factors

When seeking members it's important to take into account two other considerations. First of all, the members should enjoy each other's company. Nothing can destroy an investment club quicker than constant friction or bickering between members. The investment club should be viewed from a long-term perspective, so choose people you would want to spend time with over a period of years, even decades.

Second, a variety of occupations, backgrounds, and interests brings a vitality and wider range of investment ideas to the organization. This helps your club properly diversify its portfolio and increases the opportunity for uncovering superior stock market performers.

Make sure that each prospective club member understands that every member will be expected to carry his or her fair share of responsibilities. It is important to stress active involvement, an issue that most clubs struggle with over time. Your club bylaws should spell out what is required of each member. (See the sample investment club bylaws presented later in this part of the book.) Dividing the club duties among members and rotating them periodically serves several purposes: It keeps one or two members from becoming overly burdened, and it encourages more members to "buy into" the club's success.

Member Duties

Each member should be prepared to investigate and analyze securities and report recommendations to the group. Interested individuals need to know from the start the amount of work required of each member to make the club function successfully. Remember, without proper research and analysis, it's unlikely that your club will be able to find the stocks that promise superior investment returns. While the club typically has a social aspect, it's important to remember that the main focus of the club is its investment activities and achieving enviable investment returns. Members must make a sincere commitment to holding up their end of club responsibilities if this success is to be realized.

Contribution Amount

Another major item that needs to be agreed upon before accepting membership is the amount of money to be invested and the required frequency of this investment. This policy can dramatically affect the way your club operates. Some people may be able to afford an investment of $250 per month or more, while others may not feel comfortable with an investment in excess of $50 per month.

Some clubs require each member to invest the same amount each month; other clubs let members vary their contribution within limits. Of course, each member's respective share of club ownership would be tied to the proportional investment he or she makes. The contribution amount can be structured any way the members decide. Flexibility is one of the benefits of the investment club approach.

Meeting Time and Place

Once you've formed your investment club, you'll need to select a time and place for meetings. In today's time-pressured society, it's important to arrive at a consensus on this point. Since regular attendance is crucial to successful club performance and an active membership, many investment club bylaws include fines to be assessed against tardy or frequently absent members.

Membership Issues

It's also important to consider the new-member approval process and procedures for membership withdrawals. Clubs are frequently set up similar to mutual funds, with club units that can be bought and sold. This policy helps prevent forced selling of club holdings at an inopportune time, to raise money for redemption.

To ensure active membership, some clubs employ a withdrawal fee (or back-end load) for departing members. Such a fee may help prevent dwindling membership or at least avoid the member's departure from costing the club money. Some clubs require at least 30 to 90 days' advance notice of intent to withdraw, except in emergency situations,

While certainly not a frequent occurrence, there are occasions when a club member absconds with club funds. Safeguarding club assets can be accomplished relatively inexpensively through the purchase of a fidelity bond, which is available through the NAIC.

Corporation or Partnership?

Whether to form the club as a corporation or as a partnership needs to be addressed next. As a general rule, most clubs opt for the partnership to reduce paperwork and taxes (corporations are taxed, as well as club individuals). The federal government requires each club to obtain a tax identification number and file the appropriate tax forms (corporation or partnership). Partners will have to report their share of the profits or losses on their individual tax returns.

The Treasury Department has ruled that investment clubs typically do not meet all of the requirements for being considered a corporation for tax purposes; therefore, your club may have no option but to choose the partnership form.

Investment clubs must meet at least four of the following characteristics to be able to file as a corporation:

- the existence of a group of associates
- a common objective to carry on a business and divide the resulting gains
- continuity of the organization
- centralization of management
- limited liability
- free transferability of interests

Personal liability under the corporation tax form is restricted to each member's investment interest in the club. While personal liability is not limited under the partnership form, generally speaking, it may be restricted to a partner's acts performed within the scope of his or her authority and in the course of conducting partnership business.

Officers

Once members agree to form a club and adopt the club's partnership agreement, it's time to elect officers and choose a club broker. Club bylaws must set forth the conducting of officer elections and establish their duties; see the investment club bylaws discussion later in this part of the book. Recommended officer positions include a president or presiding partner, assistant presiding partner (vice president), recording partner (secretary), and financial partner (treasurer).

Broker Selection

When it comes to selecting a broker, look for one who can deliver the level of service and information your club requires. About half of the NAIC investment clubs use a discount broker, while the other half utilizes the full-service broker. Factors influencing your club's choice include the discounted commissions you can negotiate and the level of personalized service your group desires.

Some members may already have good working relationships with a broker and can recommend one to the club. If you need to solicit a broker, inquire whether the brokerage firm has someone who specializes in handling investment club transactions. Match your broker to your investment club's philosophy and goals so that he or she can aid your club effectively. Interview several potential brokers at several different brokerage firms. Determine his or her investment experience, professional background, and education before finalizing your decision. For the disciplinary history of any brokerage firm or broker, call 800-289-9999, the National Association of Securities Dealers, Inc. public disclosure hotline.

When choosing your broker, take into account not only the commission schedule but also the transaction efficiency and other investment services available. Many discount brokers provide services such as free Standard & Poor's Stock Guides, toll-free order and stock quote lines, discounts on financial publications, and informative investment newsletters.

Ask whether the brokerage firm is a member of the Securities Investor Protection Corporation (SIPC), which provides limited consumer protection in the event the securities firm becomes insolvent. Inquire whether the brokerage firm itself provides additional insurance coverage over and above SIPC limits. For information on SIPC coverage limits, contact SIPC, 805 Fifteenth Street, N.W., Suite 800, Washington, D.C. 20005-2207, or call 202-371-8300.

Make sure your broker understands that only one or two officers (typically the president and treasurer) are authorized to make trades in your investment club's account. When the people holding those officer positions change, notify your broker in writing, including the effective date.

Registering/Safeguarding Club Assets

Once your broker has been chosen, the form of security registration must be decided. For ease of record keeping, security transfer, and safeguarding, many clubs decide to register the securities in "street name." This procedure involves having your broker establish an account in the investment club's name or in the name of the (bonded) agent or agents specified by the club. The purchase or sale of club securities will be registered in the brokerage firm's name (street name) but recorded in your club's account. The club will receive confirmations of the transactions and a monthly statement detailing club transaction activity, plus a listing of portfolio holdings and any open orders.

To prevent delays in receiving corporate news releases and earnings reports, write directly to the company's Investors Relations Department and request to be placed on its mailing list, explaining that your shares are held in "street name."

The main benefit of having the shares registered in your investment club's name is that the club now participates in the company's dividend reinvestment plan (DRIP), putting compounding and commission avoidance to work for higher total returns.

NAIC Investment Club Membership

The final step toward forming your investment club is adopting the club bylaws and selecting its name. Membership in the NAIC is optional; approximately 50 percent of all investment clubs belong.

For those interested in joining NAIC, either as an individual or as an investment club, contact the National Association of Investors Corporation at 711 West Thirteen Mile Road, Madison Heights, Michigan 48071, or call 810-583-6242.

To register your club with the NAIC and receive its *Investor's Manual* and five copies of the brochure "An Educational and Investment Opportunity for You," send a check for $14 to the above NAIC address. Club fees will be assessed once your club is organized and registered with the NAIC. The manual skillfully guides you through the process of setting up your own investment club, conducting the first meetings, finding and selecting stocks, keeping records, and preparing tax reports.

To enroll as an individual member of NAIC, send a check for $31 and you will receive the NAIC's *Investor's Manual*, a subscription to *Better Investing,* and admission to NAIC's Low Cost Investment Plan (covered in more detail later in this section). Even if you decide not to join NAIC, you can subscribe to *Better Investing* magazine for investment ideas. An annual subscription without NAIC membership is $17.

Meeting Tips

Research forms the backbone of investment clubs and their ability to deliver superior returns. Make sure a portion of each meeting is devoted to members reporting on new investment opportunities. Don't forget to include a brief update on current holdings with hold, sell, or additional purchase recommendations. To ensure proper coverage and involvement by all club members, clubs generally assign each member an individual stock or two in the group's portfolio to study in addition to researching potential investments. Members are then responsible for gathering and presenting information, including pricing, performance, and market potential.

"The NAIC Stock Selection Guide forms are designed to get investment clubs to look at the numbers and away from the hype surrounding stocks," says NAIC's Barry Murphy.

NAIC's investment guidance and materials are designed to help the investor develop skills needed to study a stock and make an informed judgment about its potential high and low prices; compare stocks and select those that appear to offer the greatest opportunity; and follow stocks already owned, making the proper decisions to hold, sell, or buy more shares.

Setting an agenda and sticking to it can help meetings move along smoothly and keep members from complaining about wasted time and meetings that drag on forever. A reading of the prior meeting's minutes and reviewing club valuation statements should set the stage for the current meeting's business.

Once the investment recommendations have been made and discussed, members should vote on the action to take regarding the various hold, buy, and sell recommendations. It is crucial that no investment be voted on unless a report has been properly prepared by the person assigned that duty. This step prevents snap judgments on "hot tips" without the proper analysis for good decision making.

Members may invite guests as prospective new members or as speakers to inform the club on new investment opportunities or other matters of interest, such as estate planning and college financing plans. Other educational programs can include investment videotapes on companies and industries.

It's also a good idea to establish an investment reference library with financial publications, investment analysis services, and computer programs for club members to use in their investigative and analysis work.

Encourage a disciplined investment program. Do your homework and upfront investigative work, invest regularly, and keep your portfolio properly diversified. A cardinal rule of successful investment clubs: When the market goes down, don't panic. Keep investing and stick to your dollar-cost-averaging guns.

No one can guarantee you or your club superior returns, but many investment clubs over decades of investing have delivered returns that beat the professional money managers.

Sample Bylaws/Partnership Agreement

The following sample bylaws provide a handy format from which to begin tailoring your own club's governing rules. Adapt them as you see fit to best run your organization.

SAVVY INVESTMENT CLUB
PARTNERSHIP AGREEMENT

This agreement of partnership, made as of (date) by and between the undersigned, (names of partners)

Witnesseth:

1. *Formation of Partnership.* The undersigned hereby form a general partnership in, and in accordance with the laws of, the state of xxxxx.

2. *Name.* The name of this partnership is Savvy Investment Club.

3. *Term.* The partnership shall begin on (date) and shall continue until December 31, 19xx, and thereafter from year to year unless terminated.

4. *Purposes.*
    A. To educate members in the fundamental principles of investing and techniques of sound investment practices.
    B. To invest the assets of the partnership in stocks (bonds and other securities and investments could also be added).

5. *Meetings.*
    A. Periodic meetings shall be held as determined by the partnership. (Overly specific detail here and in other sections of the bylaws could result in having to amend the bylaws for meeting frequency changes or other minor procedural matters.)
    B. A quorum shall consist of the majority of partners present at a meeting.
    C. Members may be represented at any meeting by proxy carried only by another member.
    D. Special meetings may be called by the officers upon written notice to the membership.

6. *Officers.* The officers and responsibilities include the following.
    A. President or Presiding Partner: shall set date and place of meetings. Shall preside over club meetings and oversee all club activities. Shall keep a list of prospective members.

B. Vice President or Assistant Presiding Partner: shall assume President's duties in the event he or she is not present. Shall be responsible for implementing the Stock Study Assignment Sheet.

C. Secretary or Recording Partner: shall keep an accurate record of the proceedings of all organization meetings. Shall maintain a file of past stock reports (up to three years). Shall be responsible for making sure an adequate supply of forms is available for members' use. Shall keep an accurate roll of members and membership applications.

D. Treasurer or Financial Partner: shall collect regular contributions and new membership fees. Shall report on club valuation at meetings. Shall assess and collect late and missed meeting fines. Shall be responsible for all collection and disbursement of club funds. Shall prepare individual statement of worth twice a year for distribution to each member. Shall maintain a proper and accurate set of books detailing the club's financial activities.

Officers shall be elected at the Annual Meeting in January, take office at the following meeting, and serve for xx year(s). Officers shall not serve more than two consecutive terms in any one office. No member shall hold more than one office at any time. Nominations shall be from the floor at the January meeting. Terms of office incomplete due to withdrawal of the officer from the club shall be served by voluntary appointment by the President. The President and Treasurer, as the partnership's agents, shall conduct the business of the partnership's two-name account. Each shall be authorized, in compliance with partnership action, to place buy and sell orders, to deal in other transactions, and to sign checks to make club disbursements.

7. *Contributions.* The partners shall make contributions to the partnership on the date of each periodic meeting, in the amount of $xxx or as the partnership determines. However, no single partner's account shall exceed more than xx percent of the total of the accounts of all partners.

8. *Valuation.* The current value of partnership assets less the current value of the debts and liabilities of the partnership (hereinafter referred to as "value of the partnership") shall be calculated as of the weekend preceding the date of each periodic meeting. The aforementioned date of valuation shall hereinafter be referred to as "valuation date." An individual member's value shall be proportional to his or her investment.

9. *Capital accounts.* There shall be maintained in the name of each partner a capital account. Any increase or decrease in the value of the partnership on any valuation date shall be credited or debited, respectively, to each partner's account on said date. Each partner's contribution to, or withdrawal from, the partnership shall be credited from, or debited respectively to, that partner's capital account.

10. *Membership.* The partnership shall consist of no more than xx or no less than xx members with equal voting membership. When there are membership openings, prospective members may be invited to attend a club meeting. Membership acceptance requires a two-thirds majority of current members. New

members must contribute an initial amount of $xxx and begin their regular donation of $xx at their first meeting following membership acceptance.

Nonattendance at two meetings shall result in a fine of $xx, and nonattendance of four meetings during any calendar year shall require removal from the partnership.

11. *Management.* Each partner shall participate in the management and conduct of the affairs of the partnership in proportion to the value of his/ her capital account. (Alternative: Each partner has equal voting rights regardless of his/her valuation proportion).

12. *Sharing of profits and losses.* Net profit and losses of the partnership shall be allocated to each partner based on the proportion of the valuation of his/her capital account to the valuation of the partnership as a whole.

13. *Books of account.* Books of account regarding the transactions of the partnership shall be kept and at all times be available and open to inspection and examination by any partner upon reasonable notice.

14. *Periodic accounting.* A full and accurate account of the condition of the partnership shall be conducted and given to each partner xx times a year by (dates).

15. *Bank account.* The partnership shall choose an appropriate financial institution for the purpose of opening a partnership account. Funds deposited in this account shall be withdrawn by checks signed by the two partners authorized by the partnership.

16. *Broker account.* The partnership may select a broker and enter into agreements as required to effect transactions in investments approved by the partnership. No partner may be a broker doing business with the partnership (this can be approved in advance).

17. *No compensation.* Officers of the partnership shall serve without any compensation except for reimbursement of documented approved expenses.

18. *Partner withdrawal.* Any partner may make a partial or full withdrawal after written notice to the Secretary. The partnership shall continue as a taxable entity. Written notice shall be deemed received as of the first meeting of the partnership at which it is presented. The distribution shall be made based on the valuation as of the first meeting following the meeting in which withdrawal notice was presented. (Clubs may make special exceptions for emergency situations).

19. *Voluntary termination.* The partnership may be dissolved by agreement of the partners whose capital accounts total a majority of the value of all partners' capital accounts. Advance notice of xx (period of time) must be given in writing to all partners. At the appropriate date, the partnership shall be terminated by the payment of all debts and liabilities of the partnership, and the distribution of the remaining assets in either cash or in kind in proportion to the capital accounts of each partner.

20. *Partner removal.* Any partner may be removed by agreement of the partners whose capital accounts total a majority of the value of all partners' capital accounts. The removal shall be effective after a proper meeting vote and upon payment of the value of the removed partner's capital account based on the valuation of the capital account on the first regular meeting following the removal.

21. *Death or incapacity of a partner.* Withdrawal due to death or incapacity of a partner shall be treated as a regular withdrawal under Item 18 above.

22. *Purchase price.* Upon the withdrawal and valuation of capital accounts, the departing member or his/her estate shall receive the full (could be reduced by a departure load) valuation of his/her capital account less the cost of security sales to obtain sufficient cash to meet the withdrawal amount. Purchase price shall be made within xx weeks after the valuation date used in determining the purchase price. As an alternative, and at the discretion of the partnership, payment may be made solely in securities or a combination of cash and securities.

23. *Unit sales.* As an alternative to repurchase of the withdrawing partner's units, other partners may elect to purchase all or a portion of the units at the valuation price. They will be offered to all partners in proportion to each partner's respective share of the remaining partnership.

24. *Forbidden acts.* No partner shall:
    A. have the right or authority to bind or obligate the partnership to any extent whatsoever with regard to any matter outside the scope of partnership business.
    B. assign, transfer, pledge, mortgage, or sell any part of his/her interest in the partnership to any person whomsoever, or enter into any agreement as the result of which any person or persons not a partner shall become interested with him or her in the partnership; without the prior, unanimous consent of all the other partners.
    C. purchase an investment for the partnership where less than the full purchase price is paid for the same.
    D. use the partnership name, credit, or property for other than partnership purposes.
    E. commit any act detrimental to the interests of the partnership or which would make it impossible to carry on the business of the partnership.

This partnership agreement is hereby declared and shall be binding upon the respective heirs, executors, administrators, and personal representatives of each partner.

In witness whereof, the parties have set their hands the day and year first written above:

Partners _____

Other terms may be added to the partnership agreement as the club desires or as needs arise. The important point is to think through the club organization process as thoroughly as possible before problems or situations arise that create hard feelings and possibly result in sinking the investment club.

THE IRA INVESTMENT CLUB OPTION

You may use your regular investment contribution to your investment club as your contribution to your Individual Retirement Account (IRA) if your club permits IRAs in its partnership agreement. You will also need a bank (or other IRA custodian) to act as trustee and be a limited partner of the club. Since the trustee is a limited partner, the IRA trustee has no voice in the management of the club.

If you have trouble finding a bank or trust company to act as trustee, contact the NAIC. The NAIC has an arrangement with a bank to act as a trustee for its investment clubs. The NAIC can instruct you how to properly change your club's partnership agreement to a limited partnership, to include the bank as trustee for member IRAs.

LOW COST INVESTMENT PLAN

One of the tools of savvy investors is the NAIC Low Cost Investment Plan. To get around the problem of limited funds when first investing, the NAIC developed a plan for the small and beginning investor. The plan works equally well for start-up investment clubs that want to initiate investing at a minimum cost. NAIC charges a $5 processing fee for handling the paperwork.

The plan works like this: You invest in companies through the NAIC. The stock is purchased through an escrow account. You can purchase as little as one share to get enrolled in the company's dividend reinvestment program. After the shares are purchased, the plan administrator is notified to transfer the shares out of the NAIC account and into the names of those making the investment, you or your investment club. At this point, the NAIC relinquishes any further participation in those shares.

Once initiated in the company's DRIP, you can add to your investment at the regular investment dates either through dividend reinvestment or, more importantly, via additional cash purchases in amounts permitted by the each company's DRIP program.

This strategy accomplishes several things. First of all, it gets you started in a regular investment program despite having limited initial funds. Second, it eliminates the tremendous bite of commission costs, since the sponsoring companies usually absorb all administration and commission costs of purchasing the shares. This cost break is a major benefit for beginning investors or new investment clubs because commissions can represent a large percent-

age of their small investments—up to 10 percent of their monthly contribution. Third, the strategy helps improve your investment returns with the
compounding of your earnings through reinvested dividends.

NAIC Low Cost Investment Plan Company Participants

Currently, you can invest in more than 120 companies through the NAIC
Low Cost Investment Plan. In addition, the NAIC is continually working to
add new company participants to broaden the plan's investment options. The
following companies are program participants. Telephone numbers are for
the Administration or Shareholder Services Departments or the trust company handling the DRIP plans, where available.

AFLAC Incorporated
1932 Wynnton Road
Columbus, GA 31999
800-227-4756
CODE: M, No A or C

American Business Products, Inc.
P.O. Box 105684
Atlanta, GA 30348
800-633-4236
CODE: M, Fee, No C

Aquarion Company
835 Main Street
Bridgeport, CT 06601
800-526-0801
CODE: M, No A or C

Ashland Oil, Inc.
P.O. Box 391
Ashland, KY 41101
606-264-7165
CODE: Q, No A or C

AT&T
295 N. Maple Ave., RM 3346B2
Basking Ridge, NJ 07920
800-348-8288
CODE: M, Fee, No C

ALLIED Group, Inc.
701 Fifth Avenue
Des Moines, IA 50391-2000
515-280-4617
CODE: M, No A or C

American General Corporation
2929 Allen Parkway
Houston, TX 77019-2155
800-446-2617
CODE: M, No A or C

Ashland Coal Company
P.O. Box 6300
Huntington, WV 25701
800-446-2617
CODE: M, No A or C

Atmos Energy Corporation
P.O. Box 650205
Dallas, TX 75265-0205
800-382-8667
CODE: S-M, No A or C, Disc.

Avery Dennison Corporation
150 N. Orange Grove Blvd.
Pasadena, CA 91103
800-522-6645
CODE: M, No A or C

Barnett Banks Inc.
50 N. Laura St.
Jacksonville, FL 32257
800-524-4458
CODE: M, No A or C

BB&T Financial Corporation
223 W. Nash St.
Wilson, NC 27893
919-399-4219
CODE: M, No A or C, Disc.

Bob Evans Farms, Inc.
3776 S. High St.
Columbus, OH 43207
614-491-2225
CODE: S-M, No A or C

Central Maine Power Company
Edison Drive
Augusta, ME 04336
800-695-4267
CODE: M, No A or C

Central Vermont Public Service
77 Grove Street
Rutland, VT 05701
802-773-2711
CODE: M, No A or C

Chase Manhattan Corporation
1 Chase Plaza
New York, NY 10081
800-284-4262
CODE: M, No A or C, Disc.

Cincinnati Gas & Electric Co.
P.O. Box 960
Cincinnati, OH 45201-0960
800-325-2945
CODE: 45, No A or C

Bay State Gas Company
300 Friberg Parkway
Westborough, MA 01581-5039
800-442-2001
CODE: M, No A or C

Beneficial Corporation
P.O. Box 911
Wilmington, DE 19899-0911
212-791-6422
CODE: M, No A or C

Brown-Foreman Corporation
P.O. Box 1080
Louisville, KY 40201-1080
502-585-1100
CODE: M, No A, Fee

Central & SW Corporation
1616 Woodall Rodgers Freeway
Dallas, TX 75202
800-527-5797
CODE: S-M, No A or C

Century Telephone Enter., Inc.
100 Century Park Drive
Monroe, LA 71203
800-527-7844
CODE: M, No A or C

Cincinnati Bell Inc.
201 E. Fourth St.
Cincinnati, OH 45201
800-321-1355
CODE: M, No A or C

Colgate-Palmolive Company
300 Park Avenue
New York, NY 10022-7499
212-791-6422
CODE: M, No A or C

CML Group
524 Main Street
Acton, MA 01720
508-264-4155
CODE: Q, No A or C

CNB Bancshares, Inc.
20 NW Third St.
Evansville, IN 47739-0001
812-464-3416
CODE: M, No A or C

Colonial Gas Company
44 Market Street
Lowell, MA 01852
508-458-3171
CODE: M, No A or C, Disc.

Connecticut Energy Corporation
855 Main Street
Bridgeport, CT 06604
800-442-2001
CODE: M, No A or C

Connecticut Natural Gas Corp.
100 Columbus Boulevard
Hartford, CT 06144-1500
203-727-3203
CODE: Q, No A or C

Connecticut Water Service Inc.
93 W. Main St.
Clinton, CT 06413
203-669-8636
CODE: Q, No A or C, Disc.

Consolidated Natural Gas Company
615 Liberty Avenue, CNG Tower
Pittsburg, PA 15222-3199
412-227-1125
CODE: Q, No A or C

Consumers Water Corporation
Three Canal Plaza
Portland, ME 04101
800-292-2925
CODE: M, No A or C

Dana Corporation
4500 Dorr Street
Toledo, OH 43697
800-537-8823
CODE: M, No A or C

Dial Corporation
1850 N. Central Ave.
Phoenix, AZ 85077-1424
800-453-2235
Code: M, No A or C

Diebold, Inc.
P. O. Box 8230
Canton, OH 44711
216-489-4000
CODE: M, No A or C

D & N Financial
400 Quincy Street
Hancock, MI 48674
906-482-2700
CODE: M, No A or C

Dow Chemical Company
2030 Dow Center
Midland, MI 48674
517-636-1463
CODE: M, No A or C

DQE Company
Box 68
Pittsburgh, PA 15279
800-247-0400
CODE: M, Fees

Duke Realty Investments, Inc.
8888 Keystone Crossing, #1150
Indianapolis, IN 46240-4620
800-753-7107
CODE: M, No A or C

Eastern Utilities Associates
P.O. Box 2333
North Boston, MA 02107-2333
617-357-9590
CODE: M, No A or C, Disc.

Equitable Resources Inc.
420 Boulevard of the Allies
Pittsburgh, PA 15219-1393
412-553-5877
CODE: M, No A or C

Federal Realty Invest. Trust
4800 Hampden Lane, Suite 500
Bethesda, MD 20814
301-652-3360
CODE: M, No A or C

First Union Corporation
Two First Union Center
Charlotte, NC 28288
704-374-6782
CODE: M, No A or C, Disc.

Fuller (H. B.) Company
2400 Energy Park Drive
St. Paul, MN 55108
612-450-4064
CODE: N, No A or C

Great Lakes Bancorp
401 E. Liberty St.
Ann Arbor, MI 48104
800-522-6645
CODE: M, No A or C

EMC Insurance Group Inc.
717 Mulberry Street
Des Moines, IA 50309
515-280-2581
CODE: Q, No A or C

Energen Corporation
2101 Sixth Avenue
Birmingham, AL 35203
205-326-8421
CODE: M, No A or C

Federal-Mogul Corporation
P.O. Box 1966
Detroit, MI 48235
800-521-8607
CODE: M, Fees

Figgie International Inc.
4420 Sherwin Road
Willoughby, OH 44094
800-953-1505
CODE: M, No A or C

First Western Bancorp, Inc.
P.O. Box 1488
New Castle, PA 16103-1488
412-652-8550
CODE: M, No A or C

General Signal Corporation
P.O. Box 10010
Stamford, CT 06904
203-357-8800
CODE: M, No A or C

Green Mountain Power Corporation
P.O. Box 850
South Burlington, VT 05403
802-864-5731
CODE: M, No A or C, Disc.

Guardsman Products, Inc.
3033 Orchard Vista Drive, SE
Grand Rapids, MI 49546
616-957-2600
CODE: Q, No A or C

Hannaford Bros. Company
145 Pleasant Hill Road
Scarborough, ME 04074
207-883-2911
CODE: M, No A or C

John H. Harland Company
P.O. Box 105250
Decatur, GA 30348
404-588-7822
CODE: M, No A or C

Health Equity Properties
P.O. Box 348
Winston-Salem, NC 27102
919-723-7580
CODE: M, No A or C

Houston Industries Inc.
4400 Post Oak Parkway, Ste. 2700
Houston, TX 77027
800-231-6406
CODE: M, No A, Fees

Idaho Power Company
P.O. Box 70
Boise, ID 83707
800-635-5406
CODE: Q, No A or C

Insteel Industries, Inc.
1373 Boggs Drve
Mount Airy, NC 27030
704-383-5183
CODE: M, No A or C

Hanna (M. A.) Company
1301 E. 9th St., Ste. 3600
Cleveland, OH 44114-1860
216-589-4085
CODE: M, No A or C

Hanson Industries
410 Park Avenue
New York, NY 10022
212-826-0096
CODE: M, Fees

Hawaiian Electric Industries, Inc.
P.O. Box 730
Honolulu, HI 96808
808-532-5841
CODE: M, No A or C

Houghton Mifflin Company
One Beacon Street
Boston, MA 02108
617-575-2900
CODE: 45, Fees

Huntington Bancshares Inc.
41 S. High St.
Columbus, OH 43287
800-255-1342
CODE: M, No A or C, disc.

Illinois Central
455 N. Cityfront Plaza Drive
Chicago, IL 60611-5504
800-442-2001
CODE: M, No A or C

ITT Corporation
100 Plaza Drive
Secaucus, NJ 07096-0002
201-601-4202
CODE: M, No A or C

Johnson Controls, Inc.
P.O. Box 591
Milwaukee, WI 53201-0591
414-287-3956
CODE: Q, No A or C

Kaman Corporation
P.O. Box 1
Bloomfield, CT 06002
203-243-6307
CODE: Q, No A or C

Keithley Instruments, Inc.
28775 Aurora Road
Solon, OH 44139
216-248-0400
CODE: M, No A or C

Kellogg Company
P.O. Box 3599
Battle Creek, MI 49016-3599
800-323-6138
CODE: M, No A or C

Kerr-McGee Corporation
P.O. Box 25861
Oklahoma City, OK 73125
405-231-6711
CODE: M, No A or C

KeyCorp
127 Public Square
Cleveland, OH 44114-1306
800-542-7792
CODE: M, No A or C

KN Energy, Inc.
P.O. Box 281304
Lakewood, CO 80228-8304
303-989-1740
CODE: M, No A or C

Knape & Vogt Manufacturing
2700 Oak Industrial Drive, NE
Grand Rapids, MI 49505
616-461-2545
CODE: M, No A or C

La-Z-Boy Chair Company
1284 N. Telegraph Rd.
Monroe, MI 48161
718-921-8283
CODE: M, No A or C

Louisiana Land & Exploration Co.
P.O. Box 60350
New Orleans, LA 70160
800-446-2617
CODE: M, No A or C

Lukens, Inc.
50 S. First Ave.
Coatesville, PA 19320
215-383-2601
CODE: M, No A or C

Maytag Corporation
403 W. Fourth St, N
Newton, IA 50208
515-791-8344
CODE: M, No A or C

McDonald's Corporation
One Kroc Drive
Oak Brook, IL 60521
800-621-7825
CODE: S-M, No A or C

MCN Corporation
500 Griswold Street
Detroit, MI 48226
800-257-1770
CODE: M, No A or C

MDU Resources Group, Inc.
400 N. Fourth St.
Bismarck, ND 58501
701-222-7621
CODE: Q, No A or C

Merry Land & Investment Co., Inc.
P.O. Box 1417
Augusta, GA 30903-1417
800-829-8432
CODE: Q, No A or C, Disc.

Michigan National Corporation
27777 Inkster Road
Farmington Heights, MI 48333
313-473-3076
CODE: M, No A or C

Mid Am, Inc.
222 South Main Street
Bowling Green, OH 43402
718-921-8200
CODE: Q, No A or C

Minnesota Power & Light Company
30 W. Superior St.
Duluth, MN 55802
218-723-3974
CODE: M, No A or C

Mobil Corporation
3225 Gallows Road
Fairfax, VA 22037-0001
800-648-9291
CODE: M, No A or C

Modine Manufacturing Company
1500 DeKoven Avenue
Racine, WI 53403
718-921-8283
CODE: M, No A or C

Motorola, Inc.
1303 E. Algonquin Rd.
Schaumburg, IL 60196
708-576-4995
CODE: M, No A or C

National City Corporation
1900 E. Ninth St.
Cleveland, OH 44114-3484
216-575-2532
CODE: M, No A or C, Disc.

Newell Company
29 E. Stephenson St.
Freeport, IL 61032-4251
800-446-2617
CODE: M, No A or C

New Jersey Resources Corporation
1350 Campus Parkway
Wall, NJ 07719
908-938-1230
CODE: M, No A or C

NICOR, Inc.
1844 Ferry Road
Naperville, IL 60563
708-305-9500
CODE: M, No A or C

Northwest Natural Gas Company
220 NW Second Avenue
Portland, OR 97209
503-220-2591
CODE: M, No A or C

Norwest Corporation
6th & Marquette
Minneapolis, MN 55479-1016
612-667-1234
CODE: M, No A or C

Old National Bancorp
420 Main Street
Evansville, IN 47708
812-464-1434
CODE: Q, No A or C, Disc.

OM Group, Inc.
3800 Terminal Tower
Cleveland, OH 44113-2204
216-781-0083
Code: M, No A or C

ONEOK Inc.
P.O. Box 871
Tulsa, OK 74102
800-242-2662
CODE: M, No A or C

Otter Tail Power Company
215 S. Cascade St.
Fergus Falls, MN 56537
218-739-8481
CODE: M, No A or C

Pacific Enterprises
P.O. Box 60043
Los Angeles, CA 90071
800-722-5483
CODE: M, No A or C

Pacific Telesis Group
130 Kearney Street
San Francisco, CA 94108
800-637-6373
CODE: M, No A or C, Disc.

Panhandle Eastern Corporation
P.O. Box 1642
Houston, TX 77251-1642
800-225-5838
CODE: M, No A or C

Peoples Energy Corporation
122 S. Michigan Ave.
Chicago, IL 60603
800-228-6888
CODE: M, No A or C

Pioneer-Standard Electronics, Inc.
4800 E. 131st St.
Garfield Heights, OH 44105
216-587-3600
CODE: M, No A or C

PLY-GEM Industries Inc.
777 Third Avenue
New York, NY 10007
312-461-3932
CODE: M, No A or C

PMC Capital
18301 Biscayne Blvd., 2nd FL S
North Miami Beach, FL 33160
305-933-5858
CODE: M, No A or C, Disc.

Providence Energy Corporation
100 Weybosset Street
Providence, RI 02903
401-272-9191
CODE: M, No A or C

Public Service Co. of Colorado
1225 17th Street
Denver, CO 80202
800-635-0566
CODE: M, No A or C, Disc.

Pub. Service Co. of N. Carolina
P.O. Box 1398
Gastonia, NC 28053-1398
704-864-6731
CODE: M, No A or C, Disc.

Quaker Oats Company
P.O. Box 049001
Chicago, IL 60604-9001
800-344-1198
CODE: M, No A or C

Quanex Corporation
1900 W. Loop South, #1500
Houston, TX 77027
800-231-8176
CODE: M, No A or C

Questar Corporation
P.O. Box 11150
Salt Lake City, UT 84147
801-534-5804
CODE: M, No A or C

RLI Corporation
9025 N. Lindbergh Dr.
Peoria, IL 61615
309-692-1000
Code: M, No A or C

Rochester Telephone Corporation
180 S. Clinton Ave.
Rochester, NY 14646
800-836-0342
CODE: M, No A or C

RPM, Inc.
2628 Pearl Road
Medina, OH 44256
216-273-5090
CODE: M, No A or C

Ryder System, Inc.
3600 NW 82nd Avenue
Miami, FL 33166
305-593-3726
CODE: M, No A or C

St. Paul Companies, Inc.
385 Washington Street
St. Paul, MN 55102
612-221-7911
CODE: M, No A or C

SCE Corp.
2244 Walnut Grove
Rosemead, CA 91770
800-347-8625
CODE: M, No A or C

ServiceMaster Company
2300 Warrenville Road
Downers Grove, IL 60515
708-964-1300
CODE: M, No A or C

Southeastern Mich. Gas Enter. Inc.
405 Water Street
Port Huron, MI 48061-5026
800-255-7647
CODE: M, No A or C

Southwestern Bell Corporation
One Bell Center
St. Louis, MO 63101
800-351-7221
CODE: M, No A or C

SPX Corporation
700 Terrace Point Drive
Muskegon, MI 49440
616-724-5564
CODE: M, No A or C

Synovus Financial Corporation
P.O. Box 120
Columbus, GA 31901
706-649-2387
CODE: M, No A or C

Texaco, Inc.
2000 Westchester Avenue
White Plains, NY 10650-0001
800-283-9785
CODE: M, No A or C

United Cities Gas Company
5300 Maryland Way
Brentwood, NJ 37027
615-373-0104
CODE: M, No A or C, Disc.

US West, Inc.
7800 E. Orchard Rd.
Englewood, CO 80155-6508
800-537-0222
CODE: M, No A or C

Volvo (AB)
535 Madison Avenue
New York, NY 10022
800-551-6161
CODE: M, No A or C

Wendy's International Inc.
4288 W. Durbin-Granville Rd.
Dublin, OH 43017
212-936-5100
CODE: M, No A or C

Whirlpool Corporation
2000 U.S. 33 North
Benton Harbor, MI 49022
616-923-5000
CODE: M, No A or C

Tribune Company
435 N. Michigan Ave.
Chicago, IL 60611
312-222-9100
CODE: M, No A or C

Upjohn Company
7000 Portage Road
Kalamazoo, MI 49001
616-461-5535
CODE: M, No A or C

Valley Resources, Inc.
1595 Mendon Road
Cumberland, RI 02864-0700
401-333-1595
CODE: M, No A or C, Disc.

Washington Gas Light Company
1100 H Street, NW
Washington, DC 20080
800-221-9427
CODE: M, No A or C

Western Resources, Inc.
P. O. Box 889
Topeka, KS 66601-0889
800-648-8165
CODE: M, No A, Fees

CODE:

M   Monthly reinvestment or contribution

S-M   Semimonthly reinvestment or contribution

Q   Quarterly reinvestment or contribution

45   45-day reinvestment or contribution

No A   No administration charges

No C   No commission charges

Fees   Some administrative and/or commission fees; contact plan administrator for details

Disc   Discount available on stock purchased; contact plan administrator for details

NOTE:

A number of companies charge an administration fee or commissions when you sell shares of company stock through their dividend reinvestment programs.

Plan details can change over time, so contact the plan administrator for an updated copy of the DRIP before investing.

The Low Cost Investment Plan gets your investment program started at a minimal cost while you build your investment resources. The earlier you begin, the longer compounding can work to increase your investment return.

STOCK SELECTION GUIDE

The NAIC's Stock Selection Guide (SSG) is one of the most effective tools for ferreting out attractive investment candidates for superior returns. The Canadian Shareowner's Association uses a similar approach adapted from the NAIC.

The Stock Selection Guide uses operating data and financial ratios to evaluate prospective purchases. The NAIC recommends the use of the SSG prior to every purchase to help make an informed decision. The guide uses past performance to predict the company and its stock's future potential. The discussion that follows will provide you with the basics of the SSG and its completion. Refer to the NAIC's *Investor's Manual* for a more in-depth review and detailed instructions for completing the report.

It is important to remember that the SSG is only one tool in your investor's investigative and analysis kit. Use it in conjunction with other fundamental research tools such as financial ratio analysis, industry and competition review, management evaluation, and economic scenario projections.

Using Pacific Scientific Company as our prospective investment, we will walk through completion of the SSG. Refer to Chart 3–1 as we discuss each section and its meaning.

Much of the information required to complete the SSG is readily available from company financial reports (annual report and 10K), *Standard & Poor's Stock Guide,* and *Value Line Investment Survey.* The top section of Page 1 records some basic company and stock information including company name, exchange traded on, major product/service, and capitalization data. In the case of Pacific Scientific, you can see that the company manufactures motors and that its stock trades on the New York Stock Exchange.

Chart 3–1 Pacific Scientific Co. Stock Selection Guide

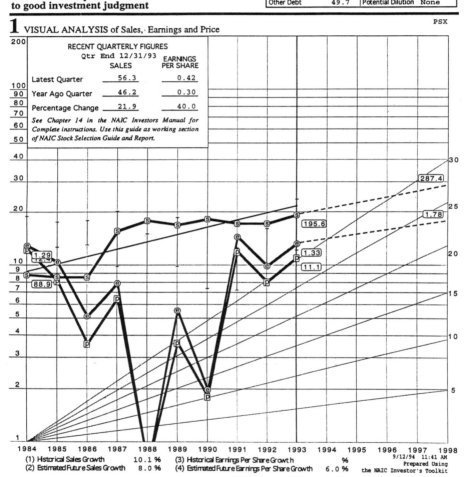

STOCK SELECTION GUIDE

The most widely used aid to good investment judgment

NATIONAL ASSOCIATION OF INVESTORS CORPORATION

NAIC

INVESTMENT EDUCATION SINCE 1951

Company __PACIFIC SCIENTIFIC__ Date __9/9/94__

Prepared by ___SPC___ Data taken from __S & P ()__

Where traded __NYSE__ Main product/service __MOTORS__

CAPITALIZATION	Authorized	Outstanding
Preferred	0.0	0.0
Common	0.0	5.4
Other Debt	49.7	Potential Dilution None

PSX

1 VISUAL ANALYSIS of Sales, Earnings and Price

RECENT QUARTERLY FIGURES

Qtr End 12/31/93

	SALES	EARNINGS PER SHARE
Latest Quarter	56.3	0.42
Year Ago Quarter	46.2	0.30
Percentage Change	21.9	40.0

See Chapter 14 in the NAIC Investors Manual for Complete instructions. Use this guide as working section of NAIC Stock Selection Guide and Report.

(1) Historical Sales Growth 10.1 %
(2) Estimated Future Sales Growth 8.0 %
(3) Historical Earnings Per Share Growth %
(4) Estimated Future Earnings Per Share Growth 6.0 %

9/12/94 11:41 AM
Prepared Using
the NAIC Investor's Toolkit

Source: National Association of Investors Corporation

Chart 3–1   Pacific Scientific Co. Stock Selection Guide

2 EVALUATING MANAGEMENT Company ___PACIFIC SCIENTIFIC___ 9/9/94

		1984	1985	1986	1987	1988	1989	1990	1991	1992	1993	LAST 5 YEAR AVE.	TREND UP	DOWN
A	% Pre-tax Profit on Sales (Net Before Taxes ÷ Sales)	13.9	9.5	4.2	4.2	-2.6	2.2	1.0	6.9	4.7	5.7	4.1	↑	
B	% Earned on Invested Capital (E/S ÷ Book Value)	13.0	9.9	4.9	7.2	-8.4	4.9	1.7	11.2	7.4	8.9	6.8	↑	

3 PRICE-EARNINGS HISTORY as an indicator of the future

PRESENT PRICE ___22.875___ HIGH THIS YEAR ___28.500___ LOW THIS YEAR ___14.625___

	Year	A PRICE HIGH	B PRICE LOW	C Earnings Per Share	D Price Earnings Ratio HIGH A ÷ C	E Price Earnings Ratio LOW B ÷ C	F Dividend Per Share	G % Payout F ÷ C X 100	H % High Yield F ÷ B X 100
1	1989	18.5	9.8	0.56	33.0	17.4	0.000	0.0	0.0
2	1990	16.4	7.4	0.20	81.9	36.8	0.000	0.0	0.0
3	1991	12.5	7.2	1.46	8.6	5.0	0.030	2.1	0.4
4	1992	16.0	9.8	1.00	16.0	9.8	0.120	12.0	1.2
5	1993	23.9	12.1	1.33	17.9	9.1	0.120	9.0	1.0
6	TOTAL								
7	AVERAGE		9.2		31.5	15.6		7.7	
8	AVERAGE PRICE EARNINGS RATIO		23.5		9	CURRENT PRICE EARNINGS RATIO		17.2	

Current P/E Based upon Last 12 mo. Earnings [1.33]
Proj. P/E [16.2] Based upon Next 12 mo. Earnings [1.41]

4 EVALUATING RISK and REWARD over the next 5 years

A HIGH PRICE - NEXT 5 YEARS
Avg. High P/E ___31.5___ (3D7) x Estimated High Earnings/Share ___1.78___ = Forecast High Price B-1 $ ___56.0___ (4A1)

B LOW PRICE - NEXT 5 YEARS
(a) Avg. Low P/E ___15.6___ (3E7) x Estimated Low E/Share ___1.33___ = $ ___20.8___
(b) Avg. Low Price of Last 5 Years = ___9.2___ (3B7)
(c) Recent Severe Market Low Price = ___7.2___
(d) Price Dividend Will Support Present Divd. / High Yield (H) = ___0.120___ / ___1.2___ = ___9.8___
Selected Estimated Low Price _____ B-2 $ ___9.2___ (4B1)

C ZONING
___56.0___ (4A1) High Forecast Price Minus ___9.2___ (4B1) Low Forecast Price Equals ___46.8___ (C) Range. 1/3 of Range = ___15.6___ (4CD)
Lower 1/3 = ___9.2___ (4B1) To ___24.8___ (Buy) (4C2)
Middle 1/3 = ___24.8___ To ___40.4___ (Maybe) (4C3)
Upper 1/3 = ___40.4___ To ___56.0___ (4A1) (Sell) (4C4)
Present Market Price of ___22.9___ is in the --- **Buy** --- (4C5) Range

D UP-SIDE DOWN-SIDE RATIO (Potential Gain vs. Risk of Loss)
High Price ___56.0___ (4A1) Minus Present Price ___22.9___ = ___33.2___ / ___13.6___ = ___2.4___ (4D) = To 1
Present Price ___22.9___ Minus Low Price ___9.2___ (4B1)
Relative Value: 73.0 %
Projected Relative Value: 68.9 %

5 5-YR POTENTIAL

A Present Full Year's Dividend $ ___0.120___ / Present Price of Stock $ ___22.9___ = ___0.005___ x100 = ___0.5___ Present Yield or % Returned on Purchase Price

B AVERAGE YIELD OVER THE NEXT 5 YEARS
Avg. Earn. Per Share Next 5 Years ___1.58___ x Avg % Payout ___7.7___ (3G7) = ___0.5___ %
Present Price $ ___22.9___
Total Return: 19.9 %

Source: National Association of Investors Corporation

Capitalization information lets you know how many shares are outstanding and the level of long-term debt. Potential dilution via convertible issues, stock options, or other dilution prospects alerts you to lower per-share earnings possibilities. Authorized but not outstanding stock may be used for a variety of purposes, including raising additional capital and acquisitions.

The quarterly figures and percentage changes for sales and earnings per share provide a quick summary of the company's recent track record. This information can be found in the upper left-hand corner of the chart. Such data can be an early warning sign of trouble ahead. You can compare the recent data with the trendline (constructed below) to determine whether recent performance is on target, above, or below. Pacific Scientific is experiencing growth rates of 21.9 percent and 40.0 percent for sales and earnings per share, respectively, for the latest quarter in comparison with the year-ago quarter.

Next, you plot revenues, earnings, and stock price to obtain a visual picture of the company and stock's historical performance and respective trendlines. This exercise allows you to determine the rate of revenue and earnings growth plus the relationship of earnings to company stock price. The graph allows plotting of 10 years of historical performance. As you can see from Pacific Scientific's chart and trendlines, the company's stock price dropped drastically with the earnings decline in 1988. The stock price has been up and down with the company's earnings rebounds in 1989 and again in 1991. The trendlines to the right of the chart divider (heavier line) are used for predicting sales, earnings, and stock price results five years into the future.

The bottom of Page 1 contains four important numbers: historical sales growth, estimated future sales growth, historical earnings per share growth, and estimated future earnings per share growth. While the historical numbers come directly from company annual reports or other sources of historical information, the estimated sales and earnings per-share growth figures can be derived from several sources, including independent research reports, projection of the historical trendline over a period of years into the future, and projection of more-recent historical trendline experience (more recent year or several quarters) ahead.

Of course, these projections can be tempered by other analysis of the company's and industry's prospects. This study can lead to projected trendlines and growth rates above or below historical performance. For example, Pacific Scientific's historical sales growth is 10.1 percent; the estimated future sales growth is only 8.0 percent despite the most recent quarterly sales growth of 21.9 percent over last year's similar period. In this case, the company's inconsistent track record outweighs recent strong gains.

Moving on to Page 2, the Evaluating Management Section uses pretax margin and return on stockholder's equity as two measures of management ability. As indicated by recent performance, Pacific Scientific's pre-tax margin and return on stockholder's equity are both in an upward trend, a good sign.

Section 3, Price-Earnings History, allows you to calculate average price-earnings ratios and projected price/earnings ratios based on available historical information. For example, the average price-earnings ratio for Pacific Scientific is determined by adding together the average high and the average low price-earnings ratio and dividing by two ([(31.5 + 15.6)/2] = 23.5). Likewise, the current price/earnings ratio is calculated by dividing the current selling price by earnings for the most recent 12 months (22.9/1.33 = 17.2).

Section 4, Evaluating Risk and Reward over the next 5 years, uses the information generated above to predict possible pricing scenarios and the upside potential and downside risk. The potential high price over the next five years is derived by multiplying the average high price-earnings ratio (Line D7) by the amount shown on the Page 1 Visual Analysis graph where the projected earnings pershare trendline crosses the vertical line for five years in the future (31.5 × 1.78 = 56.0).

On the downside, the posible low price over the next five years is found by multiplying the average low price-earnings ratio (Line E7) by the amount shown on the Page 1 Visual Analysis graph where the projected earnings per-share trendline crosses the vertical lines at the lowest point over the next five years (15.6 × 1.33 = 20.8).

Zoning helps determine whether the stock's current price is reasonable. Subtracting the low forecast price of 9.2 from the high forecast price of 56.0 equals 46.8. This number is then split into three to obtain buy, hold, and sell ranges as follows:

Lower ⅓ Range	9.2 to 24.8 (9.2 + 15.6)	Buy
Middle ⅓ Range	24.8 to 40.4 (24.8 + 15.6)	Hold/Maybe Purchase
Upper ⅓ Range	40.4 to 56.0 (40.4 + 15.6)	Sell

Since Pacific Scientific's current stock price is 22.9, the company is in the Buy Range.

Section 4D evaluates the relative odds of the potential gain versus the risk of loss. The NAIC prefers a ratio equal to or in excess of 3 to 1. In this case, Pacific Scientific, with a ratio of 2.4 to 1, fails to meet this benchmark. Investors willing to assume a higher risk posture may still purchase this stock.

Section 5, 5-Year Potential, uses yield calculations to help you determine your total return potential. While the NAIC stresses growth stock investing for superior returns, available dividends do boost the total return prospects.

This exercise gives you one way to use the SSG. There are other approaches to projecting earnings and stock prices for the years ahead for use with the SSG. The NAIC *Investor's Manual* explains these alternatives in detail.

Once you have completed Stock Selection Guides for several companies, you can compare them to decide on the stocks best situated to outperform the others you're considering for purchase. This comparison can be done informally or by using the Stock Comparison Guide forms provided by the NAIC.

THE COMPUTERIZED APPROACH

Of course, in today's computer age, many of the above tools and more are available in software packages from the NAIC and elsewhere. The American Association of Individual Investors publishes a handy and informative desk reference book, *The Individual Investor's Guide to Computerized Investing*. The book sells for $24.95. Information on ordering this comprehensive computer reference guide can be obtained by contacting the American Association of Individual Investors, 625 North Michigan Avenue, Chicago, Illinois 60611-3110, or by calling 312-280-0170.

NAIC investment software include the following:

Investor's Toolkit-SSG Master Module

Contains computerized versions of the Stock Selection Guide (SSG), Stock Comparison Guide, and Portfolio Management Guide. These indiviual software programs can also be purchased separately, but the module is the most economical buy.

NAIC/S&P Datafiles

Contains company datafiles on more than 3,300 company files arranged by stock ticker symbol. Also includes information on *Better Investing*'s Top 200, and Low Cost Investment Plan participants.

SSG Plus

Contains the Stock Selection Guide, Stock Selection Guide and Report, and Stock Comparison Guide programs plus other helpful analysis reports such as the Stock Sort Report, which allows you to sort company files by a number of variables.

SSG Combined

Contains the Stock Selection Guide, Stock Comparison Guide, PERT (Performance Evaluation and Review Technique), Company Balance Sheet, and

Personal Portfolio tracking features. It provides five ways to estimate earnings per share.

Take $tock

Contains the Stock Selection Guide, Stock Comparison Guide, PERT, and Portfolio Management Guide. The evaluator report provides a number of "Reasons to Buy" and "Items to Check" to aid the novice investor's analysis. Ratios and calculations back up the evaluations.

PERT (Performance Evaluation Review Technique) for DOS

Contains methods of monitoring and evaluating individual stocks within a portfolio. Helps determine if growth, profitability, and valuation characteristics that attracted the investor to a stock still remain valid.

STB Prospector

Features a stock screening program designed to use the 3,300 company NAIC datafiles to search out investment prospects based on your investment selection criteria. The Prospector uses more than 60 selection parameters for screening prospective purchase candidates for further analysis.

NAIC Club Accounting Software

This package eases the burden of keeping accurate track of your investment club activities. It has the ability to capture extensive security information and generate crucial reports such as Member Status Reports, Distribution of Earnings Statements, Members Cash Contributions, and Member Valuation Units Ledger.

For information on current software pricing (demonstration diskettes are also available) and computer hardware requirements, contact NAIC Software, P.O. Box 220, Royal Oak, Michigan 48068, or call 810-583-6242.

Now you have all the tools at your disposal to develop and initiate a solid investment strategy to beat the pros and deliver superior investment returns over the long term. Part 4, Investment Club Top Picks, takes a look at *Better Investing*'s Top 100 holdings of investment clubs to help you begin building your portfolio. Good luck.

Investment Club Top Picks

Without a doubt, many of the NAIC's investment clubs get a number of their stock picks from the association's *Better Investing* magazine. A review of the lifetime performance of *Better Investing*'s Stocks to Study (cover stocks) versus the performance of the Dow Jones Industrial Average indicates an impressive track record. Using overlapping five-year study periods from 1952 through 1993, the NAIC's investment magazine's featured stocks outperformed the Dow Jones Industrial Average in more than 68 percent of the five-year periods.

Better Investing's Securities Review Committee has encouraged this competition over the years to highlight longer-term performance rather than focus on how the market will perform in the weeks and months ahead. In the monthly cover story selections, the Securities Review Committee strives for diversification, in terms of company size as well as by industry, to provide greater diversification to protect investor's portfolios from unnecssary risk. See Table 4–1 for a review of performance for specific time periods.

Further analysis of the performance records show that the DJIA decreased during nine of those five-year time frames; the cover stories only decreased during five of those periods. Since 1970 there have been 20 five-year comparison periods during which the cover stories outperformed the Dow stocks 75 percent of the time.

The cover story stocks also posted the largest five-year percentage gain of 298 percent, versus 113 percent for the Dow during the same period (1982-86). Another plus: The cover story stocks scored gains of 100 percent or more nine times since the competition began; the Dow achieved a better than 100 percent gain only twice.

Another fertile ground for unearthing top performers is *Better Investing*'s Top 100 List. The Top 100 ranks the holdings of the NAIC clubs across the nation by the number of investment clubs holding a company's stock and the number of shares held by NAIC members. See Table 4–2.

In the remainder of *Main Street Beats Wall Street,* we will evaluate a number of the Top 100 stocks held by investment clubs for potential superior overall returns.

Table 4-1   Lifetime Performance Record:
BI's Stocks to Study vs Dow Jones Industrial Avg.

Five-Year Performance Period	Increase/(Decrease) in the Dow Jones Industrial Average	Average Increase/ Decrease in Price of BI Cover Stocks
1952–56*	+ 85%	+ 147%
1953–57*	+ 59	+ 64
1954–58	+ 71	+ 46
1955–59*	+ 56	+ 92
1956–60*	+ 25	+ 59
1957–61*	+ 55	+ 129
1958–62	+ 34	+ 7
1959–63	+ 22	+ 15
1960–64*	+ 41	+ 61
1961–65	+ 41	+ 35
1962–66*	+ 22	+ 58
1963–67*	+ 28	+ 44
1964–68*	+ 14	+ 146
1965–69*	(13)	+ 102
1966–70	(3)	(20)
1967–71*	+1	+ 34
1968–72*	(13)	0
1969–73	(3)	(28)
1970–74	(23)	(25)
1971–75	(3)	(43)
1972–76*	+ 5	+ 40
1973–77*	(10)	+ 34
1974–78*	+ 8	+ 43
1975–79*	+ 3	+ 93
1976–80*	(2)	+ 64
1977–81*	(1)	+ 54
1978–82*	+ 29	+ 118
1979–83*	+ 50	+ 120
1980–84*	+ 35	+ 145
1981–85*	+ 66	+ 72
1982–86*	+ 113	+ 298
1983–87	+ 62	+ 37
1984–88*	+ 85	+ 112
1985–89	+ 105	+ 65
1986–90	+ 45	(1)
1987–91*	+ 39	+ 71
1988–92*	+ 59	+ 66
1989–93	+ 52	+ 34

*Five-year periods during which BI's stocks outperformed the Dow Jones Industrial Average

Source of Data: National Association of Investors Corporation

Table 4–2 Better Investing's Top 100 for 1994

Company	Rank by # of Clubs Holding Stock	# of Clubs	Rank by Total Shares Held by NAIC Members	# of Shares Held by Members
McDonald's	1	4,273	3	2,277,785
Wal-Mart	2	3,566	2	2,478,224
PepsiCo	3	3,481	6	1,478,294
AFLAC Inc.	4	3,125	1	4,782,770
Merck & Co	5	3,060	5	1,709,142
American Tel	6	2,770	4	1,774,156
Walt Disney	7	2,517	9	997,280
WMX Tech	8	2,438	11	858,208
Abbott Lab	9	1,971	7	1,450,354
RPM, Inc.	10	1,891	8	1,147,491
Philip Morris	11	1,678	16	719,935
ConAgra, Inc.	12	1,656	14	730,482
Sara Lee	13	1,603	10	885,493
Bristol-Myers	14	1,554	19	486,846
Coca-Cola Co.	15	1,470	15	728,471
Boeing	16	1,452	20	478,934
General Elec.	17	1,421	22	437,842
Kellogg Co.	18	1,243	46	210,520
Home Depot	19	1,184	17	509,157
Glaxco Hold.	20	1,024	18	494,916
Biomet, Inc.	21	1,017	13	801,574
Colgate-Pal.	22	999	35	268,901
Rubbermaid	23	959	31	334,612
TelMex	24	924	30	349,290
St. Jude Med.	25	919	36	264,928
Motorola	26	910	81	120,616
Dana Corp.	27	889	27	363,920
Microsoft	28	888	50	195,390
Archer-Dan	29	871	21	456,264
Quaker Oats	30	857	66	151,625
Ryder Sys.	31	836	24	407,577
Procter & Gam.	32	817	48	198,934
Wendy's Intl.	33	801	12	826,860
Huntington	34	783	23	414,316
John. & John.	35	781	28	361,731
H.J. Heinz	36	759	39	260,925
Hannaford	37	724	29	349,388

Table 4–2 Better Investing's Top 100 for 1994 (continued)

Company	Rank by # of Clubs Holding Stock	# of Clubs	Rank by Total Shares Held by NAIC Members	# of Shares Held by Members
Ionics, Inc.	38	693	62	157,922
Cin. Bell	39	685	40	250,071
Toys "R" Us	40	685	49	196,483
Newell Co.	41	677	91	101,866
SW Bell	42	676	63	156,474
Anheuser-Busch	43	674	51	191,315
Upjohn Co.	44	671	85	111,458
Novell, Inc.	45	670	45	213,280
Hershey Foods	46	669	57	168,045
Eli Lilly	47	668	76	130,749
Synovus Finl.	48	665	41	247,164
Price/Costco	49	664	61	158,575
Pfizer, Inc.	50	662	53	180,779
Bob Evans	51	661	25	399,212
Mylan Labs	52	660	26	378,749
Sysco Corp.	53	657	43	233,978
Stryker Corp.	54	656	34	280,885
Amer. Grtgs.	55	655	44	223,817
Thermo Elec.	56	651	54	179,967
Banc One	57	648	38	263,390
Texaco, Inc.	58	640	73	146,812
Liz Claiborne	59	636	84	113,926
Intel Corp.	60	634	86	108,385
IBM	61	633	95	87,819
Safety-Kleen	62	632	52	184,880
US WEST, Inc.	63	630	99	64,882
Hillenbrand	64	628	56	177,288
Blockbuster	65	627	60	159,388
Caremark Intl.	66	612	98	72,072
Cracker Bar.	67	611	37	264,864
Cooper Tire	68	609	47	200,844
Mattel, Inc.	69	607	100	49,377
Amgen, Inc.	70	606	88	107,466
Mobil Corp.	71	591	94	93,116
Walgreen Co.	72	587	58	162,757
Office Depot	73	585	55	178,717
The Limited	74	583	79	123,593

Table 4–2 Better Investing's Top 100 for 1994 (continued)

Company	Rank by # of Clubs Holding Stock	# of Clubs	Rank by Total Shares Held by NAIC Members	# of Shares Held by Members
Gerber Prod.	75	580	97	78,084
GTE Corp.	76	561	71	147,599
Sigma-Aldrich	77	555	89	103,209
Kmart Corp.	78	532	69	149,830
Am. Home Prod.	79	500	80	122,148
Exxon Corp.	80	483	64	155,472
Baxter Intl.	81	461	59	161,346
Food Lion	82	446	32	322,517
Tyson Foods	83	403	70	149,830
Ford Motor	84	387	87	107,853
Ball Corp.	85	376	82	118,541
Pall Corp.	86	321	42	237,828
ADP, Inc.	87	318	68	150,220
H.B. Fuller	88	300	96	80,163
Browning-Fer.	89	284	90	102,761
Hanson PLC	90	263	78	130,203
Figgie Intl.	91	251	67	151,312
ALLIED Grp.	92	230	77	130,218
Gen. Motors	93	219	93	93,120
Worthington In.	94	217	33	295,259
RJR Nabisco	95	215	72	147,266
Russell Corp.	96	211	83	117,962
Lukens, Inc.	97	208	75	132,318
Pub. Ser. Colo.	98	207	65	155,205
Chrysler	99	205	92	98,169
PacifiCorp	100	202	74	144,512

Source: National Association of Investors Corporation

A quick perusal of the list shows that investment clubs practice what they preach in terms of diversification. You'll find companies in which they invest representing a wide variety of industries, from food service to office supplies and from toys to pharamaceuticals. In addition, an international flavor is creeping into investment club portfolios in the form of American Depositary Receipts (ADRs) of such companies as Hanson PLC, Telefonos de Mexico (one of most frequently traded securities on the New York Stock Exchange), and Glaxco Holdings.

Just because a company is on the Top 100 list doesn't mean it's an attractive purchase right now. You must still investigate the underlying fundamentals of the company and its industry with a long-term perspective. After all, many of the investment clubs may be starting to shed some of the stocks on the list due to poor performance and less-than-attractive future prospects, or they may be getting rid of stocks that have had a strong price rise and may be overpriced based on projected revenues and earnings performance.

One method of discovering investment prospects is to study NAIC lists of companies in which investment clubs are showing increased interest. Table 4–3 lists firms that have advanced dramatically since 1993 in terms of the number of investment clubs holding positions in their stock. For example, Southwestern Bell advanced 46 positions to the 42nd-place ranking, and Biomet, Inc. advanced 30 positions to the 21st place.

Similarly, Table 4–4 indicates ample investment club interest in these companies to vault them into the prestigious listing. For example: Motorola,

Table 4–3 *Top 100 Companies Advancing Five or More Positions*

Company	1994 Ranking	# Of Positions Advancing
SW Bell	42	46
Stryker Corp.	54	32
Biomet, Inc.	21	30
Price/Costco	49	25
Kmart Corp.	78	20
Telefonos de Mexico	24	19
Novell, Inc.	45	19
Synovus Finl.	48	19
Microsoft Corp.	28	16
American Grtgs.	55	13
Texaco, Inc.	58	12
Colgate-Palmolive	22	11
Toys "R" Us	40	10
Kellogg Company	18	9
Mylan Laboratories	52	9
Cooper Tire & Rubber	68	7
Banc One Corp.	57	6
Boeing Corp.	16	5
Home Depot, Inc.	19	5
Huntington Banc.	34	5

Source: National Association of Investors Corporation

Table 4–4   Companies New to the Top 100 This Year

Company	1994 Ranking
Motorola, Inc.	26
Ionics, Inc.	38
Newell Company	41
Thermo Electron Corp.	56
Intel Corporation	60
US WEST, Inc.	63
Caremark International	66
Mattel, Inc.	69
Mobil Corporation	71
Office Depot, Inc.	73
H. B. Fuller Company	88
Russell Corporation	96
Chrysler Corporation	99

Source: National Association of Investors Corporation

Inc., Ionics Inc., and Newell Company made it into the top 50 companies owned by investment clubs with rankings of 26th, 38th, and 41st; respectively. Ten other companies broke into the Top 100 list for 1994.

As these tables indicate, many NAIC investment clubs have achieved impressive track records over the years. It would be wise to consider some of the stocks favored by a great number of the clubs. With that in mind, we offer the following objective analysis of a cross-section of the clubs on the Top 100 listing. A number of these stocks, including Home Depot (19), McDonald's (1), Microsoft (28), Mylan Laboratories (52), Synovus Financial (48), and Wal-Mart Stores (2), have already been covered in Part 2 and won't be repeated here. Feel free to refer to those pages for other interesting investment candidates for superior returns.

TOP 100 COMPANY PROFILES

COMPANY PROFILE

AFLAC Incorporated
1932 Wynnton Road
Columbus, Georgia 31999

Stock Exchange: NYSE
Ticker Symbol: AFL
Telephone 706-324-6330

Company Business
AFLAC Incorporated, through its principal subsidiary, American Family Life Assurance Company of Columbus, specializes in supplemental insurance coverage. It is the world's largest provider of supplemental medical

benefit insurance. AFLAC also sells accident, life, Medicare supplement, and long-term convalescent care policies.

The insurance carrier operates in 47 states and seven foreign countries. Its Japanese business accounts for 75 percent of revenues and earnings.

Shareholder Information

Outstanding shares	102,794,000
Insider ownership	Approximately 6 percent
DRIP program	Yes

Financial Information (July 1994)

Total assets	$19 billion
Cash and temporary investments	$16 billion
Long-term debt	$206 million
Equity ratio	91 percent
Dividend rate	46 cents per share annual basis
Yield	1.3 percent
Price/earnings ratio	14

Stock Price History (through mid-September 1994)

	1992	1993	1994
Low	$19\frac{1}{8}$	$24\frac{3}{4}$	$25\frac{1}{4}$
High	$27\frac{7}{8}$	34	$36\frac{1}{8}$

Revenue and Earnings History (through July 30, 1994)

	1992	1993	1st Half 1993	1st Half 1994
Revenue	$3,986	$5,001	$2,358	$2,873
Net income	183	244*	112*	139
Earnings per share	1.79	2.32*	1.07	1.34

In millions, except per-share amounts
*Excludes gain of $11 million, or 11 cents per share, due to accounting changes

Key Growth Rates (past five years)

Investment income	12.5%
Earnings	15.0%

DRIP Details

The AFLAC Incorporated dividend reinvestment program permits automatic reinvestment of cash dividends and optional cash purchases of shares of company stock in amounts from $20 to $5,000 per month. For information on AFLAC's DRIP, contact AFL Stock Plan, AFLAC Incorporated, 1932 Wynnton Road, Columbus, Georgia 31999, or call 800-227-4756.

Company Prospects

AFLAC Incorporated ranked only fourth in the number of investment clubs holding its stock (3,125) but garnered first place in the number of shares held by investment clubs (4,782,770 shares) and the value of those shares ($136,308,945).

AFLAC is well on its way to its fifth year of consecutive earnings increases, with projected record earnings in 1994 of $2.75 per share. For 1995, earnings projections are as high as $3.40 per share.

Peter Lynch touted AFLAC in the March 1994 issue of *Worth* as a premier company most people know absolutely nothing about. Lynch cited earnings increases 12 times out of the past 13 years and an earnings growth rate moving ahead at a 15 percent annual clip. Moreover, the stock has outperformed the market 15 times out of the past 19 years. Despite all this, AFLAC represents a classic undervalued stock ripe for the picking.

Besides being a money machine, AFLAC takes a conservative investment stance. In a ranking of the 50 largest life insurance companies by The National Association of Insurance Commissioners, AFLAC rated first in terms of credit safety, with zero junk bonds, zero problem mortgages, and a 9 percent debt ratio. The company's financial strength is rated A+ "Superior" by A.M. Best.

Revival of the Japanese economy, new product introductions, investment income growth, and a growing market position will keep AFLAC's planned 15 percent revenue and earnings growth on target. Look for the company's 10-year total shareholder return in excess of 22 percent to proceed full steam ahead. Cash dividends have grown at a compounded rate of 13.5 percent over the past five years.

COMPANY PROFILE

Biomet, Inc.
Airport Industrial Park
P.O. Box 587
Warsaw, Indiana 46581-0587

Stock Exchange: NASDAQ
Ticker Symbol: BMET
Telephone 219-267-6639

Company Business

Biomet, Inc. designs, manufactures, and markets products used primarily by orthopedic medical specialists in both surgical and nonsurgical therapy. Product lines include reconstructive and trauma devices, electrical bone growth stimulators, orthopedic devices, powered surgical instruments, oral-maxillofacial implants and instruments, arthroscopy products, and operating room supplies.

The company operates facilities in California, Florida, Indiana, and New Jersey, and in England, Germany, Italy, and Puerto Rico. Foreign business accounts for approximately 15 percent of annual revenues.

Biomet advanced 30 positions in the Top 100 listing, jumping to the 21st slot in 1994. More than 1,000 investment clubs owned some 801,000 shares of Biomet common stock.

Shareholder Information

Outstanding shares	3,061,353
Insider ownership	More than 12 percent
DRIP program	No

Financial Information (May 31, 1994)

Total assets	$418 million
Cash and temporary investments	$141 million
Working capital	$288 million
Long-term debt	-0-
Equity ratio	100 percent
Book value	$3.12 per share
Dividend rate	–
Yield	–
Price/earnings ratio	18

Stock Price History (through mid-September 1994)

	1992	*1993*	*1994*
Low	$13\frac{7}{8}$	$8\frac{3}{8}$	9
High	$30\frac{1}{2}$	$16\frac{1}{2}$	$11\frac{7}{8}$

Revenue and Earnings History (through fiscal year ended May 31, 1994)

	1992	*1993*	*1994*
Revenue	$275	$335	$373
Net income	52	64	70
Earnings per share	.46	.56	.61

In millions, except per-share amounts

Key Growth Rates (past five years)

Revenue	27.0%
Cash flow	32.0%
Earnings	33.0%

Company Prospects

Biomet, Inc.'s stock prices plummeted from a high of $32\frac{3}{8}$ per share in late 1991, bottoming out in the third quarter of 1993 at $8\frac{3}{8}$ per share. Since then, the stock price has treaded water between $8 to $12 per share (see Chart 4–1). Concern over healthcare reform and a slowing in Biomet's

Chart 4–1 Biomet, Inc. Stock Chart

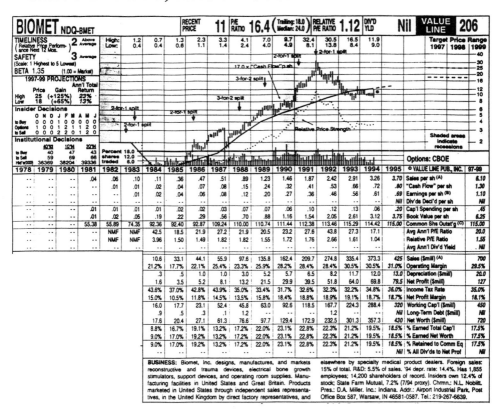

BIOMET NDQ-BMET	RECENT PRICE **11**	P/E RATIO **16.4** (Trailing: 18.0 / Median: 24.0)	RELATIVE P/E RATIO **1.12**	DIV'D YLD **Nil**	VALUE LINE **206**

TIMELINESS **2** Above Average (Relative Price Performance Next 12 Mos.)
SAFETY **3** Average
BETA 1.35 (1.00 = Market)

1997-99 PROJECTIONS — Ann'l Total Return
High: Price 25, Gain (+125%), Return 23%
Low: Price 18, Gain (+65%), Return 13%

Options: CBOE

Target Price Range 1997 1998 1999

	1978	1979	1980	1981	1982	1983	1984	1985	1986	1987	1988	1989	1990	1991	1992	1993	1994	1995	© VALUE LINE PUB., INC. 97-99
Sales per sh (A)				.04	.06	.10	.11	.36	.47	.51	.89	1.23	1.46	1.87	2.42	2.91	3.26	3.70	8.10
"Cash Flow" per sh					.01	.01	.02	.04	.07	.08	.15	.24	.32	.41	.53	.66	.72	.80	1.30
Earnings per sh (B)						.01	.02	.04	.06	.08	.12	.20	.27	.36	.46	.56	.61	.69	1.10
Div'ds Decl'd per sh																		Nil	Nil
Cap'l Spending per sh				.01	.01	.01	.01	.02	.02	.03	.07	.07	.06	.10	.12	.13	.06	.20	.45
Book Value per sh				.01	.01	.02	.05	.19	.22	.29	.56	.70	.88	1.16	1.54	2.05	2.61	3.12	3.75	6.25
Common Shs Outst'g (C)				55.38	55.89	74.35	92.36	92.40	92.87	109.24	110.00	110.74	111.44	112.38	113.46	115.29	114.42	115.00	115.00
Avg Ann'l P/E Ratio				NMF	NMF	42.5	18.5	21.9	27.2	21.9	20.5	23.2	27.6	43.8	27.3	17.1			20.0
Relative P/E Ratio				NMF	NMF	3.96	1.50	1.49	1.82	1.82	1.55	1.72	1.76	2.66	1.61	1.04			1.55
Avg Ann'l Div'd Yield																			Nil

															1992	1993	1994	1995	97-99
Sales ($mill) (A)	10.6	33.1	44.1	55.9	97.6	135.8	162.4	209.7	274.8	335.4	373.3	425							700
Operating Margin	21.2%	17.7%	22.1%	25.4%	23.3%	25.9%	28.2%	28.4%	28.4%	30.5%	30.5%	31.0%							29.5%
Depreciation ($mill)	.3	.5	1.0	1.0	3.0	5.2	5.7	6.5	8.2	11.7	12.0	13.0							20.0
Net Profit ($mill)	1.6	3.5	5.2	8.1	13.2	21.5	29.9	39.5	51.8	64.0	79.5	127							127
Income Tax Rate	43.6%	37.0%	42.8%	43.9%	35.0%	33.4%	31.7%	32.6%	32.3%	32.2%	34.8%	36.0%							35.0%
Net Profit Margin	15.0%	10.5%	11.8%	14.5%	13.5%	15.8%	18.4%	18.8%	18.9%	19.1%	18.7%	18.7%							18.1%
Working Cap'l ($mill)	16.0	17.7	23.1	52.4	45.8	63.0	92.6	118.5	167.7	224.3	288.4	320							450
Long-Term Debt ($mill)	.9	.5	.3	.1	1.2	--	--	--	1.2	--	Nil								Nil
Net Worth ($mill)	17.6	20.4	27.1	61.3	76.6	97.7	129.4	172.9	232.5	301.3	357.3	430							720
% Earned Total Cap'l	8.8%	16.7%	19.1%	13.2%	17.2%	22.0%	23.1%	22.8%	22.3%	21.2%	19.5%	18.5%							17.5%
% Earned Net Worth	9.0%	17.0%	19.2%	13.2%	17.2%	22.0%	23.1%	22.8%	22.3%	21.2%	19.5%	18.5%							17.5%
% Retained to Comm Eq	9.0%	17.0%	19.2%	13.2%	17.2%	22.0%	23.1%	22.8%	22.3%	21.2%	19.5%	18.5%							17.5%
% All Div'ds to Net Prof																			Nil

BUSINESS: Biomet, Inc. designs, manufactures, and markets reconstructive and trauma devices, electrical bone growth stimulators, support devices, and operating room supplies. Manufacturing facilities in United States and Great Britain. Products marketed in United States through independent sales representatives, in the United Kingdom by direct factory representatives, and elsewhere by specialty medical product dealers. Foreign sales: 15% of total. R&D: 5.5% of sales. '94 depr. rate: 14.4%. Has 1,855 employees; 14,200 shareholders of record. Insiders own 12.4% of stock; State Farm Mutual, 7.2% (7/94 proxy). Chrmn.: N.L. Noblitt. Pres.: D.A. Miller. Inc.: Indiana. Addr.: Airport Industrial Park, Post Office Box 587, Warsaw, IN 46581-0587. Tel.: 219-267-6639.

growth are overblown and the dramatic drop in Biomet's stock price is overdone.

A smaller player in the large-company-dominated orthopedic market, Biomet has consistently gained market share. The firm is a low-cost competitor and extremely aggressive in both product introduction and marketing. Biomet has around 20 products awaiting FDA approval. The firm recently inked a five-year contract with Health Services Corporation of America (HSCA), making Biomet one of two preferred providers of orthopedic products to HSCA and its 1,160 member hospitals.

On the acquisition front, the merger with Kirschner Medical Corporation portends additional growth through other future mergers in strategic markets and product lines., Demographics also favor Biomet: With an aging population, the $5 billion orthopedic market is expected to continue its impressive growth rate.

The company has plenty of cash (in excess of $140 million and no long-term debt) for market opportunities, top-notch management, excellent research and development, a gross margin over 65 percent, and a solid growth plan.

Institutional interest in Biomet peaked with ownership of approximately 62 percent of the outstanding common stock shares. Institutional ownership currently stands around 36 percent. Once the jitters over Biomet's performance dissipate in the wake of revenue and earnings gains in the years ahead, the company's stock price should rebound strongly. The Biomet bears are wrong. Purchase for superior long-term gains.

COMPANY PROFILE

Colgate-Palmolive Company   Stock Exchange: NYSE
300 Park Avenue   Ticker Symbol: CL
New York, New York 10022-7499   Telephone 212-310-2000

Company Business

Colgate-Palmolive Company, one of the world's most widely known consumer products firms, ranks as the second-largest domestic manufacturer of detergents, toiletries, and other household products. Major well-known brand names in addition to Colgate and Palmolive include Ajax, Dynamo, Fab, Fresh Start, and Ultra Brite.

Foreign business accounts for approximately 65 percent of annual revenues, and the company is experiencing rapid growth in populous Asia and developing countries. Strong population growth in these regions and an increasing use of household and personal care products bodes well for Colgate-Palmolive in the decades ahead.

Shareholder Information

Outstanding shares	152,880,000
Insider ownership	—*
DRIP program	Yes

*ESOP (Employee Stock Ownership Plan) owns approximately 8 percent of common stock.

Financial Information (June 1994)

Total assets	$ 6.1 billion
Cash and temporary investments	$239 million
Working capital	$848 million
Long-term debt	$ 1.8 billion
Equity ratio	39 percent
Book value	$12.01 per share

Dividend rate	$1.64 per share annual basis
Yield	3.0 percent
Price/earnings ratio	15

Stock Price History (through mid-September 1994)

	1992	*1993*	*1994*
Low	45⅛	46¾	49½
High	50⅝	67¼	65⅜

Revenue and Earnings History (through June 30, 1994)

	1992	*1993*	*1st Half 1993*	*1st Half 1994*
Revenue	$7,007	$7,141	$3,478	$3,661
Net income	477	548*	283*	297**
Earnings per share	2.92	3.38*	1.71*	1.95**

In millions, except per-share amounts

*Before effects of accounting change for postretirement benefits in the amount of $358.2 million, or $2.25 per share

** Before effects of a charge of $5.2 million, or 4 cents per share, for the sale of a non-core business

Key Growth Rates (past five years)

Revenue	3.5%
Cash flow	14.0%
Earnings	15.0%

DRIP Details

The Colgate-Palmolive dividend reinvestment program permits the automatic reinvestment of common stock cash dividends in company stock with no administrative or commission cost to the shareholder. There's another unique feature to the Colgate-Palmolive DRIP: It allows shareholders of the firm's $4.25 preferred stock to reinvest their preferred cash dividends in company common stock at no charge. In addition, company shareholders may elect to purchase additional Colgate-Palmolive common stock in cash amounts ranging from $20 to $60,000 per year on a monthly basis. For information on this DRIP, contact First Chicago Trust Company of New York, Dividend Reinvestment Plan, Colgate-Palmolive Company, P.O. Box 2598, Jersey City, New Jersey 07303-2598, or call 201-324-0498.

Company Prospects

Despite facing an extremely competitive environment, Colgate-Palmolive Company posted worldwide unit volume increases of 9 percent for the first half of 1994. Another plus: New product innovations have helped the company boost its global personal care product sales by 55 percent in the past two years.

The company has established market leadership positions through growing acceptance of its portfolio of strong brand names worldwide. Colgate-Palmolive is ranked number one globally in liquid soaps, second globally in deodorants/antiperspirants and baby care, third in bar soap, and fourth in shampoos.

The 1992 acquisition of Mennen made Colgate-Palmolive one of the two largest companies in the $3.8 billion global underarm deodorant/antiperspirant market. With more than $230 million in cash and ample credit facilities, other strategic major acquisitions can help boost market share and bring on board new product lines.

Higher gross margins and earnings increasing at a double-digit clip will keep shareholders happy. In addition, higher dividend payments have been voted by the Board of Directors for 32 consecutive years, the most recent being a 14 percent increase in the common stock cash dividend.

An investment of $100 in Colgate-Palmolive stock on December 31, 1988, would have been worth more than $300 at the end of 1993 (assuming dividend reinvestment) versus only $197 for the S&P 500. Trading below the midpoint of its 52-week trading range of $65\frac{3}{8}$ to $49\frac{1}{2}$ per share, Colgate-Palmolive rates a good look; see Chart 4–2.

The NAIC's *Better Investing* magazine featured Colgate-Palmolive in its November 1993 issue. The company moved up 11 places on the 1994 Top 100 list, to number 22, with 999 investment clubs owning nearly 269,000 company common shares.

COMPANY PROFILE

Cooper Tire & Rubber Company
P. O. Box 550
Findlay, Ohio 45839-0550

Stock Exchange: NYSE
Ticker Symbol: CTB
Telephone 419-423-1321

Company Business

Cooper Tire & Rubber Company rates as a growing player in the global tire market. Ranked as the ninth-largest tire manufacturer, the company successfully boosted revenues from less than $900 million as recently as 1990 to an estimated $1.3 billion in 1994.

The company sells 50 percent of its production output under its own Cooper and Falls brand names and the balance under private label customer programs. It targets the tire replacement market versus the original equipment manufacturer (OEM) market with tight competition and lower product margins.

Automobile and truck tires and tubes account for 85 percent of annual revenues; the balance comes from industrial rubber products business. Industrial rubber products include hose and hose assemblies, vibration control products, automotive sealing systems, and specialty seating components.

Chart 4–2   Colgate-Palmolive Company Stock Chart

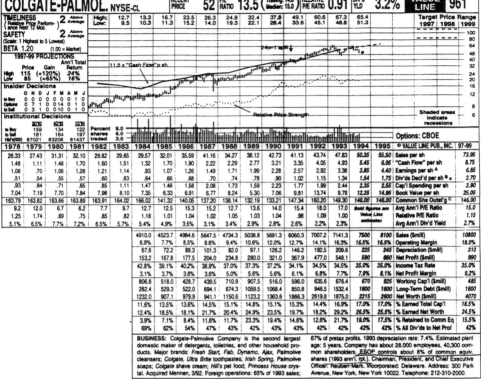

Source: ©1994 by Value Line Publishing, Inc. Reprinted by permission; All Rights Reserved.

Shareholder Information

Outstanding shares	83,624,539
Insider ownership	2 percent*
DRIP program	No

*Plus profit sharing plans own approximately 9 percent of common stock

Financial Information (June 1994)

Total assets	$960 million
Cash and temporary investments	$ 29 million
Working capital	$251 million
Long-term debt	$ 38 million
Equity ratio	91 percent

Book value	$7.12 per share
Dividend rate	24 per share annual basis
Yield	.9 percent
Price/earnings ratio	20

Stock Price History (through mid-September 1994)

	1992	1993	1994
Low	22⅛	20	22½
High	35⅝	39⅝	29½

Revenue and Earnings History (through June 30, 1994)

	1992	1993	1st Half 1993	1st Half 1994
Revenue	$1,175	$1,193	$573	$659
Net income	108*	102	49	54
Earnings per share	1.30*	1.22	.59	.65

In millions, except per-share amounts
*Before effects of accounting change in the amount of $65 million, or 78 cents per share

Key Growth Rates (past five years)

Revenue	11.0%
Cash flow	23.0%
Earnings	28.0%

Company Prospects

I rated Cooper Tire & Rubber Company as a turnaround company in the December-January 1994 issue of *Your Money* when the stock traded around $21 per share. The recommendation was based on an expanding product line, beefed-up production capacity, and an improving economy to reinflate Cooper's stock price.

Since then the stock rose to a high of $29½ per share before settling back to the $23-per-share level. Cooper's fundamentals are still impressive, with rising revenues and earnings. Strong demand and higher tire prices bode well for the future, as does a rebounding economy. Automotive manufacturing remains robust, creating increased demand for Cooper's industrial rubber products. The company has scheduled overtime to meet demand. Facility expansion and equipment renovations will add to capacity and improve efficiency.

The company's financial position, with nearly $29 million in cash and only $38 million in long-term debt, provides operating flexibility. The board of directors raised the cash dividend 9 percent in mid-1994.

Investment clubs have taken notice of Cooper's prospects. The company moved up 7 spots to 68 on the Top 100 list. More than 200,000 shares of Cooper Tire & Rubber Company common stock is owned by 609 investment clubs. The stock may be forming a base for a price runup with improved earnings (see Chart 4–3).

COMPANY PROFILE

H. B. Fuller Company   Stock Exchange: NASDAQ

2400 Energy Park Drive   Ticker Symbol: FULL

Saint Paul, Minnesota 55108   Telephone 612-645-3401

Company Business

The H. B. Fuller Company operates in the global adhesives, coatings, and sealings market segment, which is expanding at a rate twice as fast as the gross national product. Its products are used in a wide variety of industries, from packaging to furniture and from construction to insulated glass.

Chart 4–3   *Cooper Tire and Rubber Company Stock Chart*

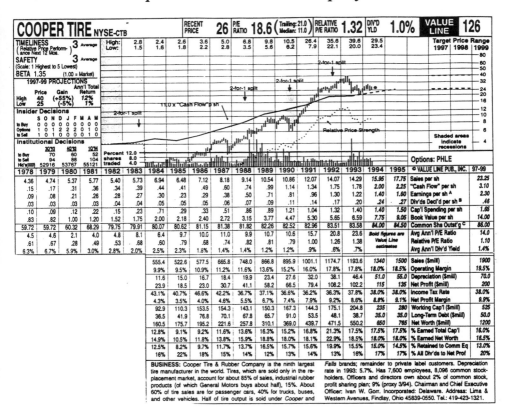

Source: ©1994 by Value Line Publishing, Inc. Reprinted by permission; All Rights Reserved.

Foreign business accounts for 46 percent of annual revenues, and the company operates modern manufacturing, distribution, and sales facilities in Asia, Europe, and Latin America as well as North America.

A progressive management team made H. B. Fuller the first specialty chemical company and only the second Fortune 500 company to affirm the CERES Principles, a 10-point environmental code of conduct authored by the Coalition for Environmentally Responsible Economies.

Shareholder Information

Outstanding shares	14,034,000
Insider ownership	More than 28 percent
DRIP program	Yes

Financial Information (May 1994)

Total assets	$689 million
Cash and temporary investments	$3 million
Working capital	$126 million
Long-term debt	$111 million
Equity ratio	68 percent
Book value	$18.48 per share
Dividend rate	58 cents per share annual basis
Yield	1.8 percent
Price/earnings ratio	20

Stock Price History (through mid-September 1994)

	1992	1993	1994
Low	$34\frac{1}{2}$	$31\frac{1}{4}$	$33\frac{3}{4}$
High	$53\frac{1}{4}$	$42\frac{3}{4}$	$42\frac{1}{4}$

Revenue and Earnings History (through May 31, 1994)

	1992*	1993*	1st Half 1993	1st Half 1994
Revenue	$942	$975	$475	$515
Net income	36	28**	11**	13
Earnings per share	2.55	1.93**	.82**	.95

In millions, except per-share amounts

*Fiscal years ended Nov 30

**Before effects of restucturing charge of $6 million, or 38 cents per share, and effects of accounting changes of $12 million, or 84 cents per share.

Key Growth Rates (past five years)

Revenue	9.5%
Cash flow	10.5%
Earnings	7.0%

DRIP Details

The H. B. Fuller Company dividend reinvestment plan allows for automatic cash dividend reinvestment with no fees or commissions charged to shareholders. Approximately 69 percent of shareholders participate in the plan. Additional cash purchases of company common stock stock can be made in amounts from $10 to $6,000 quarterly. For information, contact H. B. Fuller Company, Administration, 2400 Energy Park Drive, St. Paul, Minnesota 55108-1591, or call 612-647-3401.

Company Prospects

H. B. Fuller Company represents another turnaround company poised to perform well as a result of restructuring efforts. The firm took a $6-million or 38-cents-per-share, charge in 1993 after revamping its North American and international operations. Consolidation of the firm's adhesivies business in Canada, Mexico, and the United States promises synergistic benefits and improved efficiencies. Overseas, the company moved from a geographic structure to one better aligned to serve its industrial customers.

Key acquisitions such as Fana Produkte, AG in Germany and Timminco, Inc. in Canada deliver broader product lines and greater market share. H. B. Fuller has successfully acquired more than 50 companies over the past 15 years.

From 1983 through 1993, the company delivered an annual return to shareholders of 12.4 percent. An investment of $10,000 in Fuller stock when the company went public in 1968 would have been worth a tad over $432,000 in May 1994 (assuming reinvestment of all dividends). The company has paid dividends for 42 consecutive years and raised them every year since going public in 1968.

The stage is set for an earnings rebound. H. B. Fuller's stock price dropped from an all-time high of $53\frac{1}{3}$ per share in 1992 to bottom out at $31\frac{1}{4}$ per share in 1993. The stock continues to languish in the low $30-per-share range (see Chart 4-4). Purchase for the stock price's eventual upside move as earnings surge once again. Investment club interest in H. B. Fuller vaulted the company into the Top 100 listing's 88th spot, with 300 investment clubs owning more than 80,000 shares of company stock.

COMPANY PROFILE

Kellogg Company	Stock Exchange: NYSE
One Kellogg Square	Ticker Symbol: K
Battle Creek, Michigan 49016-3599	Telephone 616-961-2000

Company Business

Kellogg Company leads the ready-to-eat cereal industry with 43 percent of the global market, including a 38 percent share of the domestic market, 47

Chart 4–4   H.B. Fuller Company Stock Chart

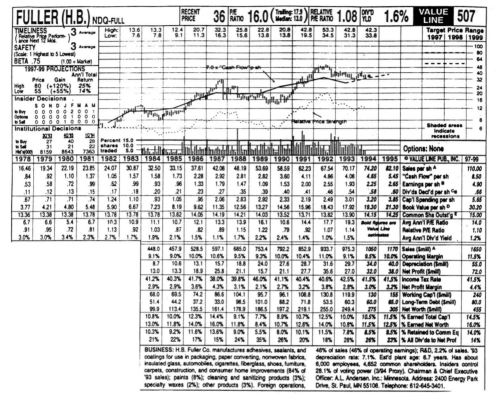

| FULLER (H.B.) NDQ-FULL | | RECENT PRICE 36 | P/E RATIO 16.0 (Trailing: 17.9 / Median: 13.0) | RELATIVE P/E RATIO 1.08 | DIV'D YLD 1.6% | VALUE LINE 507 |

BUSINESS: H.B. Fuller Co. manufactures adhesives, sealants, and coatings for use in packaging, paper converting, nonwoven fabrics, insulated glass, automobiles, cigarettes, fiberglass, shoes, furniture, carpets, construction, and consumer home improvements (84% of '93 sales); paints (8%); cleaning and sanitizing products (3%); specialty waxes (2%); other products (3%). Foreign operations,

46% of sales (46% of operating earnings); R&D, 2.2% of sales. '93 depreciation rate: 7.1%. Est'd plant age: 6.7 years. Has about 6,000 employees, 4,652 common shareholders. Insiders control 28.1% of voting power (3/94 Proxy). Chairman & Chief Executive Officer: A.L. Andersen. Inc.: Minnesota. Address: 2400 Energy Park Drive, St. Paul, MN 55108. Telephone: 612-645-3401.

percent of the Asia/Pacific market, 50 percent of the European market, and a 78 percent market share in Latin America. The company operates manufacturing facilities in North America, Asia/Pacific, Europe, and Latin America.

Major Kellogg brand names include such popular cereals as Corn Flakes, Frosted Flakes, Special K, Rice Krispies, Apple Jacks, and Nutri-Grain. In addition, breakfast food product extensions include Eggo (waffles) and Pop-Tarts (toaster pastries). Kellogg shed its Mrs. Smith's Frozen Foods Company and its Argentine snack foods business in early 1994.

Global ready-to-eat cereal demand is still on an upswing, with overseas growth of 5 percent to 7 percent exceeding domestic demand growth of 2 percent to 3 percent. Kellogg ranks as the industry leader in every major market.

Shareholder Information

Outstanding shares	225,900,000
Insider ownership	*
DRIP program	Yes

*W. K. Foundation controls 34 percent of common shares.

Financial Information (June 1994)

Total assets	$ 4.5 billion
Cash and temporary investments	$232 million
Working capital	$ 4 million
Long-term debt	$520 million
Equity ratio	77 percent
Book value	$7.63 per share
Dividend rate	$1.44 per share annual basis
Yield	2.7 percent
Price/earnings ratio	18

Stock Price History (through mid-September 1994)

	1992	1993	1994
Low	54⅜	47¼	47⅜
High	75⅜	67⅞	58

Revenue and Earnings History (through June 30, 1994)

	1992	1993	1st Half 1993	1st Half 1994
Revenue	$6,191	$6,295	$3,060	$3,228
Net income	683*	681	322	335
Earnings per share	2.86*	2.94	1.38	1.49

In millions, except per-share amounts

*Before effects of accounting change in amount of $252 million, or $1.05 per share

Key Growth Rates (past five years)

Revenue	11.0%
Cash flow	12.5%
Earnings	11.0%

DRIP Details

The Kellogg Company dividend reinvestment plan allows for automatic reinvestment of cash dividends at no administration or commission cost to the company shareholder. In addition, cash investments in amounts between $25 and $25,000 per year may be made in company common stock. For information on the Kellogg DRIP, contact Harris Trust and Savings Bank,

Dividend Reinvestment Service, P.O. Box A3309, Chicago, Illinois 60690 or call 800-323-6138.

Company Prospects

Kellogg Company has embarked on cost cutting programs to become more efficient. That, coupled with strong overseas demand and its commanding market share, will keep earnings on the rise at a double digit pace. A share repurchase program will also enhance future per-share comparisons.

New plants in China and India will expand the company's network for tapping global demand for ready-to-eat cereals. New product introductions promise to keep the competition at bay and Kellogg's market share intact.

Kellogg advanced nine places to the 18th spot on the Top 100 ranking. Some 1,243 investment clubs own more than 210,000 shares of its common stock.

With the stock trading around the midpoint of the company's 52-week trading range of $61\frac{7}{8}$ to $47\frac{3}{8}$ per share and well below its all-time high of $75\frac{3}{8}$ per share achieved in 1992, there's plenty of upside potential for the patient long-term investor; see Chart 4–5.

COMPANY PROFILE

Newell Company
29 East Stephenson Street
Freeport, Illinois 61032

Stock Exchange: NYSE
Ticker Symbol: NWL
Telephone 815-235-4171

Company Business

Newell Company manufacturers do-it-yourself hardware, housewares, and office products. It sells to high-volume customers such as The Home Depot, K-Mart, Office Depot, and Wal-Mart Stores. The firm's extensive product line includes such popular brand names as Anchor Hocking (glassware and plastic storageware), BernzOmatic (hand torches), Goody (hair accessories), Mirro (cookware), Newell (window furnishings), and Stuart Hall (school supplies and stationery).

The company accelerates its growth rate with a bevy of acquisitions. In the past decade, Newell acquired seven major businesses representing an additional $1 billion in annual revenues. Management is adept at seeking out companies with yet-unrealized profit potential and improving the acquired companies' operations to tap those resources.

Shareholder Information

Outstanding shares
Insider ownership
DRIP program

78,900,000
Approximately 7 percent
Yes

Chart 4–5   Kellogg Company Stock Chart

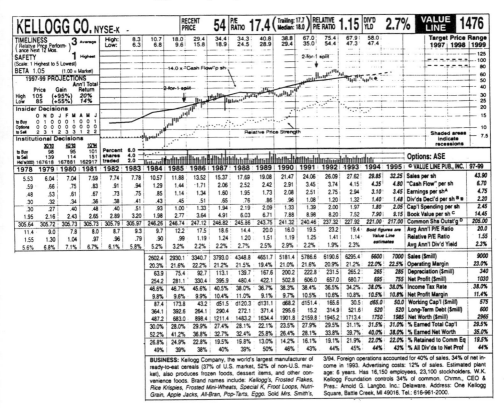

KELLOGG CO. NYSE-K	RECENT PRICE **54**	P/E RATIO **17.4** (Trailing: 17.7 / Median: 18.0)	RELATIVE P/E RATIO **1.15**	DIV'D YLD **2.7%**	VALUE LINE **1476**

| TIMELINESS **3** Average | High: | 8.3 | 10.7 | 18.0 | 29.4 | 34.4 | 34.3 | 40.8 | 38.8 | 67.0 | 75.4 | 67.9 | 58.0 | | Target Price Range 1997 1998 1999 |
| (Relative Price Perform-ance Next 12 Mos.) | Low: | 6.3 | 6.8 | 9.6 | 15.8 | 18.9 | 24.5 | 28.9 | 29.4 | 35.0 | 54.4 | 47.3 | 47.4 | | |

SAFETY **1** Highest (Scale: 1 Highest to 5 Lowest)
BETA 1.05 (1.00 = Market)

1997-99 PROJECTIONS
	Price	Gain	Ann'l Total Return
High	105	(+95%)	20%
Low	85	(+55%)	14%

Insider Decisions
	O	N	D	J	F	M	A	M	J
to Buy	0	1	0	0	1	0	0	0	1
Options	0	0	0	0	0	0	0	0	0
to Sell	2	3	1	2	3	3	1	2	2

Institutional Decisions
	1Q'93	4Q'93	1Q'94
to Buy	98	95	101
to Sell	139	114	151
Hld's(000)	167618	167881	162917

Percent shares traded 6.0 4.0 2.0

1978	1979	1980	1981	1982	1983	1984	1985	1986	1987	1988	1989	1990	1991	1992	1993	1994	1995	© VALUE LINE PUB., INC.	97-99
5.53	6.04	7.04	7.59	7.74	7.78	10.57	11.88	13.52	15.37	17.69	19.08	21.47	24.06	26.09	27.62	29.85	32.25	Sales per sh	43.90
.59	.66	.75	.83	.91	.94	1.29	1.44	1.71	2.06	2.52	2.42	2.91	3.45	3.74	4.15	4.35	4.80	"Cash Flow" per sh	6.70
.48	.53	.61	.67	.73	.75	.85	1.14	1.34	1.60	1.95	1.73	2.08	2.51	2.75	2.94	3.10	3.45	Earnings per sh^A	4.75
.30	.32	.34	.36	.38	.41	.43	.45	.51	.65	.76	.86	.96	1.08	1.20	1.32	1.40	1.48	Div'ds Decl'd per sh ^B■	2.20
.30	.27	.40	.48	.40	.51	.93	1.00	1.33	1.94	2.19	2.09	1.33	1.39	2.00	1.97	1.80	2.05	Cap'l Spending per sh	2.45
1.95	2.16	2.43	2.65	2.89	3.20	1.98	2.77	3.64	4.91	6.03	6.71	7.88	8.96	8.20	7.52	7.90	9.15	Book Value per sh ^C	14.45
305.64	305.72	305.73	305.73	305.79	305.97	248.26	246.74	247.12	246.82	245.86	243.75	241.32	240.46	237.32	227.92	221.00	217.00	Common Shs Outst'g ^D	205.00
11.4	9.0	7.8	8.0	8.7	9.3	9.7	12.2	17.5	18.6	14.4	20.0	16.0	19.5	23.2	19.4	Bold figures are		Avg Ann'l P/E Ratio	20.0
1.55	1.30	1.04	.97	.96	.79	.90	.99	1.19	1.24	1.20	1.51	1.19	1.25	1.41	1.14	Value Line estimates		Relative P/E Ratio	1.55
5.6%	6.8%	7.1%	6.7%	6.1%	5.8%	5.2%	3.2%	2.2%	2.2%	2.7%	2.5%	2.9%	2.2%	1.9%	2.3%			Avg Ann'l Div'd Yield	2.3%
						2602.4	2930.1	3340.7	3793.0	4348.8	4651.7	5181.4	5786.6	6190.6	6295.4	6600	7000	Sales ($Mill)	9000
						20.3%	21.6%	22.2%	21.2%	21.5%	19.4%	21.0%	21.6%	20.9%	21.2%	22.0%	22.5%	Operating Margin	23.0%
						63.9	75.4	92.7	113.1	139.7	167.6	200.2	222.8	231.5	265.2	265	285	Depreciation ($Mill)	340
						254.2	281.1	330.4	395.9	480.4	422.1	502.8	606.0	657.0	680.7	695	755	Net Profit ($Mill)	1030
						46.6%	46.7%	45.6%	40.5%	38.0%	36.7%	38.3%	38.4%	36.5%	34.2%	38.0%	38.0%	Income Tax Rate	38.0%
						9.8%	9.6%	9.9%	10.4%	11.0%	9.1%	9.7%	10.5%	10.6%	10.8%	10.5%	10.8%	Net Profit Margin	11.4%
						87.4	173.8	43.2	d51.5	d120.3	d131.1	d68.2	d151.4	165.6	30.5	d65.0	50.0	Working Cap'l ($Mill)	575
						364.1	392.6	264.1	290.4	272.1	371.4	295.6	15.2	314.9	521.6	520	520	Long-Term Debt ($Mill)	600
						487.2	683.0	898.4	1211.4	1483.2	1634.4	1901.8	2159.8	1945.2	1713.4	1750	1985	Net Worth ($Mill)	2965
						30.0%	28.0%	29.9%	27.4%	28.1%	22.1%	23.5%	27.9%	29.5%	31.1%	31.5%	31.0%	% Earned Total Cap'l	29.5%
						52.2%	41.2%	36.8%	32.7%	32.4%	25.8%	26.4%	28.1%	33.8%	39.7%	40.0%	38.0%	% Earned Net Worth	35.0%
						26.8%	24.9%	22.8%	19.5%	19.8%	13.0%	14.2%	16.1%	19.1%	21.9%	22.0%	22.0%	% Retained to Comm Eq	19.5%
						49%	39%	38%	40%	39%	50%	46%	43%	44%	45%	44%	43%	% All Div'ds to Net Prof	44%

BUSINESS: Kellogg Company, the world's largest manufacturer of ready-to-eat cereals (37% of U.S. market, 52% of non-U.S. market), also produces frozen foods, dessert items, and other convenience foods. Brand names include: Kellogg's, Frosted Flakes, Rice Krispies, Frosted Mini-Wheats, Special K, Froot Loops, Nutri-Grain, Apple Jacks, All-Bran, Pop-Tarts, Eggo. Sold Mrs. Smith's, 3/94. Foreign operations accounted for 40% of sales, 34% of net income in 1993. Advertising costs: 12% of sales. Estimated plant age: 6 years. Has 16,150 employees, 23,100 stockholders. W.K. Kellogg Foundation controls 34% of common. Chrmn., CEO & Pres.: Arnold G. Langbo. Inc.: Delaware. Address: One Kellogg Square, Battle Creek, MI 49016. Tel.: 616-961-2000.

Options: ASE

Shaded areas indicate recessions

Financial Information (June 1994)

Total assets	$ 2.0 billion
Cash and temporary investments	$ 1.2 million
Working capital	$149 million
Long-term debt	$240 million
Equity ratio	80 percent
Book value	$13.00 per share
Dividend rate	80 cents per share annual basis
Yield	1.8 percent
Price/earnings ratio	20

Stock Price History (through mid-September 1994)

	1992	1993	1994
Low	16½	15⅜	18⅞
High	26½	21½	23⅞

Revenue and Earnings History (through June 30, 1994)

	1992	1993	1st Half 1993	1st Half 1944
Revenue	$1,452	$1,645	$707	$937
Net income	119*	165	62	76
Earnings per share	.77*	1.05	.40	.48

In millions, except per-share amounts

*Before effect of accounting change in amount of $44 million, or 57 cents per share

Key Growth Rates (past five years)

Revenue	5.0%
Cash flow	16.0%
Earnings	22.0%

DRIP Details

Newell Company's dividend reinvestment plan allows for automatic reinvestment of cash dividends in the company's common stock plus additional cash investments by shareholders in amounts between $10 and $30,000 annually. For information on the Newell Company DRIP, contact Newell Company, Investor Relations, 4000 Auburn Street, Rockford, Illinois 61101, or call 815-235-4171.

Company Prospects

Newell Company specializes in purchasing companies with good product lines and market potential and turning them around to perform better under the Newell umbrella of companies. Combined with internal growth, acquisitions help Newell more than achieve its targeted earnings growth of 15 percent.

By streamlining the operations of 1993 acquisitions Goody, Levolor, and Lee/Rowan and increasing the marketing of their product lines, Newell's gross margin and bottom lines should improve beginning in 1994.

A surge of interest in Newell during 1993 pushed the company into the Top 100 list with a ranking of 41. At the end of 1993, 677 investment clubs owned nearly 102,000 shares of its common stock.

The stock has rebounded from a low of $15⅜ per share (adjusted for a 2-for-1 stock split in September 1994) in mid-1993 and has been testing its 52-week high of $23⅞ per share (see Chart 4-6). Look for Newell's internal growth and key acquisitions to boost earnings and the firm's stock price.

Chart 4–6 Newell Company Stock Chart

NEWELL CO. NYSE-NWL	RECENT PRICE **45**	P/E RATIO **18.4** (Trailing: 20.9 Median: 14.0)	RELATIVE P/E RATIO **1.24**	DIV'D YLD **1.8%**	VALUE LINE **966**

TIMELINESS	2	Above Average	High:	5.8	4.4	5.7	9.2	10.8	14.8	25.3	35.5	45.8	53.0	43.0	46.6	Target Price Range 1997 1998 1999
(Relative Price Perform- ance Next 12 Mos.)			Low:	3.3	3.3	3.8	5.3	5.3	6.9	12.8	17.8	23.0	33.0	30.8	37.6	
SAFETY	3	Average														

2-for-1 split

14.0 x "Cash Flow" p sh — 2-for-1 split

BETA 1.40 (1.00 = Market)

1997-99 PROJECTIONS

	Price	Gain	Ann'l Total Return
High	100	(+120%)	23%
Low	65	(+45%)	11%

Insider Decisions

	O	N	D	J	F	M	A	M	J
to Buy	0	0	0	0	0	0	0	0	0
Options	0	0	0	0	0	0	0	0	0
to Sell	0	0	1	0	0	0	0	0	0

2-for-1 split

Institutional Decisions

	3Q'93	4Q'93	1Q'94	Percent	7.5	
to Buy	107	84	89	shares	5.0	
to Sell	90	103	102	traded	2.5	
Hld's(000)	44517	46837	49444			

Relative Price Strength

Shaded areas indicate recessions

Options: NYSE

1978	1979	1980	1981	1982	1983	1984	1985	1986	1987	1988	1989	1990	1991	1992	1993	1994	1995	©VALUE LINE PUB., INC.	97-99
4.32	4.95	5.58	6.73	5.39	6.93	8.97	10.12	8.76	15.56	21.09	19.01	18.00	18.01	18.53	20.92	24.70	28.05	Sales per sh	41.45
.28	.38	.43	.52	.37	.53	.63	.79	.75	1.20	1.95	2.12	2.24	2.44	2.77	2.92	3.30	3.70	"Cash Flow" per sh E	5.55
.20	.29	.32	.38	.34	.38	.41	.52	.54	.69	1.01	1.41	1.58	1.81	2.10	2.10	2.45	2.75	Earnings per sh A	4.40
.08	.08	.10	.11	.13	.13	.13	.13	.19	.21	.28	.43	.50	.60	.60	.69	.78	.89	Div'ds Decl'd per sh B	1.40
.13	.11	.13	.14	.07	.23	.16	.28	.15	.24	.59	.43	.61	.92	.99	.75	.65	.65	Cap'l Spending per sh	.85
1.38	1.58	1.79	2.02	2.32	2.56	2.67	3.04	3.99	4.39	5.32	7.51	8.39	9.76	10.97	12.45	14.10	16.00	Book Value per sh C	23.85
24.56	24.60	24.84	25.33	33.14	34.18	34.38	34.60	45.82	46.24	46.85	59.06	59.57	62.13	78.34	78.63	79.00	79.00	Common Shs Outst'g D	79.00
8.3	3.9	4.1	5.2	6.4	11.7	9.3	8.5	13.1	12.3	10.7	13.7	16.1	19.7	19.8	17.8	Bold figures are Value Line estimates		Avg Ann'l P/E Ratio	18.5
1.13	.56	.54	.63	.71	.99	.87	.69	.89	.82	.89	1.04	1.20	1.26	1.20	1.05			Relative P/E Ratio	1.40
4.6%	7.5%	7.7%	5.6%	5.7%	2.8%	3.3%	3.0%	2.6%	2.5%	2.5%	2.2%	2.0%	1.7%	1.4%	1.8%			Avg Ann'l Div'd Yield	1.7%

						308.4	350.0	401.4	719.7	988.2	1122.9	1072.6	1118.9	1451.7	1645.0	1950	2215	Sales ($mill)	3275
						12.7%	12.6%	14.5%	14.7%	16.2%	18.3%	19.8%	21.2%	21.2%	21.3%	21.5%	21.5%	Operating Margin	21.5%
						7.6	8.5	11.2	23.5	39.7	40.7	38.4	39.5	53.9	64.3	70.0	75.0	Depreciation ($mill)	95.0
						14.2	18.9	24.0	37.2	61.4	85.4	95.9	112.2	163.3	165.3	190	220	Net Profit ($mill)	350
						44.8%	42.6%	46.5%	44.6%	41.2%	41.4%	40.1%	39.9%	41.2%	40.0%	41.0%	41.0%	Income Tax Rate	41.0%
						4.6%	5.4%	6.0%	5.2%	6.2%	7.6%	8.9%	10.0%	11.2%	10.1%	9.7%	8.9%	Net Profit Margin	10.7%
						75.3	82.9	88.3	185.7	142.1	149.3	194.1	122.4	219.5	76.7	210	330	Working Cap'l ($mill)	250
						51.5	58.3	38.2	239.2	153.6	100.2	89.3	176.6	176.8	218.1	250	250	Long-Term Debt ($mill)	250
						106.9	120.1	198.0	354.6	400.3	455.8	508.7	606.4	859.4	979.1	1110	1260	Net Worth ($mill)	1885
						10.7%	12.4%	11.3%	7.5%	13.0%	16.6%	17.2%	15.4%	16.7%	14.3%	14.5%	15.0%	% Earned Total Cap'l	16.5%
						13.3%	15.7%	12.1%	10.5%	15.3%	18.7%	18.9%	18.5%	19.0%	16.9%	17.0%	17.5%	% Earned Net Worth	18.5%
						10.5%	12.7%	8.5%	11.0%	15.7%	13.4%	13.1%	12.4%	13.6%	11.3%	11.5%	11.5%	% Retained to Comm Eq	12.5%
						32%	29%	35%	40%	37%	30%	32%	33%	28%	33%	32%	32%	% All Div'ds to Net Prof	32%

BUSINESS: Newell Co. makes and markets do-it-yourself hardware, housewares & off. prods. Acu'd. Anchor Hocking, 7/87; Sanford, 2/92; Stuart Hall, 7/92; Intercraft, 10/92; Levelor, 4/93; Lee/Rowan, 9/93; Goody, 11/93. Prods. incl. alum. cookware & bakeware, cabinet & window hardware, window furnishings, jar caps & closures, glassware, paint sundries, & other cons. goods, in-dustrial lighting components and toiletry bottles, and plastic indl. goods. Divested W.E. Wright & Carr-Lowrey, '89; closures unit, 10/92. Has about 3,500 stockholders. '93 depr. rate: 11.4%. Top managers control about 7% of shares (3/94 proxy). Chrmn., Pres. & C.E.O.: D.C. Ferguson. Inc.: DE. Add.: Newell Center, 29 E. Stephenson St., Freeport, IL 61032. Tel.: 815-235-4171.

COMPANY PROFILE

Novell, Inc.
122 East 1700 South
Provo, Utah 84606

Stock Exchange: NASDAQ
Ticker Symbol: NOVL
Telephone 801-429-7000

Company Business

Novell, Inc. is the leading computer networking company worldwide. It designs, manufactures, and markets high-performance LANs (local area networks). It is also the fourth-largest software company in the world. Foreign business accounts for 48 percent of annual revenues.

Novell's products serve a wide variety of needs from integrating small workgroups of desktop computers to linking departmental systems to interconnecting enterprisewide information environments.

Shareholder Information

Outstanding shares	368,313,000
Insider ownership	Approximately 11 percent
DRIP Program	No

Financial Information (July 1994)

Total assets	$ 1.86 billion
Cash and temporary investments	$758 million
Working capital	$936 million
Long-term debt	-0-
Equity ratio	100 percent
Book value	$3.92 per share
Dividend rate	–
Yield	–
Price/earnings ratio	21

Stock Price History (through mid-September 1994)

	1992	*1993*	*1994*
Low	$22\frac{1}{2}$	17	$13\frac{3}{4}$
High	$33\frac{1}{2}$	$35\frac{1}{4}$	$26\frac{1}{4}$

Revenue and Earnings History (through July 30, 1994)

	1992	*1993*	*9 Months 1993*	*9 Months 1994*
Revenue	$933	$1,123	$1,321	$1,512
Net income	249	(35)*	(62)*	186**
Earnings per share	.81	(.11)*	(.17)*	.51**

In millions, except per-share amounts

*Includes charges of $320 million, or $1.01 per share, due to acquisitions

**Includes charges of $129 million, or 35 cents per share, due to acquisitions

Key Growth Rates (past five years)

Revenue	28.0%
Cash flow	49.0%
Earnings	50.5%

Company Prospects

Novell, Inc. is hot on the acquisition trail. In fiscal 1993, the company acquired UNIX System Laboratories, a move which resulted in charges of $320 million, or $1.01 per share, and masked a 13 percent gain in net income. This year, Novell acquired WordPerfect and Quattro Pro and incurred a charge of $129 million, or 35 cents per share.

The company will also take further charges in the fourth quarter of fiscal 1994 and later for restructuring and employee separations related to the acquisitions as management attempts to mold the companies into one smoothly functioning unit.

The acquisition strategy is geared toward making Novell the predominant force in the industry for decades to come. However, this involves not a small degree of risk. Many things can go wrong in mergers and product introductions (as evidenced by Storage Technology's long-delayed Iceburg product).

Novell jumped 19 places to secure the 45th spot on the Top 100 list. At the end of 1993, 670 investment clubs owned more than 213,000 Novell shares. For my money, the profit opportunities are not sufficient to offset the risks (see Chart 4-7). Don't jeopardize your hard-won investment earnings with excess risk. Look elsewhere for equal or better potential returns with substantially less risk.

Chart 4–7   Novell, Inc. Stock Chart

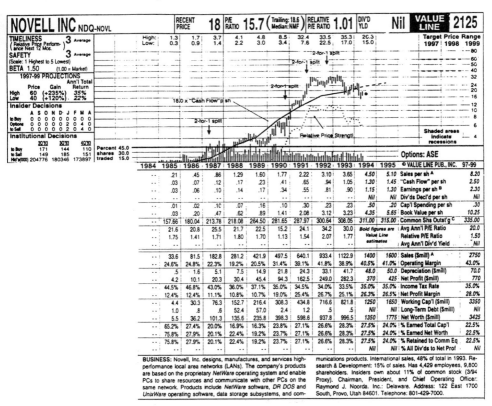

Source: ©1994 by Value Line Publishing, Inc. Reprinted by permission; All Rights Reserved.

COMPANY PROFILE

RPM, Inc.   Stock Exchange: NASDAQ
2628 Pearl Road   Ticker Symbol: RPOW
P.O. Box 777   Telephone 216-273-5090
Medina, Ohio 44258

Company Business

RPM, Inc. manufactures coatings, sealants, and specialty chemicals for industrial and consumer markets worldwide. Its industrial products are used in general maintenance, corrosion control, waterproofing, and other applications. RPM's do-it-yourself consumer products serve the automotive repair, hobby, home maintenance, leisure, and marine market segments. The firm's products are sold in more than 100 countries and manufactured at 45 facilities in the United States, Belgium, Canada, Luxembourg, and the Netherlands. Foreign business generates approximately 12 percent of annual revenues.

Like Newell Company, RPM specializes in purchasing companies with specialized products and unique market niches and works hard to improve their operating efficiencies and marketing thrust.

Shareholder Information

Outstanding shares	56,717,000
Insider ownership	5 percent
DRIP program	Yes

Financial Information (May 1994)

Total assets	$661 million
Cash and temporary investments	$ 25 million
Working capital	$227 million
Long-term debt	$233 million
Equity ratio	57 percent
Book value	$5.54 per share
Dividend rate	52 cents per share annual basis
Yield	2.9 percent
Price/earnings ratio	19

Stock Price History (through mid-September 1994)

	1992	*1993*	*1994*
Low	$12\frac{5}{8}$	$16\frac{1}{4}$	$16\frac{1}{4}$
High	$18\frac{1}{2}$	$19\frac{3}{8}$	$19\frac{3}{8}$

Revenue and Earnings History (through fiscal year ended May 31,1994)

	1992	*1993*	*1994*
Revenue	$680	$768	$816
Net income	38	40	53
Earnings per share	.73	.74	.93

In millions, except per-share amounts

Key Growth Rates (past 5 years)

Revenue	10.0%
Cash flow	13.0%
Earnings	11.0%

DRIP Details
The RPM, Inc. dividend reinvestment plan permits automatic reinvestment of cash dividends in company shares of common stock plus additional cash investments between $25 to $5,000 per month. There are no administration or commission charges to shareholders for stock purchases through the plan. For information on the RPM DRIP, contact RPM, Inc., RPM Dividend Reinvestment Plan, P.O. Box 777, Medina, Ohio 44258, or call 216-273-5090.

Company Prospects
A longtime favorite of investment clubs, RPM captured the number 10 slot based on the number of clubs owning the stock (1,891) and eighth in the number of shares held by investment clubs (1,147,491). There's good reason investment clubs love RPM. For starters, the company delivers consistent performance,with 47 consecutive years of record revenues and earnings. In addition, RPM has boosted its cash dividend for 20 straight years.

RPM broke the ranks of the Fortune 500 based on results through fiscal year ended May 31, 1993. It ranked 491st based on sales but 104th in return on sales, 111th in return on shareholder's equity, and 87th in return to shareholders over a 10-year period.

A 1,000-share purchase of RPM stock back in 1974 at $10 per share would have been worth more than $700,000 by the end of fiscal 1994 and paid out $21,000 in annual cash dividends. A 1,000 share investment in 1984 at $16 per share would be worth approximately $90,000 today, with a cash dividend payout of $2,600 annually., Looking ahead, the fiscal 1994 acquisitions of Stonehard, Inc. and Dynatron/Bondo plus the fiscal 1995 acquisition of Rust-Oleum Corporation add nearly $250 million in annual revenues. Rust-Oleum complements RPM's already strong presence in the do-it-yourself market as well as in its industrial segment.

Stonehard, the worldwide leader in industrial and commercial polymer flooring, gives RPM an entree into this new market. Dynatron/Bondo, a manufacturer of automotive repair coatings, provides synergistic benefits with RPM's consumer automotive product lines.

RPM takes a unique approach to acquisitions. Instead of replacing management of the acquired company, RPM prefers to keep them running the company under RPM guidelines, with salaries tied to incentive performance benchmarks. RPM is poised to deliver the revenue, dividend, and earnings growth that has already made it a solid favorite of investment clubs across the nation. Recently, the stock price has languished between its 52-week trading range of $19⅜ to $16¼ per share (see Chart 4-8). Patient investors should purchase for superior long-term total return.

Chart 4–8 RPM, Inc. Stock Chart

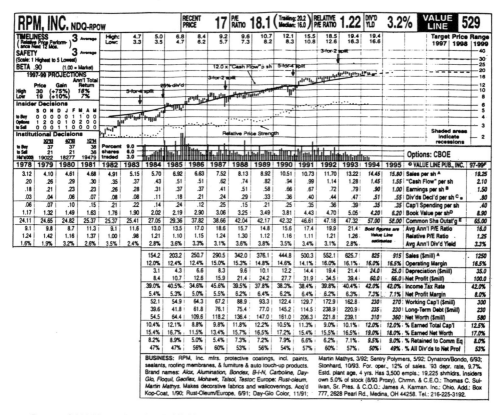

Source: ©1994 by Value Line Publishing, Inc. Reprinted by permission; All Rights Reserved.

COMPANY PROFILE

Stryker Corporation
2725 Fairfield Road
P.O. Box 4085
Kalamazoo, Michigan 49003-4085

Stock Exchange: NASDAQ
Ticker Symbol: STRY
Telephone 616-385-2600

Company Business

Stryker Corporation develops, manufactures, and markets specialty surgical and medical products including endoscopic systems, orthopedic implants, powered surgical instruments, and patient handling equipment for the global market. The company generated approximately 34 percent of annual revenues from overseas business in 1993. Surgical products account for around 80 percent of revenues and medical devices another 20 percent.

Shareholder Information

Outstanding shares	48,358,000
Insider ownership	More than 33 percent
DRIP program	No

Financial Information (June 1994)

Total assets	$490 million
Cash and temporary investments	$145 million
Working capital	$233 million
Long-term debt	$ 35 million
Equity ratio	90 percent
Book value	$6.69 per share
Dividend rate	7 cents per share annual basis
Yield	.2 percent
Price/earnings ratio	26

Stock Price History (through mid-September 1994)

	1992	*1993*	*1994*
Low	26¼	21	23¾
High	52¼	39¾	7½

Revenue and Earnings History (through June 30, 1994)

	1992	*1993*	*1st Half 1993*	*1st Half 1994*
Revenue	$474	$557	$275	$303
Net income	48	60	28	34
Earnings per share	1.00	1.25	.59	.71

In millions, except per-share amounts

Key Growth Rates (past 5 years)

Revenue	24.5%
Cash flow	27.0%
Earnings	28.5%

Company Prospects

Concern over healthcare reform and growth prospects for healthcare companies has put Stryker Corporation's stock price under considerable pressure. From an all-time high of $52¼ per share in late 1991, Stryker's market price tumbled to a low of $21 per share in 1993 before rebounding. The price trendline is once again on the upswing, with a $15-per-share rise from its 1993 low (see Chart 4–9).

Chart 4–9   Stryker Corporation Stock Chart

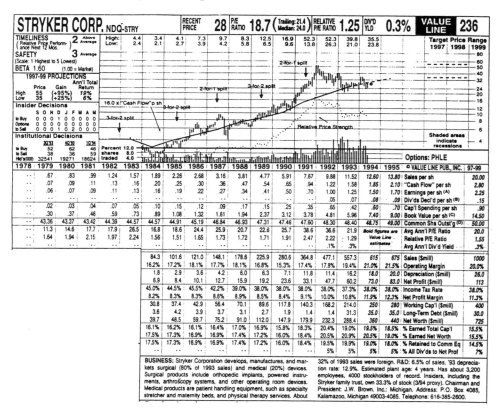

Source: ©1994 by Value Line Publishing, Inc. Reprinted by permission; All Rights Reserved.

Stryker is proving the naysayers wrong. For the first half of 1994, the company posted revenue growth of 10 percent and an earnings-per-share rise of 20 percent.

The company takes steps to continue that pace. In June 1994, Stryker entered into an agreement to purchase 31 percent of the outstanding shares of Matsumoto Medical Instruments, Inc., one of Japan's largest distributors of medical devices. That move boosts Stryker's stake in Matsumoto Medical to 51 percent. Another plus on the horizon: FDA approval of the company's spinal implant products in 1995 could add a nice boost to earnings in 1995 and beyond.

During 1993, Stryker moved up 32 positions on the Top 100 listing, taking over the 54th-place spot in terms of the number of investment clubs owing its stock. Even more impressive, Stryker captured 34th place based on the number of shares held by investment clubs. Some 656 investment clubs own 280,885 shares of Stryker common stock. Purchase on pullbacks from the $36-per-share level for long-term capital appreciation.

COMPANY PROFILE

Shaw Communications, Inc.	Stock Exchange: TORONTO
7605-50 Street	Ticker Symbol: SCLB
Edmonton, Alberta, Canada T6B 2W9	Telephone 403-468-1230

Shaw Communications Inc., although not on the NAIC's Top 100 list, is the stock the Canadian Shareowners Association uses throughout its *Stock Selection Manual* to illustrate proper completion of the Stock Selection Guide. While this distinction alone does not merit it as an attractive stock to consider purchasing for superior returns, the company's performance and future prospects do make a convincing case in that regard.

Company Business

Shaw Communications, Inc. operates in the cable television market and ranks among the largest Canadian cable television system operators. Shaw derives 92 percent of annual revenues from cable operations and the balance from the company's radio division, which operates eight radio stations.

The company benefits from the ongoing consolidation of the cable industry. Recent acquisitions have boosted Shaw's subscription base in excess of 55 percent to more than 1.6 million and propelled the company into becoming Canada's second-largest Canadian cable television operator.

Shareholder Information

Outstanding shares	63,396,000 Cl A & B
Insider ownership	Majority of Cl A & 15 percent of Cl B shares
DRIP program	No

Financial Information (Cdn$) (May 1994)

Total assets	$800 million
Cash and temporary investments	$ 43 million
Working capital	-0-
Long-term debt	$266 million
Equity ratio	35 percent
Book value	$6.69 per share
Dividend rate	7 cents per share annual basis
Price/earnings ratio	20

Stock Price History (through mid-September)

	1992	1993	1994
Low	$7\frac{1}{2}$	$8\frac{1}{2}$	$11\frac{1}{4}$
High	$9\frac{1}{2}$	$12\frac{5}{8}$	$14\frac{7}{8}$

Revenue and Earnings History (through May 31, 1994)

	1992	1993	9 Months 1993	9 Months 1994
Revenue	$166	$234	$165	$215
Net income	19	25	17	24
Earnings per share	.39	.47	.165	.22

In millions Cdn$, except per-share amounts

Key Growth Rates (past five years)

Revenue	24.5%
Cash flow	20.5%
Earnings	17.0%

Company Prospects

In August 1994, Shaw Communications Inc. signed an agreement to purchase Classic Communications Ltd. of Ontario, Canada, for C$240 million, adding another 102,000 subscribers to its cable television network and narrowing the distance Shaw trails behind Canadian industry leader Rogers Communications with 1.9 million subscribers.

The move should bolster annual revenues by at least C$50 to C$75 million and raise fiscal 1995 earnings to the $1.00 to $1.25 per share range.

Shaw represents an interesting play in the North American cable television industry. More acquisitions will help the company pick up market share. Even more interesting is the scenario of Shaw itself becoming a takeover target, substantially raising its stock market price. For most of 1994, the stock has traded in relatively narrow range (see Chart 4–10). Purchase for strong long-term growth or possible takeover activity.

Chart 4–10 Shaw Communications, Inc. Stock Chart

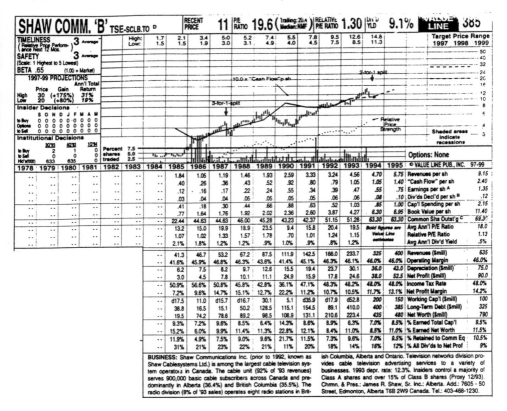

| SHAW COMM. 'B' TSE-SCLB.TO ᴰ | RECENT PRICE 11 | P/E RATIO 19.6 (Trailing: 20.4 Median: NMF) | RELATIVE P/E RATIO 1.30 | DIV'D YLD 9.1% | VALUE LINE 385 |

	High:	1.7	2.1	3.4	5.0	5.2	7.4	7.8	9.5	12.6	14.8		Target Price Range 1997 1998 1999
TIMELINESS 3 Average (Relative Price Performance Next 12 Mos.)	Low:	1.5	1.5	1.9	3.0	3.1	4.9	4.0	4.5	7.5	11.3		

TIMELINESS 3 Average
SAFETY 3 Average (Scale: 1 Highest to 5 Lowest)
BETA .65 (1.00 = Market)

1997-99 PROJECTIONS
	Price	Gain	Ann'l Total Return
High	30	(+175%)	31%
Low	20	(+80%)	19%

Insider Decisions
	S	O	N	D	J	F	M	A	M
to Buy	0	0	0	0	0	0	0	0	0
Options	0	0	0	0	0	0	0	0	0
to Sell	0	0	0	0	0	0	0	0	0

Institutional Decisions
	2Q'93	4Q'93	1Q'94
to Buy	2	1	0
to Sell	0	0	0
Hld'n(000)	633	635	0

Percent shares traded 7.5 5.0 2.5

1978	1979	1980	1981	1982	1983	1984	1985	1986	1987	1988	1989	1990	1991	1992	1993	1994	1995	© VALUE LINE PUB., INC.	97-99
							1.84	1.05	1.19	1.46	1.93	2.59	3.33	3.24	4.56	4.70	5.75	Revenues per sh	9.15
							.40	.26	.36	.43	.52	.92	.80	.79	1.05	1.05	1.40	"Cash Flow" per sh	2.40
							.12	.16	.17	.22	.24	.55	.34	.39	.47	.55	.75	Earnings per sh ᴬ	1.35
							.03	.04	.04	.05	.05	.05	.05	.06	.06	.08	.10	Div'ds Decl'd per sh ᴮ	.12
							.41	.18	.30	.44	.66	.88	.63	.52	1.03	.85	1.00	Cap'l Spending per sh	2.15
							.77	1.64	1.76	1.92	2.02	2.36	2.60	3.87	4.27	6.30	6.95	Book Value per sh	11.40
							22.44	44.63	44.63	46.00	45.28	43.23	42.37	51.15	51.28	63.30	63.30	Common Shs Outst'g ᶜ	69.30
							13.2	15.0	19.9	18.9	23.5	9.4	15.8	20.4	19.5	*Bold figures are*		Avg Ann'l P/E Ratio	18.0
							1.07	1.02	1.33	1.57	1.78	.70	1.01	1.24	1.15	*Value Line estimates*		Relative P/E Ratio	1.13
							2.1%	1.8%	1.2%	1.2%	.9%	1.0%	.9%	.8%	1.2%			Avg Ann'l Div'd Yield	.5%
							41.3	46.7	53.2	67.2	87.5	111.9	142.5	166.0	233.7	325	400	Revenues ($mill)	635
							41.6%	45.9%	46.8%	46.3%	43.6%	41.4%	45.1%	46.3%	46.1%	46.0%	46.0%	Operating Margin	46.0%
							6.2	7.5	8.2	9.7	12.6	15.5	19.4	23.7	30.1	36.0	43.0	Depreciation ($mill)	75.0
							3.0	4.5	7.8	10.1	11.1	24.9	15.9	17.8	24.6	38.0	52.5	Net Profit ($mill)	90.0
							50.9%	56.6%	50.8%	45.8%	42.8%	36.1%	47.1%	48.3%	48.2%	48.0%	48.0%	Income Tax Rate	48.0%
							7.2%	9.6%	14.7%	15.1%	12.7%	22.2%	11.2%	10.7%	10.5%	11.7%	13.1%	Net Profit Margin	14.2%
							d17.5	11.0	d15.7	d16.7	30.1	5.1	d35.9	d17.9	d52.8	200	150	Working Cap'l ($mill)	100
							38.8	16.5	15.1	50.2	128.5	115.1	154.5	89.1	410.0	400	325	Long-Term Debt ($mill)	325
							19.5	74.2	78.6	89.2	98.5	108.9	131.1	210.6	223.4	435	480	Net Worth ($mill)	790
							9.3%	7.2%	9.6%	8.5%	6.4%	14.3%	8.6%	8.9%	6.3%	7.0%	8.5%	% Earned Total Cap'l	9.5%
							15.2%	6.0%	9.9%	11.4%	11.3%	22.8%	12.1%	8.4%	11.0%	8.5%	11.0%	% Earned Net Worth	11.5%
							11.9%	4.9%	7.5%	9.0%	9.6%	21.7%	11.5%	7.3%	9.6%	7.0%	8.5%	% Retained to Comm Eq	10.5%
							31%	21%	23%	22%	21%	11%	20%	18%	14%	16%	12%	% All Div'ds to Net Prof	9%

Options: None

BUSINESS: Shaw Communications Inc. (prior to 1992, known as Shaw Cablesystems Ltd.) is among the largest cable television systems operations in Canada. The cable unit (92% of '93 revenues) serves 900,000 basic cable subscribers across Canada and predominantly in Alberta (36.4%) and British Columbia (35.5%). The radio division (8% of '93 sales) operates eight radio stations in British Columbia, Alberta and Ontario. Television networks division provides cable television advertising services to a variety of businesses. 1993 depr. rate: 12.3%. Insiders control a majority of Class A shares and over 15% of Class B shares (Proxy 12/93). Chrmn. & Pres.: James R. Shaw, Sr. Inc.: Alberta. Add.: 7605 - 50 Street, Edmonton, Alberta T6B 2W9 Canada. Tel.: 403-468-1230.

Now it's your turn to put your investigative and analysis skills to work to earn superior investment returns like your investment club counterparts.

Glossary

AAAII: American Association of Individual Investors.

ACCRETED: The process of earning or growing gradually. For example, the interest on zero coupon bonds is accreted.

ADJUSTABLE RATE PREFERRED: A preferred security with its dividend payment pegged to a specific index or indices.

AMERICAN DEPOSITARY RECEIPT (ADR): A negotiable receipt for shares of a foreign corporation held in the vault of a United States depositary bank.

ANNUAL REPORT: The Securities and Exchange Commisssion-required report of the company's operations and financial position. It includes a balance sheet, income statement, statement of cash flows, description of company operations, and management discussion of company financial condition, operating results, and any events which materially impact the company.

ASSET ALLOCATION: Investment strategy of reducing risk and increasing return by investing in a variety of asset types.

ASSET PLAY: A stock investment that value investors find attractive due to asset undervaluation by the market.

AT THE MONEY: The situation when the underlying security's market price equals the exercise price.

BASIS PRICE: The cost of an investment used to determine capital gains or losses.

BEAR MARKET: A period of time during which stock prices decline over a number of months or years.

BOND: A long-term debt security that obligates the issuer to pay interest and repay the principal. The holder does not have any ownership rights in the issuer.

BOND RATIO: The measure of a company's leverage, it compares the firm's debt to total capital.

BOTTOM-UP INVESTING: Investment strategy starting with company fundamentals and then moving to the overall economic and investment environment.

BUSTED: A convertible whose underlying common stock value has fallen so low that the convertible provision no longer holds any value.

CALL OPTION: A contract providing the holder the right to buy the underlying security at a specific price during a specified time period.

CALL PROVISION: A provision allowing the security issuer to recall the security before maturity.

CASH EQUIVALENT: Asset type with maturities of less than one year.

CASH FLOW: The flow of funds in and out of an operating business. Normally calculated as net income plus depreciation and other noncash items.

CASH FLOW/DEBT RATIO: The relationship of free cash flow to total long-term indebtedness. This ratio is helpful in tracking a firm's ability to meet scheduled debt and interest payment requirements.

CASH FLOW/INTEREST RATIO: This ratio determines how many times free cash flow will cover fixed interest payments on long-term debt.

CASH FLOW PER SHARE: Represents the amount earned before deduction for depreciation and other charges not involving the outlay of cash.

CASH RATIO: Used to measure liquidity, this ratio is calculated as the sum of cash and marketable securities divided by current liabilities. It indicates how well a company can meet current liabilities.

CLOSED-END FUND: An investment fund that has a fixed number of shares outstanding and trades on exchanges like stock in regular companies.

CLUSTER INVESTING: Method of diversification recommending investing in stocks from different clusters or groups.

COMMON and PREFERRED CASH FLOW COVERAGE RATIOS: These ratios determine how many times annual free cash flow will cover common and preferred cash dividend payments.

COMMON STOCK RATIO: The relationship of common stock to total company capitalization.

CONTRARIAN: An investor seeking securities out of favor with other investors.

CONVERTIBLES: A security that is exchangeable into common stock at the option of the holder under specified terms and conditions.

COVERED CALL: An option in which the investor owns the underlying security.

CUMULATIVE: As it relates to preferred stock, any unpaid preferred dividends accrue and must be paid prior to resumption of common stock dividends.

CURRENT RATIO: Liquidity ratio calculated by dividing current assets by current liabilities.

CYCLES: Repeating patterns of business, economic, and market activity.

CYCLICAL: Industries and companies that advance and decline in relation to the changes in the overall economic environment.

DEBT-TO-EQUITY RATIO: The relationship of debt to shareholder's equity in a firm's capitalization structure.

DEFENSIVE INVESTMENTS: Securities that are less affected by economic contractions, thus offering downside price protection.

DIVERSIFICATION: The spreading of investment risk by owning different types of securities, investments in different geographical markets, etc.

DOLLAR COST AVERAGING: Investment strategy of investing a fixed amount of money over time to achieve a lower average security purchase price.

DOW JONES INDUSTRIAL AVERAGE: Market index consisting of 30 U.S. industrial companies. Used as a measure of market performance.

DOW THEORY: Investment theory that the market moves in three simultaneous movements that help forecast the direction of the economy and the market.

DRIP: Dividend reinvestment plan in which stockholder can purchase additional shares with dividends and/or cash.

EARNINGS PER SHARE: Net after-tax income divided by the number of outstanding company shares.

ECONOMIC SERIES: The complete cycle of economic period types, such as from expansion to slowdown to contraction to recession/depression to increased activity back to expansion.

ECONOMIC VALUE: The economic value of a stock represents the anticipated free cash flow the company will generate over a period of time, discounted by the weighted cost of a company's capital.

EFFICIENT MARKET: A market that instantly takes into account all known financial information and reflects it in the security's price.

EXERCISE PRICE: The price at which an option of futures contract can be executed. Also known as the striking price.

EXPIRATION DATE: The last day on which an option or future can be exercised.

FEDERAL RESERVE: The national banking system consisting of 12 independent federal reserve banks in Atlanta, Boston, Chicago, Cleveland, Dallas, Kansas City, Minneapolis, New York, Philadelphia, Richmond, St. Louis, and San Francisco.

FISCAL YEAR: The 12-month accounting period that conforms to the company's natural operating cycle, as opposed to the calendar year.

FREDDIE MAC: The nickname of the Federal Home Loan Mortgage Corporation.

FREE CASH FLOW: Determined by calculating operating earnings after taxes and then adding depreciation and other noncash expenses, less capital expenditures and increases in working capital.

FREE CASH FLOW/EARNINGS RATIO: The percentage of earnings actually available in cash. It is the percentage of free cash available to company management for investments, acquisitions, plant construction, dividends, etc.

FUNDAMENTAL ANALYSIS: Investment strategy focusing on the intrinsic value of the company as evidenced by a review of the balance sheet, income statement, cash flow, operating performance, etc.

GAP: The occurrence of a trading pattern in which the price range from one day does not overlap the previous day's price range.

GLOBAL DEPOSITARY RECEIPT (GDR): Similar to ADRs. Depositary receipt issued in the international community representing shares in a foreign company. Other designations include International Depositary Receipt (IDR) and European Depositary Receipt (EDR).

GROWTH INVESTMENTS: Companies or industries whose earnings are projected to outpace the market consistently over the long-term.

HIGH-TECH STOCK: Securities of firms in high-technology industries such as biotechnology, computers, electronics, lasers, medical devices, and robotics.

HOMETOWN INVESTMENT: An investment opportunity in the area in which you live.

HYBRID SECURITY: A security that possesses the characteristics of both stock and bonds, such as a convertible bond.

INDENTURE: The legal contract spelling out the terms and conditions between the issuer and bondholders.

INDEX: A compilation of performance for specific groupings of stocks or mutual funds such as the Dow Jones Industrial Average, S&P 500, etc.

INDICATOR: A measurement of the economy or securities markets used by economists and investment analysts to predict future economic and financial moves and direction. Indicators are classifed as leading, coincidental, or lagging. Indicator examples include interest rate changes, utility consumption, number of unemployment claims, etc.

INSIDER: Anyone having access to material corporate information. Most frequently used to refer to company officers, directors, and top management.

INSTITUTIONAL INVESTORS: Investor organizations, such as pension funds and money managers, who trade large volumes of securities.

IN THE MONEY: The situation when the price of the underlying security is above the exercise price.

INTRINSIC VALUE: The difference between the current market price of the underlying security and the striking price of a related option.

IPO (INITIAL PUBLIC OFFERING): The first public offering of a company's stock.

JUNK BONDS: Bonds with ratings below investment grade.

LEADING INDICATOR: An economic measurement that tends to be accurate in predicting the future direction of the economy or stock market.

LEAPS: Long-term equity participation securities. Long-term options with maturities up to two years.

LEVERAGE: The use of debt to finance a company's operations. Also, the use of debt by investors to increase the return on investment from securities transactions.

LIFE-CYCLE INVESTING: Developing an investment strategy based on where you are in your life cycle.

LIQUIDITY: The degree of ease in which assets can be turned into readily available cash.

LISTED: Investment securities that have met the listing requirements of a particular exchange.

MAINTENANCE MARGIN: The minimum equity value that must be maintained in a margin account. Initial margin requirements include a minimum deposit of $2,000 before any credit can be extended. Current Regulation T rules require maintenance margin to equal at least 50 percent of the market value of the margined positions.

MARGIN: The capital (in cash or securities) that an investor deposits with a broker to borrow additional funds to purchase securities.

MARGIN CALL: A demand from a broker for additional cash or securities as collateral to bring the margin account back within maintenance limits.

MUNICIPAL BOND: A bond issued by a local or state government or government agency.

MUTUAL FUND: An investment company that sells shares in itself to the investing public and uses the proceeds to purchase individual securities.

NAFTA: North American Free Trade Agreement.

NAIC: National Association of Investors Corporation.

NAKED OPTION: An option written when the investor does not have a position in the underlying security.

NASDAQ: National Association of Securities Dealers Automated Quotation System. Provides computerized quotes of market makers for stocks traded over the counter.

NET ASSET VALUE: The quoted market value of a mutual fund share. Determined by dividing the closing market value of all securities owned by the mutual fund plus all other assets and liablities by the total number of shares outstanding.

NUMISMATICS: The study, collecting, and investing in money and medals.

OBSOLETE SECURITY: Security that is no longer actively traded on an exchange but has collector value.

OPEC: The Organization of Petroleum Exporting Countries.

OPTION: A security that gives the holder the right to purchase or sell a particular investment at a fixed price for a specified period of time.

OUT OF THE MONEY: An option whose striking price is higher than the underlying security's current market price for a call option or whose striking price is lower than the current market price for a put option.

PARTICIPATING: As it relates to preferred stock, the preferred stockholder shares in additional dividends as the earnings ofthe company improve.

PAYOUT RATIO: The percentage of a company's profit paid out in cash dividends.

PORTFOLIO: The investment holdings of an individual or institutional investor, including stocks, bonds, options, money market accounts, etc.

PREFERRED: A security with preference to dividends and claim to corporate assets over common stock.

PRICE/EARNINGS RATIO: Determined by dividing the stock's marketprice by its earnings per common share. Used as an indicator of company performance and in comparison with other stock investments and the overall market.

PRIVATE PLACEMENT: The placement of a security directly with a person, business, or other entity without any offering to the general investing public.

PROSPECTUS: The SEC-required printed summary of the registration statement. The prospectus contains critical information about the security offering such as business, management, and financial information.

PUT OPTION: A contract giving the holder the right to sell the underlying security at a specific price over a specified time frame.

QUICK RATIO: This ratio is used to measure corporate liquidity. It is regarded as an improvement over the current ratio, which includes the usually not very liquid inventory. The quick ratio formula is computed as current assets less inventory divided by current liabilities.

RANGE: The high and low prices over which the security trades during a specific time frame: day, month, 52 weeks, etc.

RATING: Independent ranking of a security in regard to risk and ability to meet payment obligations.

REBALANCING: The process of adjusting a portfolio mix to return to a desired asset allocation level.

REIT: Real Estate Investment Trust.

RELATIVE STRENGTH: Comparison of a security's earnings or stock price strength in relation to other investments or indices.

RISK: The financial uncertainty that the actual return will vary from the expected return. Risk factors include inflation, deflation, interest rate risk, market risk, liquidity, default, etc.

RULE OF EIGHT: Diversification strategy that contends a minimum of eight stocks is necessary to properly diversify a portfolio.

SCRIPOPHILY: Collecting of antique stock and bond certificates.

SECONDARY MARKET: Market where previously issued securities trade, such as the New York Stock Exchange.

SHORT AGAINST THE BOX: Investment strategy of selling short while holding a long position in the security.

SHORT SALE: Sale of a security not yet owned in order to capitalize on an anticipated market price drop.

SHORT SQUEEZE: Rapid price rise forcing investors to cover their short positions. This drives the security price up even higher, often squeezing even more short investors.

SPECIAL SITUATION: An undervalued security with special circumstances, such as management change, new product, technological breakthrough, etc., favoring its return to better operating performance and higher prices.

SPIN-OFF: Shedding of a corporate subsidiary, division, or other operation via the issuance of shares in the new corporate entity.

SPLIT: A change in the number of outstanding shares through board of directors' action. Shareholder's equity remains the same; each shareholder receives the new stock in proportion to his/her holdings on the date of record. Dividends and earnings per share are adjusted to reflect the stock split.

S&P 500: Broad-based stock index composed of 400 industrial, 40 financial, 40 utility, and 20 transportation stocks.

STRIKING PRICE: The price at which an option or future contract can be executed according to the terms of the contract. Also called exercise price.

10K, 10Q: Annual and quarterly reports required by the Securities and Exchange Commission. They contain more in-depth financial and operating information than the annual and quarterly stockholder's reports.

TECHNICAL ANALYSIS: Investment strategy that focuses on market and stock price patterns.

TOP-DOWN INVESTING: Investment strategy starting with the overall economic scenario and then moving downward to consider industry and individual company investments.

TOTAL RETURN: The return achieved by combining both the dividend/interest and capital appreciation earned on an investment.

TRADING RANGE: The spread between the high and low prices for a given period.

TURNAROUND: A positive change in the fortunes of a company or industry. Turnarounds occur for a variety of reasons, such as economic upturn, new management, new product lines, strategic acquisition, etc.

UNDERLYING SECURITY: The security that may be bought or sold under the terms of an option agreement, warrant, etc.

UNDERVALUED SITUATION: A security with a market value that does not fully value its potential or the true value of the company.

UPTREND: Upward movement in the market price of a stock.

VALUE AVERAGING: An investment purchase method that concentrates on the investment's value, not its cost.

VOLUME: The number of units of a security traded during a given time frame.

WARRANT: An option to purchase a stated number of shares at a specified price within a specfic time frame. Warrants are typically offered as "sweeteners" to enhance the marketability of stock or debt issues.

WORKING CAPITAL: The difference between current assets and current liabilities.

YIELD: An investor's return on investment from its interest- or dividend-paying capability.

ZERO COUPON: A bond selling at a discount to maturity value and earning interest over the life of the bond but paying it upon maturity.

Index

A

AAII Journal, 35–36
AFLAC, Inc., 129, 133–135
American Depositary Receipts, 5, 16, 22, 36, 131
American Society of Individual Investors, 35–36, 124
Arrow Investment Club, 65–77, 84, 94

B

Becton, Dickinson & Company, 65, 68, 71–72
Berry, Bonnie, 78–79
Biomet, Inc., 129, 132, 135–138

C

Canadian Shareowners Association, 36, 119, 159
Carlson, Charles B., 18
Cassidy, Don, 35, 95
Cisco Systems, Inc., 52–54, 56-59
Colgate-Palmolive Company, 129, 132, 138–141
Constant dollar formula, 10–11
Constant ratio formula, 11–12
Cooper Tire & Rubber Company, 130, 132, 140–143

D

DRIP Investor, 18
Directory of Companies Offering Dividend Reinvestment Plans, 16
Direct Stock Purchase Plan, 16, 19
Diversification, 2–6
Dividend reinvestment plans, 12–29, 36, 102, 109
Dollar cost averaging, 6, 8–9, 15, 34, 103
Dow Theory Forecasts, 18

E

Edleson, Michael E., 9
Evergreen Enterprises, 16

F

Federal National Mortgage Association, 90–92
First Share, 19
Flandreau Investment Club, 90–95
Fuller, H.B. Company, 131, 133, 143–146

G–H

GRQ Investment Club, 39–53, 91
General Dynamics Corporation, 6
General Electric Company, 52–53, 59–61, 129
Glaxco Holdings, PLC, 5, 22, 131
Guide to Dividend Reinvestment Plans, 16
Home Depot, 39, 46–49, 52–53, 91, 129, 132–133, 148

I–J

Individual Retirement Account, 108
Intel Corporation, 66, 79–83, 130
International Game Technology, 3, 90, 92–94
Jacobson, Patricia, 54

K–L

Kellogg Company, 129, 132, 145–148
L-P Investors Investment Club, 50, 52–64
Life-cycle investing, 1
Lindgren, Dr. Henry Clay, 39–41
Low Cost Investment Plan, 19, 66, 102, 108–119, 124
Lynch, Peter, 90, 135

M

McCormick & Company, Inc., 5
McDonald's Corporation, 52, 62, 78, 81, 84–86, 129, 133
Microsoft Corporation, 66–70, 78, 84, 90, 94, 129, 132
Moneypaper, The, 15–19, 23
Moneypaper DRP 63 Index, 16–18
Moody's Handbook of Dividend Achievers, 27, 30

W–Y

About the Author

Richard J. Maturi is a widely respected business and investment author whose nearly 1,000 articles have appeared in such distinguished publications as *Barron's, Investor's Business Daily, Institutional Investor, Your Money, Industry Week, Kiplinger's Personal Finance, The New York Times, Your Company,* and many others. In addition, he publishes three investment newsletters, *Utility and Energy Portfolio, 21st Century Investments,* and *Gaming and Investments Quarterly* (see discount coupon offer in back of book). Mr. Maturi is the author of *Wall Street Words: The Basics and Beyond* (Chicago: Probus, 1991); *Stock Picking: The 11 Best Tactics for Beating the Market* (New York: McGraw-Hill, 1993); *Divining the Dow: 100 of the World's Most Widely Followed Stock Market Prediction Systems* (Chicago: Probus, 1993); *Money Making Investments Your Broker Doesn't Tell You About* (Chicago: Probus, 1994); and *The 105 Best Investments for the 21st Century* (New York: McGraw-Hill, 1995). Four of Maturi's books are Fortune Book Club selections.

Maturi is a member of the American Society of Journalists and Authors, Denver Press Club, and Wyoming Media Professionals. In addition to attending the University of Notre Dame, he received his bachelor's degree from the University of Minnesota-Duluth and his M.B.A. from Oregon State University. While in the corporate world, he managed company pension and profit sharing funds and served as a trustee of the Minnesota Teamsters Pension Fund. In 1993, Maturi travelled the Lincoln Highway route from Wyoming to Wall Street in his 1936 Oldsmobile, giving financial seminars and attending book signings en route. He and his wife, Mary, live in a log home in the Laramie Range of Wyoming's Rockies.

The author of
Main Street Beats Wall Street
invites you to examine these three special offers:

*Gaming & Investments Quarterly**

Covers the gambling, hotel, and entertainment industries with in-depth analysis of unique common stock investment opportunities. Regular $75 annual subscription; special price, $25 annual subscription.

*Utility & Energy Portfolio**

Includes investment ideas, discussions of where to find higher yields and safety, plus coverage of major industry trends and key players. Regular $95 annual subscription; special price, $35 annual subscription.

21st Century Investments

New investment newsletter covering investment opportunities positioned to perform well into the next century and beyond. Regular subscription $95, special six month trial offer for only $5.

* BONUS A subscription to either of these entitles you to a free copy of *Wall Street Words: The Basics and Beyond,* a $14.95 value.

TEAR HERE

Please send check or money order, or order with your Discover® card:

R. Maturi, Inc.
1320 Curt Gowdy Drive
Cheyenne, WY 82009

☐ Gaming & Investments Quarterly   @$25
☐ Utility & Energy Portfolio   @$35
☐ 21st Century Investments   @$5 (six month trial offer)

Name _____
Address _____
City _____ State _____ Zip _____
Account No. _____ Exp. Date _____

DATE DUE

GAYLORD			PRINTED IN U.S.A.

Someone Other Than a Mother

Someone Other Than a Mother

FLIPPING THE SCRIPTS ON A WOMAN'S
PURPOSE AND MAKING MEANING
BEYOND MOTHERHOOD

ERIN S. LANE

A TarcherPerigee Book

tarcherperigee

An imprint of Penguin Random House LLC
penguinrandomhouse.com

TarcherPerigee with tp colophon is a registered trademark of Penguin
Random House LLC.

Most TarcherPerigee books are available at special quantity discounts for
bulk purchase for sales promotions, premiums, fund-raising, and educational
needs. Special books or book excerpts also can be created to fit specific
needs. For details, write: SpecialMarkets@penguinrandomhouse.com.

ISBN 9780593329313
eBook ISBN 9780593329320

Printed in the United States of America
10 9 8 7 6 5 4 3 2 1

BOOK DESIGN BY KATY RIEGEL

To Janell.

And everyone who trusted me to carry this story,
which is sometimes their story. It was you
who carried me.

Author's Note

WHILE WRITING THIS book, I would wake up in the dead of night sure that I was going to break something. A water glass. Someone's trust. A million little hearts—or three.

So, here is what I did.

For those whose lives intersected with mine through no fault of their own, I have changed identifying details when in the service of protecting their privacy and dignity. Many of these individuals have been kinder to me than necessary. I tried to be likewise.

For those brave souls who consented to an interview, I used audio recordings and e-mail correspondences and sometimes memory to compose and condense their words. Any failing in the accuracy or interpretation of those words is utterly my own. Most chose to use their real names. I am a little in love with them all.

There is a charge in my religious tradition to speak the truth in love. Or, as I prefer to put it, the truth is not a tyrant. May these pages mend more than they break.

We speak as though there is one good plot with one happy outcome, while the myriad forms a life can take flower—and wither—all around us.

—REBECCA SOLNIT[1]

Contents

Preface: Mother or Mother Superior

THERE IS A belief that mother love is a superior love. Like American exceptionalism to which it is closely aligned, the worldview of maternal exceptionalism sees mothers as not just different but better, morally speaking, than those who are not mothers. Mothers are more mature. More self-less. Even more godlike. God is a parent, too, I've been told.

As a young Catholic girl who grew up in the American Midwest on white bread and Jesus, I had two options for a life well-lived: Mother or Mother Superior. I could marry a man and mother my own children, or I could marry God, so to speak, and mother the world's children. Both were good out-comes for someone else's life. Neither would fit the shape of mine.

I was born in the 1980s when motherhood was not, in fact, a given. The widespread legalization of reproductive rights was barely a decade old. Increasing numbers of women were delaying children to pursue an education or career, sometimes opting out or aging out of the traditional milestone altogether. Anxieties about this emerging future fueled conservatives' renewed emphasis on the family and women's distinct place in it.

And what was more distinct about a woman than her womb?

A pious child who picked up on religious rhetoric like it was hopscotch, I was fervently "pro-life"; all children were like hand-knit gifts from God. In elementary school, I wrote a want ad for my future husband that listed "knows the Lord" and "doesn't believe in abortion" alongside must-haves like "loves the outdoors and sports, mainly baseball." But when it came to the idea of my own children, the fervor faded. I wanted to be someone's wife more than I wanted to be someone's parent. More than anything, I think, I wanted to be whoever it was that I was.

It took some time to realize that this would be a problem. I would be a problem. At first, I didn't notice that Disney villains were nearly all childless or jealously parenting someone else's children. I didn't catch that relatives started sentences with "When you become a mother . . ." and not "If you become a mother . . ." I almost believed adults who promised with great confidence and zero evidence that my maternal instincts would kick in, despite substandard babysitting skills. But by the time I graduated from college in the South, where tradition hung as heavy as Spanish moss, the message was clear: A woman who embraced a purpose other than parenting was deficient, defiant, possibly devilish—in a word, *cursed*.

It was also clear I had become that woman.

I count it as one of life's dumb blessings that at twenty-two I married a man who was mutually, but not equally, damned. Rush may have been the "head" of our household, as the thinking went among my evangelical friends, but surely I was the controlling "neck" when it came to the question of children. On a blistering summer day in July, we wed in a church ceremony bereft of any blessing for future offspring. No reproductive fruitfulness, please. Or mention of multiplication, thank you, we told our officiants. We were purposefully, prayerfully even, what we would later call "childfree for the common good" and my grandmother would call "interesting."

Community, not parenting, is what compelled us to marry. We thought we were better together; it was as simple and shapeless as that. Like Jesus sending out his disciples, two was enough. But after our wedding day the pressure to start a family, as if we were not already a family unto ourselves, only increased. "You'll change your mind when you get married" was replaced by "You'll change your mind when you get older." The premise felt preposterous to test, as if my body was some high-stakes craps table.

Instead, we began practicing "the ministry of availability" to other people's children. This was not because we liked children per se but because we liked other people and, at a certain age, one has to accept that it's hard to love your grown-ups without learning to love their little ones. "Let us watch your kids so you can go to dinner," I told our friends. "Go grocery shopping. Go to an R-rated movie. Go to sleep." For reasons I can try to explain but change every time that I do, few people called on us. So we called the Department of Social Services, curious if there were parents who might actually need us, if we might actually need them.

Was it possible to do something more meaningful than mothering? You would think that after almost thirty years of childlessness, ten spent coupled and six devoted to earning degrees in gender and theology, the answer would be clear. But the old scripts that said women are made to mother—and made to like it—were legion. Our natural wiring would win out. Our paid work would never pay off. Besides, women are told, "You don't know love until you become a mother."

That last one really fucked with me.

AS A THEOLOGICAL anthropologist, or someone who thinks a lot about what humans (*anthropos*) think about God (*theos*), I've spent years talking to people about the stage directions they received on how to be acceptably female. These stage directions are sometimes called social scripts, and they refer to an entire choreography of language, practices, and beliefs that reinforce cultural norms. "Normal" is a community of belonging.

When I first set out to study social scripts, I was hoping to find a universal answer to what made women *women*. I was hoping to find an answer to what made me *me*. I longed for an Easy-Bake manual to my life as much as the next girl. Instead, I discovered that if women are a monolith, it's because we've had to manage some version of the mother scripts* that say our highest self is hiding in our reproductive role. Best wishes, warmest regards, and good luck unlocking your ultimate destiny.

But seriously.

Social scripts are not inherently bad; they're simply the behavioral and conversational shorthand we use to predict, control, and make sense of our mercurial reality. They are ready-made answers to the questions that churn in the night: Why are we this way and not that way? What do we want, and will it make us happy? What does happy feel like exactly? And why do we feel so far from home in these hapless human bodies? The mother scripts take a "typical" woman's body—her womb, her breasts, the anxious heart inside her chest—and promise a way out of the unknowing. A mother's love will always shine a path.

For some lucky souls, this promise pays off. Maybe for a time, maybe for always, motherhood is a revelation. This is true of my own mother, who for most of my childhood was a

---

* There are as many versions of the mother scripts as there are versions of womanhood, which is to say infinite. What follows in this book are the nine that were most alive (and would not die) in my White, cisgender, middle-class, able-bodied, American life.

single mother and worked as little as she could for as much as she could in order to spend as long as she could with my older brother and me. Her only regret is that she didn't have more children. We were that great, apparently.

But for others, the promise of experiencing fulfillment in motherhood is painful, nonsensical, exhausting. I've heard women who don't have children ask, "What's wrong with me?" and women who don't want children moan, "I can't talk to friends anymore," and mothers doing it differently sigh, "I'm tired of having to defend my life."

Along the way, I've learned that the problem with the mother scripts is not simply that they don't work for *some* women. The problem is that they're assumed to work for *all* women, thereby shaming *any* woman who lives beyond their cloud of certainty.

Take, for instance, the script, "Your biological clock is ticking." Are we saying that if you're not worried about your reproductive window or don't feel the pull to parenthood, you're unnatural? Like, maybe your body is a little bit broken?

Or consider the script that says, "Children are a gift from God." It's a lovely belief in the abstract. But I do worry about it being applied individually. Does this mean that if you don't know the blessing of offspring, you're unfortunate? Or, if you don't want the blessing of offspring, you're ungrateful? By this logic, is using contraception ungrateful?

Then there's the script that assures, "But you'd make a great mom!" which is only uttered to some women, the "right" kind of women. The word *mother*, as Alexis Pauline Gumbs has helped me see, is more often a noun that reproduces the status quo than a verb that subverts it.[1]

In some ways, the option for me to make a life as an actual Mother Superior, or regular Catholic nun, was itself subversive. I don't imagine I saw it that way when I was in catechism class. But it did undermine the broadly American notion that biological mothers are the most blessed, their homes the most "missional," their work the most patriotic. So, too, did it undermine the belief that a woman's life should and would center on romantic love, a love born and fueled by feeling rather than the tedium of faithfulness.

Still, even spiritual motherhood can perpetuate the mother scripts. I have a friend in her seventies who knew from a young age that she didn't want children and, in her words, "has wandered that alien path as quietly as possible." Yet every year, she bemoans, people persist in wishing her a happy Mother's Day. "I try to remind them—kindly—that I'm not a mother, and I am corrected, *But you have been like a mother to so many*." What's meant to be a compliment instead feels like coercion. Insisting all women find meaning in our metaphorical reproductive role is no more helpful than insisting we find meaning in our literal one.

Questions of meaning are unavoidably questions of faith. So, how does our faith influence the emphasis we put on mothering? The little evidence that exists on the topic suggests quite a lot. There is quite a lot of correlation between your childbearing attitudes and, say, how literally you read the Bible or how often you attend church or how you religiously affiliate, if at all.[2, 3, 4] It's not surprising then that, across faiths, the religious report more stigma than the nonreligious when deviating from the mother scripts.[5]

Let me be clear here about my own faith. I'm no longer a practicing Catholic, but the prayers still live under my tongue, the incense hibernates in my nostrils. Somewhere in a Las Vegas cathedral, you will still find my father serving communion in a Hawaiian shirt. My mother, on the other hand, attends the same church that I do and talks to God in bed each morning. I talk to God, too, but I have a very wide definition of what this looks like: Breathing can be talking, having a hot cry on the elliptical can be talking, studying scripture can be talking.

I have studied a lot of Christian scripture. So, the story of Jesus is one of the stories I know best, and, on the whole, I think it is a good one for the childless, childfree, and unlikely families.* And yet his followers have caused colossal harm over the last two thousand years by conflating our religious values with popular cultural ones. Even if you're not religious,

---

* A word about words here. While women use different labels (and often no labels) to describe their relationship to children, for the purposes of this book, women who don't have children (for whatever reason) will be identified as *childless*. Within that group, women who don't want children will further be identified as *childfree*. And women who don't center biological children are making *unlikely families*. Honestly, though? Many of us are over the categories completely. But we'll get there . . .

you may have been shaped by Christian idioms regarding everything from the purpose of sex to who counts as family.

"Erin, nobody is thinking about this stuff as much as you," my husband, Rush, once had to tell me.

And I might have left it at that—a writer's tendency to overwork things—had I not noticed how the mother scripts were failing a huge portion of the population. Not just the non-moms they demean. But also the conventional moms they esteem. The titles alone of popular parenting books in the last decade paint a bleak picture. *Fed Up. Maxed Out. All Joy and No Fun.*

And I might have left it at that—a writer's sympathy for other people's misery—had the promise of motherhood not eventually failed me.

ONE YEAR I was childfree, and eighteen months later, I was an adoptive parent of three. Spoiler alert: Parenting was not the shortcut to enlightenment I'd been sold.

In order to be certified as a foster parent in Durham County, North Carolina, you have to take a thirty-hour class on parenting children impacted by trauma. The crew that came together in a room where biology was not destiny and a love life was not the only life was magic. There was a broad-shouldered Black man who wanted better for the youth he pastored. There was a mixed-faith couple who had buried a son and only recently begun to unbury their faces. There was a conservative

White couple whose church took the call to love widow and orphan so seriously that they offered free childcare for anyone who followed the call to this class. How lucky we felt to practice family free from a formula.

In one getting-to-know-you exercise called "the human chain," our first facilitator stood in the middle of the conference room and proclaimed with Oprah-like pitch, "I love pasta!" The invitation was for someone else to stand and say, "I love pasta, too," and join the fledgling circle by linking arms with their new mate. That someone else then offered another benign love to the group—soccer, sewing, cats—and one by one we bound ourselves together by common interests. It was not for lack of effort that I was the last one sitting at the end, but rather firm commitment to the cause. I *liked* but did not *love* soccer, sewing, or cats, and refused to be phony about this or any other loves simply to join the human chain.

Our second facilitator had been the link before me. A more soft-spoken woman, she bobbed her wet, curly bangs left and then right before stopping on a love she thought I—surely anyone—could live with. "I love children," she purred. The blood drained from my face. I willed my bones to stack and rise. Across the circle Rush's cheeks ballooned out and in, out and in. When I finally arrived, I gave her my limp arm and conceded, "I'm getting there."

It was not children in general but children in particular that compelled us to adopt the sibling set of three school-age